SCHOOLING AND DISABILITY

SCHOOLING AND DISABILITY

*Eighty-eighth Yearbook of the
National Society for the Study of Education*

Part II

Edited by
DOUGLAS BIKLEN, DIANNE FERGUSON, AND ALISON FORD

Editor for the Society
KENNETH J. REHAGE

Distributed by THE UNIVERSITY OF CHICAGO PRESS ● CHICAGO, ILLINOIS

The National Society for the Study of Education

Founded in 1901 as successor to the National Herbart Society, the National Society for the Study of Education has provided a means by which the results of serious study of educational issues could become a basis for informed discussion of those issues. The Society's two-volume yearbooks, now in their eighty-eighth year of publication, reflect the thoughtful attention given to a wide range of educational problems during those years. In 1971 the Society inaugurated a series of substantial publications on Contemporary Educational Issues to supplement the yearbooks. Each year the Society's publications contain contributions to the literature of education from more than a hundred scholars and practitioners who are doing significant work in their respective fields.

An elected Board of Directors selects the subjects with which volumes in the yearbook series are to deal and appoints committees to oversee the preparation of manuscripts. A special committee created by the Board performs similar functions for the series on Contemporary Educational Issues.

The Society's publications are distributed each year without charge to members in the United States, Canada, and elsewhere throughout the world. The Society welcomes as members all individuals who desire to receive its publications. Information about current dues may be found in the back pages of this volume.

This volume, *Schooling and Disability*, is Part II of the Society's Eighty-eighth Yearbook. Part I, published at the same time, is entitled *From Socrates to Software: The Teacher as Text and the Text as Teacher*.

A listing of the Society's publications still available for purchase may be found in the back pages of this volume.

Library of Congress Catalog Number: 88-062760
ISSN: 0077-5762

Published 1989 by
THE NATIONAL SOCIETY FOR THE STUDY OF EDUCATION
5835 Kimbark Avenue, Chicago, Illinois 60637
© 1989 by the National Society for the Study of Education

No part of this Yearbook may be reproduced in any form without written permission from the Secretary of the Society

First Printing, 6,000 Copies

Printed in the United States of America

Officers of the
National Society for the Study of Education, 1988-1989
(*Term of office expires March 1 of the year indicated.*)

LUVERN L. CUNNINGHAM, Ohio State University (1989)
MARGARET EARLY, University of Florida (1990)
JOHN I. GOODLAD, University of Washington (1990)
PHILIP W. JACKSON, University of Chicago (1991)
ANN LIEBERMAN, University of Washington (1989)
KAREN K. ZUMWALT, Teachers College, Columbia University (1991)

KENNETH J. REHAGE, University of Chicago, Secretary-Treasurer

Contributors to the Yearbook

DOUGLAS P. BIKLEN, co-editor, Syracuse University
DIANNE L. FERGUSON, co-editor, University of Oregon
ALISON FORD, co-editor, Syracuse University
KATHY ZANELLA ALBRIGHT, University of Wisconsin, Madison
ADRIENNE ASCH, Teachers College, Columbia University
JAMES BLACK, Syracuse University
LOU BROWN, University of Wisconsin, Madison
IAN M. EVANS, State University of New York, Binghamton
PHILIP M. FERGUSON, University of Oregon
ROBERT GAYLORD-ROSS, San Francisco State University
ARNOLD P. GOLDSTEIN, Syracuse University
JACK JORGENSEN, Madison Metropolitan School District
MARA SAPON-SHEVIN, University of North Dakota
SUSAN STAINBACK, California State University, Los Angeles
WILLIAM STAINBACK, California State University, Los Angeles
PAT VANDEVENTER, Madison Metropolitan School District
ELVERA WELD, State University of New York, Binghamton

Acknowledgment

The most recent publications of the National Society for the Study of Education that deal with aspects of special education appeared in 1950 (*The Education of Exceptional Children*, the Forty-ninth Yearbook) and in 1967 (*The Educationally Retarded and Disadvantaged*, the Sixty-seventh Yearbook). It is clearly time for another look at this important component of education. Furthermore, with the passage in 1975 of the Education for All Handicapped Children Act (Public Law 94-142) special education has entered a new era.

In 1985, the Board of Directors invited Professor Douglas Biklen and his colleagues to submit a proposal for a yearbook on special education. They graciously responded with an intriguing document. The proposal was approved and since that time the editors and authors have worked diligently and effectively to produce the manuscript for this volume. The Society is grateful to all who have had a part in producing this book. They give the reader a comprehensive view of the issues that are central to discussions about special education today, especially the complicated problem of establishing closer and more meaningful relationships between special education and "regular" education. To each of the authors, and especially to the editors, we express our deepest appreciation for making it possible for us to add this significant volume to the NSSE Yearbook series.

KENNETH J. REHAGE
Editor for the Society

Editors' Preface

From the outset we realized that this yearbook would touch on more than special education. Of course, the yearbook would necessarily report on some of the most controversial, burning issues of the day related to the education of students with disabilities. But if the book was to serve the members of the National Society for the Study of Education and its reading audience, mainly educators but not principally special educators, it should explore the relationship of special *and* "regular" education. Also, the book should raise broad issues of ideology and policy and at the same time include examples of effective educational practice. If we addressed these questions, the book would concern not just special education but education in general and its principal focus would be on the place of students with disabilities in education. Hence the title, *Schooling and Disability*.

In the U.S., as in Canada, Italy, certain states of Australia, and in a number of other countries, efforts to educate students with disabilities with their nondisabled peers (in other words, mainstreaming and integration), have been central to the special education/regular education agenda. In each context, however, teachers, parents, students, school administrators, and the public readily admit and sometimes complain that such integration is just developing. Placing students in physical proximity with each other, creating programs that educate students together, and enabling students to accept and befriend each other are separate but related steps not accomplished easily. Thus we begin *Schooling and Disability* with the question: Is there any place within society where integration of people with disabilities and nondisabled people has already occurred so well and to such an extent that we could derive lessons for organizing and operating schools? The answer is "Yes." In Section One we explore this question, building a vision of what schools might look like and the principles upon which they would function if they strived to include all students. Also in this section, we describe how education in its dominant form unnecessarily stigmatizes students with disabilities.

In Section Two we attempt to define the goals of education for students with disabilities and their place in schools. For example, how have educators conceptualized the purposes of special education and how do these fit with notions of educational excellence? What is the place of students with disabilities in the educational reform movement? Each of the major reform reports has been silent about this group of students. Yet there must be areas where the reform agendas intersect with the lives of students with disabilities. Conversely, are there elements of recent reforms in special education that could instruct schooling in general? This section includes chapters on educational reform and the principles behind curricula for students with severe and mild disabilities. In addition, to conclude this section, we invited a parent of a student with a severe disability and an adult who has a disability to write about schooling and disability. They share their perspectives and analyze the personal narrative literature of other parents and people with disabilities for lessons on what they want schools to be like.

Implicit in the discussions in each chapter is the notion that experiences from the education of students with disabilities can inform all of education. For example, a newly emerging concept of community-referenced curriculum for students with severe disabilities could have its analogs for all students, with the community serving as more of a systematically used resource than is currently common. The same might be said for the concept of supported work as a form of vocational education. Similarly, it is impossible to address student aggression and school violence as an educational issue without adopting certain assumptions about student worth, behavior, educational methods, and teacher and student roles. Section Three focuses on these and other practical concerns and concludes by asking: How do we know when an educational strategy works? That is a common question in education but has not often been asked with respect to the education of students with disabilities. By asking and attempting to answer that question, we learn a great deal about educational evaluation in general.

Finally, we hoped that this book would provide a vision of educational reform that would include students with disabilities. To that end the editors collaborated to write the concluding chapter and section. It outlines how schools might redefine their perceptions of students with disabilities and develop practices for making schools inclusive communities. It reflects on the fact that the culture of schools largely determines how students with disabilities experience education.

We are grateful to Margaret Early, a member of the NSSE Board of Directors, for suggesting to the Board that we might write this book. *Schooling and Disability* was born out of our experiences in schools, particularly in schools that have endeavored to include students with disabilities as members of their communities. We thank especially the school districts of Syracuse, New York, Madison,

Wisconsin, and Eugene, Oregon. Also, we thank our colleagues at Syracuse University and the University of Oregon who read and commented on various drafts of the manuscript and Rosemary Alibrandi who typed and corrected each of the chapters. The authors deserve special recognition as well, for they willingly adjusted their busy research and writing agendas to our time schedule and made changes in substance and style to help us make their contributions a whole. In addition we wish to acknowledge the invaluable editing and guidance we received from Kenneth Rehage and his colleagues at the National Society for the Study of Education. We are pleased to have this opportunity to reach the members and audience of NSSE with our thoughts on schooling and disability.

DOUGLAS BIKLEN
DIANNE FERGUSON
ALISON FORD

January 1989

Table of Contents

	PAGE
THE NATIONAL SOCIETY FOR THE STUDY OF EDUCATION	iv
OFFICERS OF THE SOCIETY, 1988-89; CONTRIBUTORS TO THE YEARBOOK	v
ACKNOWLEDGMENT	vii
EDITORS' PREFACE	ix

Section One
The Form of Education

CHAPTER
I. REDEFINING SCHOOLS, *Douglas P. Biklen* 1

Section Two
The Goals of Education

II. SEVERITY OF NEED AND EDUCATIONAL EXCELLENCE: PUBLIC SCHOOL REFORM AND STUDENTS WITH DISABILITIES, *Dianne L. Ferguson* . 25

III. CHARACTERISTICS OF EDUCATIONAL PROGRAMS FOR STUDENTS WITH SEVERE INTELLECTUAL DISABILITIES, *Kathy Zanella Albright, Lou Brown, Pat VanDeventer,* and *Jack Jorgensen* . 59

IV. MILD DISABILITIES: IN AND OUT OF SPECIAL EDUCATION, *Mara Sapon-Shevin* 77

V. LESSONS FROM LIFE: PERSONAL AND PARENTAL PERSPECTIVES ON SCHOOL, CHILDHOOD, AND DISABILITY, *Philip M. Ferguson* and *Adrienne Asch* 108

Section Three
Practice

VI. THE COMMUNITY-REFERENCED CURRICULUM FOR STUDENTS WITH MODERATE AND SEVERE DISABILITIES, *Alison Ford* and *James Black* 141

VII. TEACHING ALTERNATIVES TO AGGRESSION, *Arnold P. Goldstein* . 168

VIII. CLASSROOM ORGANIZATION FOR DIVERSITY AMONG STUDENTS, *Susan B. Stainback* and *William C. Stainback* 195

TABLE OF CONTENTS

IX. VOCATIONAL EDUCATION FOR STUDENTS WITH HANDICAPS, *Robert Gaylord-Ross* 208

X. EVALUATING SPECIAL EDUCATION PROGRAMS: PROCESS AND OUTCOME, *Ian M. Evans* and *Elvera M. Weld* 232

Section Four
Conclusion

XI. ELEMENTS OF INTEGRATION, *Douglas P. Biklen, Alison Ford,* and *Dianne L. Ferguson* 256

NAME INDEX 273
SUBJECT INDEX 279
INFORMATION ABOUT MEMBERSHIP IN THE SOCIETY 283
PUBLICATIONS OF THE SOCIETY 285

Section One
THE FORM OF EDUCATION

CHAPTER I

Redefining Schools

DOUGLAS P. BIKLEN

Autobiographical accounts of people with disabilities speak of longed for inclusion in society, of wanting to be seen as ordinary, of hope for a society in which disability does not evoke prejudice, discrimination, and stereotyping.[1] Happily, this sought after social condition is not just a vision. There are two areas of people's lives in which the experience of ordinariness is *now* occasionally achieved. These areas are self-definition and family relationships. In a third area, namely social institutions (e.g., schools), unconditional inclusion has been more difficult, though not without some emerging form, as we will see in a later section of this chapter.

In terms of self-definition, people with disabilities frequently describe themselves as ordinary and wonder why others do not see them in the same way. Not surprisingly, one of the first national self-help organizations for people labeled retarded is called "People First." The name declares that disability is a quality, not an all-defining characteristic. In the minds of many people so labeled, it may not even exist. In his article on this question, Robert Bogdan demonstrates the error in judgment of assuming that saying "I am not disabled" is a defense mechanism, a denial of the truth. He quotes one man who had spent six years in a mental retardation institution: "I have never really

---

This article was prepared with support of the Research and Training Center on Community Integration, funded by the National Institute on Handicapped Research, U.S. Department of Education (Cooperative Agreement No. G0085C03503). The opinions expressed herein are solely those of the author and no official endorsement by the U.S. Department of Education should be inferred.

thought of myself as retarded. I never really had that ugly feeling down deep."[2] He quotes another as saying "The worst word that I have to be called is retarded. That's because I am not retarded."[3] To these people, retardation is an epithet, like calling somone dumb or bad. They have heard the term retardation used to justify their own former institutionalization, but they themselves believe they were sent away for other reasons, such as a death in the family and an absence of alternative groups with which to affiliate. They believe that the term retardation denies their humanness, their diversity, and their feelings. In Bogdan's words, people labeled retarded who reject the label "have come to understand the caricature painted by the name retardate."[4] This is a view shared among many disability rights spokespersons. For example, Anne Peters writes: "Many of us reject being called either 'handicapped' or 'disabled'—neither feels right to us—we don't consider ourselves to be the kind of person such a word conjures up in our minds."[5]

One of the truly remarkable aspects of labeled people's abilities to define themselves as able, as fully human beings, is that they do it in the face of a literal barrage of opposite messages. Leonard Kriegel discussed this dilemma in his classic article on the social meaning of disability.[6] He recounts an incident in which he got into a heated argument with another boy in his neighborhood. Angered by something the boy said, Kriegel challenged him to a fight:

He agreed, but most reluctantly. Fighting a cripple would not reflect creditably on him in the neighborhood, but, true to the obligations of adolescence, he knew that not to have accepted would be a sign of weakness and sentimentality.[7]

So they had their fight and true to expectations, the other boy won. But Kriegel remembers feeling satisfied: "It enabled me to forget momentarily the fact that I was a cripple. We met if not as equals then at least as combatants on the same battleground."[8] The feeling of ordinariness lasted only moments, however, until Kriegel overheard the other boy's mother instructing him never to fight with a "cripple." A fight between two boys was redefined as a fight between a boy and a cripple.

Denise Karuth, a person with multiple sclerosis and one of the contributors to Brightman's *Ordinary Moments*, echoes this theme of preserving a sense of self in the face of all kinds of contradictory attitudes including excessive solicitude, pity, and despair. She describes a humorous account with a plumber who was nearly overwhelmed by pity when he discovered that she used a wheelchair, is blind, and has a seeing eye dog:

Holy Jesus! God bless you, ma'am. I'm really sorry. God bless you. If you ever have any trouble with your sink or electricity you just call this number. Call any time, even at night. Just tell them you're a handicapped apartment and they'll come right out. God bless you. Jesus God![9]

If given the opportunity, Karuth would like the world to know how she thinks about herself. And it is not at all the way the plumber sees it:

Look, I appreciate your concern, but my life isn't that bad. Sure, It's not quite uninterrupted bliss, but whose life is? It's a good life. I work and play and have friends and make love and mistakes and get bored now and again just like you. So put your handkerchiefs away. First impressions aside, I'm a lot more like you than you probably imagine.[10]

The importance of disability as a defining characteristic puzzles the person who sees his or her humanness as a dominant reason for assuming peer status with other people. Why does disability get in the way of other people seeing this point of view?

Next, let us consider relationships. People labeled disabled are not alone in their perception of disability as a quality rather than a separate status (i.e., "the disabled"). In relations with friends and families we can sometimes see the same theme, acceptance of humanness and rejection of disability as all-defining. The attitudes of parents on this topic may be reflected in their response to the question, "Would you like your child normal?" Featherstone speaks about people labeled disabled and families when she writes: "[T]he disability is . . . woven into their past; it is bound up with what they have lived through and what they are. They could not remove the painful threads without ripping out the whole fabric of their existence. To have the best you must take the worst."[11]

Certainly some parents have great difficulty raising a child with a disability, particularly when society often seems to be at odds with the goal of accepting the child. But most parents of children with disabilities, like parents in general, come to know, respect, and love their children. What other people see in their children is not necessarily what they see. A mother, Mary Lou, for example, disputes what professionals say about her son Mel:

They had said that he was severely retarded, severely behaviorally disordered, hyperactive, epileptic, depending upon which reports you read. He had about ten different labels. But I always had the sense that there was a bright little kid under there.[12]

This mother is not saying that her son does not have a disability. Rather, she seems to be saying "give him a chance, see him as a person, let him into your world." She views her son as someone who, like other people, interacts with the environment. She remembers that he would cry and throw himself on the floor of the car if he thought he was being taken back to the institution out of which she had adopted him. "He has a tantrum," she relates, "whenever he sees a little can of pudding" because little cans of pudding were commonly used rewards in behavior modification programs at the institution. When he first moved out of the institution, he would hoard food:

He will tell you how big people used to steal his food. When he first moved in with me, he used to hide food every night under his mattress and pillow. He would try to hide food under his shirt and sneak up to his room and hide it under his mattress. We kept telling him there was plenty of food. Eventually he went from hiding things to opening cupboards and looking to make sure there was food. He was amazed that food came from the store; he would tell you it came on the elevator. At the institution that was his experience; it came on a cart off the elevator.

She explains that when he left the institution he could not talk and that he knew only five signs: eat, run, more, music, and help. With her instruction he learned 200 signs within the first three months outside the institution. Also, he loves to go to the symphony with his mother. Thus while he might be called a difficult or challenging child, a child who has severe tantrums, a child who has alternative ways of communicating, he is not easily categorized.

Would Mary Lou's attitudes toward her son be different if her son had not learned so many signs, if he did not enjoy the symphony, and if we were unable to explain his behavior on the basis of his institutional experiences? Of course, we cannot know for certain. Yet it appears that Mary Lou has an unconditional love for her son and that attitude certainly plays a large part in her ability to understand him. In other words, what matters is not how much students know but who they are and how people see them. As Ferguson and Asch convey in their chapter in this book, parents are a rich and available resource not merely to advocate for their children, although that is a crucial role, but also to help others understand who they are. The idea, for example, that a student with a severe intellectual disability has a sense of humor, has clearly defined interests, and can communicate, albeit in unconventional ways, may surprise us but should hopefully also delight us. It certainly contrasts with the stark, clinical terms (e.g., retarded, autistic, disturbed) by which such a student is often described and defined. Other parents who have not seen the dramatic progress in their children that Mary Lou conveys about Mel nevertheless often speak exuberantly about their humanness and of their participation in life.

By saying "forget the labels," parents, friends, or people labeled disabled are not saying "we do not have what you say we have" but rather, "it's not exactly as you think it is," or "we are not just that," or "don't make it into more than it is." Mary Lou typifies this perspective and spirit when she speaks of her son Mel's disability: "Labels. It is so easy to label a kid. And, yes, functionally Mel was behaving as a severely retarded kid. It would have been easy to dismiss him through all of those labels rather than to see what was beyond them."

A central reason that parents talk and write about their children is so that others, including people in schools, can see what they see. To view their children only as "disabled" misses their humanity. As Mary Lou's stories of Mel suggest, this humanness comes through in unexpected ways:

He was sitting on the couch quietly with the book open and just crying. I couldn't imagine what was happening. He had never had quiet moments like that at that point, or at least very rarely. He was looking at Burt Blatt's book *Christmas in Purgatory* (an exposé of abuse in mental retardation institutions). He looked up and said "big house." It was like he recognized that this was about where he had been. I sat down and we went through the book together. He just cried. At this point he had very little language. It was just amazing to me. . . . He has shown me time and time again, "don't underestimate me and don't judge me by your outside perceptions."

Schools: Special, Not Ordinary

Many parents want schools to approximate the inclusive society that is envisioned in the autobiographies of people with disabilities and in firsthand accounts of parents such as Mary Lou. Some want and expect only that schools merely recognize their children with disabilities as more than the clinical terms that have been attached to them. But how well have the schools done? Put another way, what is the place of disability in schools and of students classified as disabled?

Suppose for a moment that schools had not yet been created and that it was our task to invent them. And suppose we wanted schools to be instruments for discriminating against certain groups of people, for example, those with somewhat less than average intellectual abilities, those with more than 80 decibel hearing loss in both ears, those who use wheelchairs for mobility, those who seem inattentive in formal learning situations, and so forth. Ironically, many of the elements in such schools might closely resemble the structure, processes, and content of today's schools. This is not to say that public education has been purposely designed to discriminate against students labeled "disabled" or that it always has this effect. But, intention aside, many elements of schooling separate those labeled "disabled" from others, identify and often intensify differences between this group and others, and treat them differentially.

STRUCTURE

The principal mechanism by which schools educate students they perceive as different is special education. That the concept of special education has burgeoned into a field with its own separate structures, often a school within a school, a district within a district, or in some instances an altogether separate district (e.g., an intermediate school district) probably reflects several factors. Among the explanations are these: (a) special classes for mildly disabled students serve as a safety valve for the school's lack of success with certain students—42 percent of all special education students are labeled "learning disabled," all are referred from regular classes as a result of difficulties in regular classrooms, and together they are not distinguishable from students in regular classes who are labeled "slow learners"; (b) special education accommodates those perceived as abnormal (e.g., students labeled "severely retarded"); (c) special education also seems to attract minority and male students whom it identifies as "emotionally disturbed"; (d) special education offers special techniques (e.g., sign language instruction, mobility training, and adapted physical education); and (e) special education promises to individualize instruction. Tomlinson demonstrates how the rise of special education occurred simultaneously with the elaboration of professional psychological assessment, each survey of students leading to an expansion of special education ranks.[13] Education's pursuit of professionalism coincided with and made popular the growth of special education. In chapter 2 of this book, Ferguson examines how professionalism continues to shape the field. Special education identified students on the margin of school culture and made them its own. Thus, not surprisingly, passage in the U.S. of P.L. 94-142, the Education for All Handicapped Children Act, prophesied and realized an expansion of the percentage of public school students labeled "disabled" from 6 to 12 percent.[14] Similarly, Great Britain's recent national study of special education envisioned 20 percent of the school population labeled.[15]

The organization of special education services bespeaks its separation and differentiation from regular education. Large school districts typically identify a senior administrator as special education director. Very small districts that cannot afford a separate administrator locate the coordination of special education in the office of the director of pupil personnel, who is then characterized as doing double duty by attending to special and regular students. In some states, special education is not a part of the local school district at all. Rather, intermediate, regional, or special school districts provide special education, sometimes in separate special schools or in the local schools where the special school district may rent space. Regional program teachers who work in local schools report that they feel like intruders, *in* the school but not *of* it, responsible to a regional school board rather than the local school, often serving students who because they have been congregated from multiple districts are themselves outsiders. Not surprisingly, states in which the intermediate or regional school districts have the authority to construct or own school buildings are also the states that are high users of separate disability schools (e.g., New York, Ohio, Missouri). Together, America's school districts employ 240,000 special education teachers and 224,000 other specialists or support staff.[16] Such administrative arrangements and special staffing encourage a perception that the education of students identified as "disabled" is not the business of "regular education."

Students perceived as having problems in the regular class find themselves referred out to resource room programs or special classes. Typically, 90 percent of those referred are placed. Ironically, the popularity of "refer-and-place" runs counter to knowledge about its effectiveness. Criticisms of such practices include the following: (a) separate classes have not been proven educationally superior to regular class instruction, (b) separate classes may impose stigma on referred students, (c) resource and other special classes do not address the possibility that a student's difficulties in the typical class stem from ineffective educational practices in the regular class, (d) assessment practices yield greater than expected referrals of minority students, and (e) resource programs and other mild disability programs are populated by students indistinguishable from other students in regular classes who have not been labeled.[17]

Special education might be likened to the repair shop. Students perceived as having problems, like something broken, are sent to resource rooms, special classes, even special schools or institutions, to be repaired and later returned. Often there are special classes for each category—emotionally disturbed, learning disabled, hearing impaired, and visually handicapped—although some states and districts now offer noncategorical classes that group students with different labels. Unlike a real repair shop, however, in special education many students, indeed the preponderance of them (excluding those with speech impairments that are either cured or simply disappear by the time students reach the secondary level), never escape the "special" label. They stay in the repair shop.

Other forms of special services include physical therapy, occupational therapy, speech therapy, and adaptive physical education. These activities called related services can be integrated into the subject area curricula and into the ebb and flow of classroom activities. But typically they are not. More usually, students accompany a specialist to a corner of the classroom, leave the regular classroom, or even leave the school building to receive these related services or therapies.

Just as the structure of programs and the organization of professionals differentiate students labeled "disabled" as special, so too do school finance practices. Public education typically relies on three sources of financing: local property tax revenues, state funds, and federal funds. Local revenues provide the initial support for education, but since local communities vary tremendously in their ability to tax themselves, state and federal allocations to public education often help to equalize community differences. Poor communities may receive proportionately more funds per child or per program than rich ones. The standard state funding mechanisms for special services include one of the following: direct subsidy for specific services (e.g., transportation, counseling, resource room programs); funding of types of personnel (e.g., special teachers, itinerant teachers); or per capita student funding. The latter may be a set amount per labeled student, a percentage of the extra cost that is presumed associated with educating a special as opposed to a regular student, or a weighted amount, based on a different percentage for each type of disability. Each mechanism, whether for specific services, personnel, or students, differentiates education funding for students labeled "disabled" from that of their nondisabled peers. States *could* fund the education of all students without identifying any students or programs as special, but they do not. Persistence in funding labeled students or programs may reflect concern that students with disabilities would not receive much needed special services if unlabeled.

It is not hard to imagine the programmatic imperatives that can derive from such funding mechanisms. If state reimbursement rates provide more funding for learning disabilities than for "slow learners" or underachievers, for example, the ranks of students labeled "learning disabled" can be expected to expand. Similarly, if a state provides near total funding for certain types of services (e.g., for private or state residential schools), and a far less substantial allotment for serving students in their home districts, local school boards might be tempted to "place" more students outside the district. These effects of fiscal incentives have been well documented.[18]

By establishing special funding mechanisms to support special education, state and federal government attempted to ensure equal access to educational opportunity. Ironically, however, earmarked funds for special education may confirm the impression that the education of students labeled "disabled" is an add-on to an already existing system of education. In other words, is disability a quality that automatically differentiates students, or is it that our ways of thinking about, organizing, and *funding* education and other social relations merely make it so?

PROCESS

Special education is intended to identify and remediate individual needs, to ensure the student "an appropriate education." Its processes comprise what is commonly called a clinical or individual model. By law, states and local school districts must look for students suspected of having disabilities. Then, they must evaluate them individually. Specific guidelines delineate acceptable evaluation methods: tests and evaluation materials must be in a child's native language or mode of communication; tests must examine specific areas of learning and not simply produce a general intelligence quotient; professionally trained personnel must administer the assessment; no single test or procedure may constitute the entire evaluation; and a "multidisciplinary team," including at least one teacher or other specialist with expertise in the suspected area of disability, must be involved in the evaluation. The evaluation is to be comprehensive in examining all aspects of learning related to the suspected disability. Further, the evaluation team is to consider information from a broad range of sources, including home, teacher recommendations, social and cultural factors, physical examinations, and so forth.[19]

Interestingly, the process of evaluation is seen as leading to *placement*. Federal law specifically instructs evaluation teams to "interpret evaluation data" and to make "placement decisions." In other words, placement is synonymous with special treatment. Nonplacement can only occur if the student is found nondisabled or if the state allows specialized services in the typical class as an integrated part of the typical program. Such practices are rare, in part at least because the law does not envision them.

P.L. 94-142 requires that states "insure that a continuum of alternative placements is available to meet the needs of handicapped children for special education and related services." The law envisions at least the following special services in the placement continuum: regular classes with supports (e.g., resource rooms, consultants in the classroom, and itinerant instruction); special classes; special schools; home instruction; and instruction in hospitals and institutions. By articulating such a continuum, the law legitimizes this range of placements, including disabled-only classes, disabled-only schools, and institutionalization.

What are the implicit assumptions of these evaluation and placement processes? Obviously, the law presumes that some children have distinctly different needs than their peers and that these needs are best identified as different and remediated in a distinct fashion. Further, there is the assumption that certain types of educational placements, different in location and composition (i.e., student characteristics, content) from regular education, can best serve students with perceived disabilities. With the continuum of special services ranging from a combination of the regular class and resource assistance to institutionalization, and regulatory language that links integrated placements to the student's ability to benefit from the instructional setting, severity of disability is commonly associated with greater degrees of separation from "regular" education. The location of a student's placement is seen as a function of the student's individual characteristics more than of the school's nature or performance.

In such a context, integration and, therefore, ordinariness does not come easily. Students with disabilities, cast in the role of outsiders, must prove themselves in order to gain a place in the mainstream. Thus the most common form of integration finds one teacher working out an arrangement with another teacher (we call this a "teacher deal,") to move a student with a disability from the special class back into the regular class. The condition of the deal is that the student must succeed, albeit with help or special consideration. It is an agreement that more often than not lacks institutional support. It is a kind of experiment in which, if the student stumbles, the hypothesis is thought wrong.

A number of recent studies on the evaluation and placement process and on actual placements raise serious doubts about both the correctness of individual placements and the legitimacy of the continuum of placements. In one study, Algozzine and Ysseldyke presented school personnel from a variety of different disciplines with referral information.[20] Each subject was given data on one individual randomly chosen from a pool of sixteen cases. Additional data were available on request. The data for each of the sixteen cases were all within the range of normal development and behavior. Yet more than half of the professionals identified the cases as disabled and eligible for special education. These findings appear to concur with actual referral practice. When researchers have applied the standards used to identify learning disabled students to the typical school population, in this case third, fifth, and twelfth graders, they found that 85 percent of the students qualified for learning disabilities classification and treatment.[21] Similarly, when they compared low-achieving fourth graders with fourth graders classified as learning disabled, they could not distinguish the groups. As we will see in the next major section of this chapter as well as in subsequent chapters, what Ysseldyke and his colleagues found for students with mild disabilities has parallels for students with severe disabilities. While students with severe retardation, autism, and other more demonstrable differences cannot easily be mistaken for the "regular" education student, the rightfulness of separate placement has not gone unquestioned. Indeed, surveys of "promising practices" for educating students with severe disabilities argue for schooling that brings together disabled and nondisabled students.[22]

National data on classification and placement practices suggest little clarity about who is disabled and how and where particular students ought to be educated.[23] The confusion concerns not only students labeled "learning disabled," but virtually every disability category. California, for example, places less than 1 percent of all students labeled "mentally retarded" in separate disability-only schools, while Delaware and New York place more than 30 percent in separate schools and Maryland over 40 percent.[24] Of the students labeled "emotionally disturbed," Ohio educates 4 percent in regular classes while Wisconsin keeps 88 percent in regular classes.[25] New York has 50 percent more students labeled "emotionally disturbed" than any other state and Ohio has 10,000 more students labeled "retarded" than any other state.[26] Obviously clinical decisions regarding special education placement and whether a student is integrated or segregated may reflect different theoretical predispositions of the professionals who make them. But, the national data on school placements compel us to consider the causative power of nonclinical factors as well. These other factors include: the prior existence of disabled-only schools; state funding practices that encourage segregated or integrated placements; separate-school lobbies; and expanding or declining enrollments in typical schools (i.e., are labeled students the last admitted to and first excluded from typical schools under conditions of limited space?) From this viewpoint, in the matter of integrated or segregated schooling, it is more instructive to know where students live than the predispositions of their assessors.

The absence of consistency in special education classifications and placements has caused a number of leading scholars in the field to question special education's legitimacy or usefulness. They have tended to recommend moderating its separate status, cutting back on the numbers and enrollments of special classes, and integrating more students in regular classes. Dunn, for example, asked if special education for students with mild disabilities was justifiable.[27] Reynolds warned: make education as least special as possible.[28] Government policy holds out as a goal integration as the placement of preference. And a few educators have discussed and even advocated the dissolution of special education as a separate enterprise, urging instead a special/regular education merger.[29] Ysseldyke, Algozinne, and Epps "question the basis of special education" placements and by implication, special education itself.[30] Similarly, Wang, Reynolds, and Walberg, as well as Will, speak of "rethinking" special education.[31]

CONTENT

Educators talk about special education as if it were different than "regular" education and as if students classified or labeled "disabled" are basically different than unlabeled students. The initial step in rendering a student different is in the referral. The act of referral suggests that the child is "suspected" of having a problem. Then, with classification comes a label that takes on an encompassing quality. A student who was having difficulties in learning becomes a "mentally retarded student," a "learning disabled student," an "emotionally disturbed student," a "blind student." The disability, once a suspected characteristic, then an identified quality, now becomes *the* defining factor of the student. With the label and a placement to go with it, disability achieves what sociologists call "master status." Those who interact with or observe the labeled person have trouble seeing a person; they see instead a disabled person and all of the stereotypes associated with that status.

Consider, for example, some of the ways that disability labels permeate the culture of a school. Students with disabilities may be transported to and from school in special buses for the handicapped. They may attend special classes, perhaps called the "emotional disturbance," the "trainable," or the "L.D." classes rather than being named by subject area or grade level, perhaps congregated in one wing of the school. Special students may have a shorter school day. They may eat their lunches in their classrooms rather than in the cafeteria. They may be the only groups in the school not required to participate in annual achievement testing. When all other students have homework, they may have none. They often do not participate in extracurricular activities. The labels they wear may target them for both derisive humor and patronizing solicitude from their nonlabeled peers. Terms like "clinical treatment," "therapy," "intervention," "disorders," and "diagnosis" evoke images of medicine and laboratories rather than of education and schools. In the characteristic situation of any identified minority group, students labeled "disabled" become at once invisible (i.e., not recognized as one of the normal group) and highly visible (i.e., on stage, being evaluated, unusual, and therefore not ordinary).

Some, but not all, of these problems are challenged by P.L. 94-142. Students with disabilities cannot legally be prohibited from extracurricular programs, for example, or educated for a shorter time than nondisabled students. But many of the practices, (e.g., separate transportation, labeling) are allowable or at least arguable under the law.

The individual educational programming (IEP) requirements of the federal special education law specify an individualized approach that has become synonymous with special education:

(A) a statement of the present levels of educational performance of such child, (B) a statement of annual goals, including short-term instructional objectives, (C) a statement of the specific educational services to be provided to such child, and the extent to which such child will be able to participate in regular educational programs, (D) the projected date for initiation and anticipated duration of such services, and (E) appropriate objective criteria and evaluation procedures and schedules for determining, on at least an annual basis, whether instructional objectives are being achieved.[32]

The positive aspects of individualized planning include: teacher emphasis on students' unique needs; recognition that students have different styles of learning and paces for learning; opportunity to consider alternative strategies of instruction; a structure by which parents, teachers, and other personnel can share ideas and plan together; a process that links student abilities with instructional goals and objectives; and the requirement that student progress be evaluated.

Despite these benefits, however, the IEP creates two problems for students with disabilities. First, as the principal framework within P.L. 94-142 for characterizing special education, the individual focus of this approach tends to shift attention from school programs and school performance to individual performance. As Ferguson explains in chapter 2, this has a potential "blame-the-victim" effect, placing responsibility on individual students to achieve within the individually prescribed opportunity available to them rather than focusing attention on the effect of school philosophy, school environment, peer groupings, and instructional approaches, and overall school performance. While we have observed some schools using IEPs in a more integrated fashion with the school program, an all too common approach is to view the IEP as an individual document, somehow separated from the culture of the school as a whole. This approach reinforces the perception of the student with a disability as broken, needing special intervention or a special technique to work. It separates student performance from school performance.

Second, because a similarly detailed, individual approach is not applied to all students, the IEP becomes another of the many structural ways in which students with disabilities are differentiated from the typical student. With the introduction of P.L. 94-142, schools now have IEP and non-IEP students.

An example may help explain the dilemma of the IEPs. In educating a student with a hearing impairment, for example, a major focus is on communication. Curricula are likely to include instruction in sign language or oral communication. Techniques, methods, and materials might include: "speech, language, and auditory training instruction from a specialist; amplification systems;... special seating;... captioned films, good acoustics, and reduction of background noise, special tutoring and review; someone to take notes in class;" and modified curricula.[33] The IEP will specify each of these items. But, the IEP will leave many unanswered questions, all related to the student's place in school. How does the student's curriculum fit with the curriculum of the other students, the curricular goals of the school, and the educational atmosphere of the school? What are the attitudes of teachers and peers about disability and other perceived differences? How obtrusively or unobtrusively are special services presented?

As Evans and Weld explain in their chapter on evaluation in this volume, educators have tended to evaluate regular education through individual and program measures but to evaluate special education in terms of individual performance (i.e., IEP goal achievement) alone or not to evaluate it at all. This probably reflects the perception of special education content as expert technique applied to fix individuals rather than as concepts and approaches that could transform education in general. We make an icon of individualization. Put another way, in terms of the example noted above, the student who has a severe hearing impairment deserves the kind of individualizing adaptations described above but the quality of the labeled student's education cannot be understood individually apart from its relation to the school context. Technique is never context free. We can wonder at least what the student's experience in school would be like if the school struggled to learn about the culture of deafness, if students could take sign language as a subject, if the study of literature and social studies incorporated analyses of materials and issues related to being deaf in a hearing society, in other words, if the education of a deaf student meant not only modifying one student's program but meant changing a school.

In light of the civil rights origins of P.L. 94-142, it is ironic now to suggest that the law and the practices that flow from it may be partially responsible for the stereotyping, discrimination, and isolation that labeled students experience. Much of special education's recent development has been conceived of as an expression of civil rights.

The federal law guarantees students "with handicapping conditions" the right to an "appropriate education." The IEP requirement is clearly a response to prior conditions in which students with disabilities were either excluded from school altogether or were forced to accept inappropriate placements in available school programs. Parents have filed scores of lawsuits to win due process rights, the right to an education, and the right to integrated education. Nevertheless, as we have seen, the structures, processes, and content of special education which emanate from the law and from the profession of special education manifest many of the hallmarks of stereotyping and discrimination. Guarantees of smaller class size, explicit learning contracts (IEPs), multidisciplinary teaching and program planning, instructional strategies geared to student abilities and so forth are not in and of themselves stigmatizing and do not have to effect the wholesale segregation of students with disabilities; in fact they may well be valuable educational strategies for all students. But if they are accompanied by negative labeling, assignment of students to separate routines and spaces, devaluation of students so served, discontinuity in a student's education, with labeled students losing touch with the regular curriculum, and failure to integrate the special techniques into the life of the school, then they may have a discriminatory effect. Thus we may ask, despite a civil rights motivation, has society promoted the physical and psychological exclusion of labeled students from their unlabeled peers and from the mainstream of education? If it has, could it be otherwise? Is there a progressive role for special education technique? Is it possible to educate students in such a way that certain students are *not* rendered outsiders? Can students labeled "disabled" ever be provided the adaptive education they need and yet achieve the ordinariness they desire?

Schools: A New and Different Vision

Is there an alternative to a system of special and regular education which separates students, making one group the insiders and another the outsiders? Is it possible, in other words, to educate all students in a way that makes none an outsider? To be more specific, can we create classes so that they accommodate a broad range of differences? Can education individualize in a way that is normative rather than exclusionary and deviancy making? Can instruction in basic language or speech skills, for example, be provided to students in the same manner as instruction in writing or reading? Can community-based instruction in independent living skills become comparable in status as social studies? If the answer to any of these questions is "yes," then we must surely rethink and reformulate special education.

Our earlier discussion of schools' experiences with integration has suggested that integration has not always come easy; not all schools have embraced it as a value or goal. But more than a few schools *have* made integration central to their ethos. In effect, some schools have declared integration a value to which they are as committed as to educating both boys and girls or as to providing mathematics and reading as core instructional subjects. In these settings, integration is new, so much so that the teachers and administrators openly admit they are searching for what works rather than applying the known and proven. Yet in these examples we find data that begin to approximate the spirit and vision of a refashioned society that is so vividly portrayed in the autobiographies of people with disabilities. Through two examples drawn from observations of integration programs, including teachers' accounts of their own experiences with integrating individual children and parent perspectives on what integration means to them and their children, we begin to encounter some of the practices that make such a vision more than mere fantasy.

The first example concerns a lower-middle-class district which we shall call Elmwood Center. Recognized by the National Diffusion Network as an exemplary program, the Elmwood model cannot easily be characterized as a particular approach, although teachers and administrators speak of their attempt to apply educational research to day-to-day practice. They refer to elements of schooling (for example, school and classroom climate, teacher involvement in curriculum design, team teaching, experiential learning, instructional grouping, and measurement of student performance [outcomes]). Eighteen months before we visited the district, it brought eighty-nine mildly and moderately disabled students back into the schools. These students had previously been in classes operated by a special intermediate school district. Initially, Elmwood merely replicated the traditional approach, educating students with disabilities in "satellite" or special classes. At the beginning of the second year, the district abandoned disability labels and special education groupings. One administrator explains the school's approach, "We believe in inclusion, so we have to ask ourselves, how do we manifest that? You have to create the organizational structure for inclusion, or for any belief, otherwise you are constantly finding that you are compromising on your values." Applying this philosophy to the education of students with disabilities, he explained, "you don't create change (i.e., inclusion) by changing special ed (i.e., part of the system). The change process must look at philosophy (of education) overall."

In the fifth grade in Elmwood Center, as in all of the elementary grades, there are no students called emotionally disturbed, retarded, or learning disabled. Ask the English teacher if there are any special education students in the class and she responds, "three, the young lady in the pink sweatshirt, and the boy in the striped shirt, and the young fellow in the blue shirt; I think that's about it here." There are no resource rooms. All students are assigned to a homeroom; there is no special homeroom for classified students. There is no special room to which to send students who are perceived as disruptive: "You can't get kids out of your room because they act out. That's a big change; it requires problem solving." The fifth grade includes five teachers, one of whom is a special education teacher. But all of the teachers teach a combination of "classified" and typical students in the standard subject areas, reading, language arts, mathematics, and social studies. Strategies often associated with special education abound (e.g., process consultation, individualizing of instruction, small-group instruction, team teaching, and affective education). None of the groupings of students, whether classes or groups in classes, is designed to include only "classified" students. The special education teacher teaches in the subject areas. An administrator declares: "The special educator is not a resource person to the team. She's a teacher on the team." Interestingly, there seems to be no effort to dissociate the specialist from special techniques or to deny students with disabilities the uniqueness of some of their needs, only to minimize the different status of particular students and teachers. This practice of making the specialist an ordinary team member mimics the delabeling of students.

A teacher reports, "Last year when I was called a special ed teacher, my kids were constantly being told 'Oh, you're one of those kids'." Then, on the first day of school, one of her students from the previous year's class (it had been a traditional resource program) came up to her and announced proudly, "Guess what, I'm in a regular class now." The teachers report similar changes in their own relations in school: "What's nice is that I'm just another teacher, not a special ed teacher," one teacher declared. These anecdotal comments confirm a finding that has been noted in other integrated programs, namely that physical proximity as well as strategies to minimize stigma and to foster interaction yield improved attitudes and interaction.[34]

Our second example is of an urban elementary school that we shall call the Washington School. More as a result of intense pressure and encouragement brought by parents of students with severe disabilities, Washington developed a variety of what it calls integrated classes where special and regular education teachers combine to co-teach classes of nondisabled and autistic students. These classes have the same space and number of students as two classes. A regular education teacher and a special education teacher and one or two teaching assistants team to create one class. They have two classrooms for their use, thus making it possible to have large- and small-group instruction. This approach has been described by Knoblock and also by Biklen.[35] Unlike the Elmwood approach, students are still labeled, although the staff avoid using traditional disability labels, referring instead to "typical" and "special" students. Also, the teachers refer to students' abilities or disabilities descriptively (e.g., Mary communicates by sign and gestures—she knows a dozen signs; Jack does better with hands-on materials than with abstract presentations or materials—he's very social but he lacks appropriate social skills). The classes are not called "special classes" but rather "integrated classes." Interestingly, one of the nondisabled students told us: "They shouldn't call them integrated classes, they're just classes." An obvious difference from Elmwood, which integrates students with mild disabilities, these classes serve severely disabled, even some multiply handicapped students, alongside nondisabled students. Curricular strategies include such concepts as partial participation, cooperative learning, parallel programming (students working on the same subject area but at different levels), peer tutoring, peer modeling, integrated therapies, group projects, cooperative goal structuring, "hands-on materials," in-school jobs for all students, small-group and individual learning centers, educational field trips, matching of teaching methods to learner styles, integrated "specials" such as art and music, and "community-based" and "functional" programming, use of "natural environments" with "natural cues," all of which are described more fully in chapters in this book by Zanella et al., Stainback and Stainback, Ford and Black, and in the concluding chapter. When asked what integration means to her, one mother of a student in the program explained that it was more than one thing: integration meant her son David is learning how to tolerate change; it meant he is learning from fellow, nondisabled students how to behave, and what behavior would not be accepted; and it meant that fellow students might see him as more than their abstract stereotype of a disabled (i.e., incompetent) student:

It's nice to have typical children have the experience of being very impressed with someone whom they regard as handicapped. When he was in third grade he could spell better than many of the third graders. They were impressed that he could do that. I think they had a sense of his intellectual capacity, and yet they thought, "look how he spells." Occasionally I have heard stories of kids being impressed by his effort when something was clearly so hard for him, yet he mastered it. And sometimes they're impressed that he controls his behavior. David had a period at his elementary school when he could not sit next to someone. It was an automatic poke. I remember being told that after that period was over, one child remarked: "It is nice I can sit by David. He doesn't poke any more." They were pleased with that.

At the secondary school level, David's program was a "community curriculum," including a job in a university office where he helped package admissions materials, and recreation at the local YMCA where he went jogging along with business people. As a curriculum strategy, his integration experiences were extending from the school into his future environment, the community.

The theme of securing a place in the nondisabled world surfaces time and again in parent discussions about school integration. Mary Lou Accetta, the parent of Melvin who was mentioned earlier, recalls an incident in which the students in her son's class were to receive levels tests in mathematics. As the teacher readied the tests Melvin became agitated. He started to run around the room, laughing and throwing things. His teacher immediately understood that he was probably uncomfortable about the levels test. She said to him, "All of the fourth graders are going to take levels tests, Mel. Are you going to take levels tests?" "I don't know" he responded. The fact that he responded with a sentence was in itself a kind of breakthrough for a child who typically communicated with signs or one or two words. As the teacher surmised, Mel wanted to be one of the group. If other students were going to take the levels tests, then he too wanted to take one. And so the teacher proceeded to give him a levels test along with the other youngsters, although his was at a different skill level. Mary Lou recounts the incident as it was told to her by the teacher:

He ran around telling everybody he was taking levels tests and then Mel, who usually has no attention span to speak of (seven minutes) sat for an hour and a half taking the levels test. Every time the teacher suggested that he might want to take a break he said: "No, more work." Even after he got beyond questions and problems that he was able to answer, he sat marking the test and saying: "Same as the kids, same as the kids."

Obviously, accounts of integration for students such as Mel or David are tentative. Teachers and schools are exploring what integration means, in terms of curricula, in terms of helping students relate to each other, in allowing students to feel part of the group, and in relation to their own attentiveness to student feelings and experiences. At times, the vision of what parents and a few teachers and school administrators want seems clearer than the practices to achieve it. For example, how much should teachers focus on student's social experiences and emotional growth? Are there ways of organizing learning and student groups in schools so that students with more unique needs are not treated as fundamentally different? What are the curricula that pay attention to the future skills that students with disabilities need and how do these fit with the so-called regular education curricula? Is there a clear relationship between curriculum thought for disabled and nondisabled students? If there are progressive, integrating curricula that promise to bring disabled and nondisabled students together in a unified educational experience, and if there are curricula that address the challenges of students who are failing in regular classes, of the students with the most severe and multiple disabilities, and of students with emotional problems, what are the key principles behind these curricula?

In each of the subsequent chapters, we address these and related issues. Ferguson, for example, explores the social history of special education and its place in the larger context of education. She addresses the difficult question of how to interpret special education practice, as professional/technical enclave or fundamental equity reform. She discusses the social functions of special education in schools and society, then asks what a future agenda for special and regular education might look like. In two subsequent chapters, we look at the assumptions behind special education for students with severe as well as mild disabilities. Zanella, Brown, and their colleagues outline concepts to bring students with the most severe disabilities into the heart of educational reform. Sapon-Shevin explains the tortuous history of mild disability labels and offers a new framework for reconceptualizing mild disabilities education and, by definition, general education as well.

To ensure that our conversation about the nature of education for students with disabilities is grounded in the experiences of affected people, namely students with disabilities and their parents, as well as professional educators, we asked Philip Ferguson (a parent) and

Adrienne Asch (a person with a disability) to survey their own experiences as well as the autobiographical literature on disability and schooling. What emerges is not only a consciousness about the consumer perspective but also an urgency for fundamental reform in special education and general education.

In Section Three we address issues of practice. How can schools and teachers rethink classrooms and education so that a diverse student body receives an education, with none labeled? What are the curricula for students with severe disabilities and how do they relate to the existing curricula in schools? How can schools accommodate students who have aggressive, disruptive behavior? How should the new, integrated classroom look? How would it be organized? Who would be in it? What materials and teaching strategies would we find in it? Stainback and Stainback address these and related questions in their chapter on classroom organization. In their chapter, Evans and Weld ask how schools should evaluate the educational experiences of students with disabilities. Most special education programming has not been evaluated, presumably because of the difficulties of standardizing assessment of programs that emphasize individualization. If evaluation is possible, should it occur for individual students or programs, or both? And finally, if schools can conceivably approximate a vision of the integrated society articulated by parents and by people with disabilities, what are the elements of that vision? What are the accommodations that schools could make to accomplish the inclusion of students with disabilities into the educational mainstream? The editors of this volume explore that question in the final chapter when they ask, "What are these elements of integration?"

FOOTNOTES

1. Alan J. Brightman, ed., *Ordinary Moments: The Disabled Experience* (Baltimore, MD: University Park Press, 1985); Children's Defense Fund, *Children Out of School in America* (Washington, DC: Washington Research Project, 1974); Barbara Cutler, *Unraveling the Special Education Maze* (Champaign, IL: Research Press, 1981); P.L. 94-142, *Education for All Handicapped Children Act, 1975*): U.S. Department of Education, *Seventh Annual Report to Congress on the Implementation of Public Law 94-142* (Washington, DC: Government Printing Office, 1985).

2. Robert Bogdan, "What Does It Mean When a Person Says, 'I Am Not Retarded'?" *Education and Training of the Mentally Retarded* 15 (February 1980): 76.

3. Ibid.

4. Ibid., p. 77.

5. Anne Peters, "Do We Have to Be Named?" *Disability Rag* 7 (November/December 1986): 31.

6. Leonard Kriegel, "Uncle Tom and Tiny Tim: Some Reflections on the Cripple as Negro," *American Scholar* 28 (Summer 1969): 428.

7. Ibid.

8. Ibid., p. 429.

9. Denise Karuth, "If I Were a Car, I'd Be a Lemon," in *Ordinary Moments*, ed. Brightman, p. 12.

10. Ibid.

11. Helen Featherstone, *A Difference in the Family* (New York: Penguin, 1982), p. 230.

12. This quotation and all other unreferenced quoted passages in this chapter are taken from records of my interviews with parents and school officials.

13. Sally Tomlinson, *The Sociology of Special Education* (Boston: Routledge and Kegan Paul, 1982).

14. P.L. 94-142, *Education for All Handicapped Children Act*.

15. Department of Education and Science, *Special Educational Needs: The Warnock Report* (London: HMSO, 1978).

16. U.S. Department of Education, *Eighth Annual Report to Congress on the Implementation of the Education of the Handicapped Act* (Washington, DC: U.S. Department of Education, 1986), pp. G21, G24.

17. Douglas Biklen and Nancy Zollers, "The Focus of Advocacy in the Learning Disabilities Field," *Journal of Learning Disabilities* 19 (December 1986): 579-86.

18. Burton Blatt, "Public Policy and the Education of Children with Special Needs," *Exceptional Children* 38, no. 7 (1972): 537-45.

19. P.L. 94-142.

20. Bob Algozzine and James E. Ysseldyke, "Special Education Services for Normal Children: Better Safe Than Sorry?" *Exceptional Children* 48, no. 3 (1981): 238-43.

21. James Ysseldyke, Bob Algozzine, and Susan Epps, "A Logical and Empirical Analysis of Current Practice in Classifying Students as Handicapped," *Exceptional Children* 50 (October 1983): 160-66.

22. Steven Taylor and Dianne Ferguson, "A Summary of Strategies Utilized in Model Programs and Resource Materials," in *Integration of Students with Severe Handicaps*, ed. Susan Stainback and William Stainback (Reston, VA: ERIC Clearinghouse on Handicapped and Gifted Children, Council for Exceptional Children, 1985), pp. 125-45.

23. U.S. Department of Education, *Eighth Annual Report to the Congress on the Implementation of the Education of the Handicapped Act*.

24. Ibid., p. 242.

25. Ibid., p. 243.

26. Ibid.

27. Lloyd Dunn, "Special Education for the Mildly Retarded: Is Much of It Justifiable?" *Exceptional Children* 35, no. 1 (1968): 5-22.

28. Maynard Reynolds, "A Framework for Considering Some Issues in Special Education," *Exceptional Children* 28, no. 7 (1962): 367-70.

29. William Stainback and Susan Stainback, "A Rationale for the Merger of Special and Regular Education," *Exceptional Children* 51, no. 2 (1984): 102-11.

30. Ysseldyke, Algozzine, and Epps, "A Logical and Empirical Analysis of Current Practice in Classifying Students as Handicapped."

31. Margaret C. Wang, Maynard C. Reynolds, and Herbert J. Walberg, eds., *Handbook of Special Education, Research and Practice* (Oxford: Pergamon Press 1986); Madeleine Will, *Educating Students with Learning Problems: A Shared Responsibility* (Washington: DC: U.S. Department of Education, 1986).

32. P.L. 94-142.

33. William L. Heward and Michael D. Orlansky, *Exceptional Children*, 2d ed. (Columbus, OH: Charles E. Merrill, 1984).

34. For a discussion of research on acceptance and interaction, see Luanna Meyer Voeltz, "Program and Curriculum Innovations to Prepare Children for Integration," in *Public School Integration of Severely Handicapped Students*, ed. Nick Certo, Norris Haring, and Robert York (Baltimore: Paul Brookes, 1984), pp. 155-83.

35. Peter Knoblock, *Teaching and Mainstreaming Autistic Children* (Denver: Love Publishing, 1982); Douglas P. Biklen, *Achieving the Complete School* (New York: Teachers College Press, 1985).

Section Two
THE GOALS OF EDUCATION

CHAPTER II

*Severity of Need and Educational Excellence:
Public School Reform and Students with Disabilities*

DIANNE L. FERGUSON

American public schooling in the 1980s once again finds itself caught up in an era of reform. Arising from a variety of political and ideological sources, and carried on a wave of hundreds of reports, studies, and reform initiatives, the overriding message of the current reform discourse is that something is terribly wrong with our schools, but it can be fixed. As artfully put by Seymour Sarason, schools are both the "scapegoat and salvation" for the nation's current social and economic ills.[1]

Of course, all reports are not created equal, either in their critiques or their recommendations. While there is a general level of agreement that something is amiss in American public education, there is less similarity in the various discussions of specific problems or solutions. Despite the range of detail contained in the analyses of various examples, the current school reform literature generally emerges from one of three identifiable perspectives. Perhaps the most dominant in the public media are those reports widely perceived as "conservative" in orientation, and here, *A Nation at Risk* by the National Commission on Excellence seems to have received the most attention.[2] A second group of reports, reflecting a more "liberal" perspective, has appeared in the form of book-length studies rather than commission or task-force reports. Two examples that have received national prominence are Goodlad's *A Place Called School* and Boyer's *High School*.[3] Finally, while achieving much less national exposure, there is a third group—small but significant—of critical responses to both the conservative and liberal critiques that adopts a more progressive and theoretical approach to understanding the processes and functions of schooling reform.[4]

In addition to the general indictment of schools in all this literature, another note of striking agreement is the almost unanimous silence about the extent to which the analyses and recommendations apply to, or affect, students with handicaps in public special education. Although a few examples[5] make mention of "mildly" handicapped students (including those typically labeled "mildly mentally retarded," "learning disabled," and "emotionally disturbed"), even a thorough search of the reform literature leaves one with the overwhelming impression that special education is not even part of public schooling. This silence is particularly surprising since a major result of the 1970s effort at national educational reform explicitly expanded public schooling's mandate to previously excluded students, especially those most severely handicapped. While the reforms of the 1960s do not escape comment in the current spate of reports and monographs, any vision of a different future school experience for students with handicaps is entirely absent.

For its part, special education seems almost as completely to have ignored the schooling debates.[6] Policy debates in special and regular education, for both historical and administrative reasons, tend to occur in parallel tracks—in isolation from each other. However, the increasing physical presence of students with disabilities in the schools and classrooms of our public education system suggests that the issues raised by the current reform discussions must intersect with the experiences of special education if a comprehensive understanding of schools in America is ever to result.

In this chapter I try to locate the areas of intersecting interests between the general reform efforts and special education in the public schools by (a) briefly summarizing some of the major themes to be found in the current reform literature, (b) outlining the implications of both the reports and their critiques for public special education, and (c) describing some of the promising developments within the area of educational reform for students with handicaps (especially those with severe handicaps) that have potential implications for ongoing critical reform in other areas of public schooling.

Current Context of Reform

The form and language of the current reform documents are as important as what those documents actually say. Many of them, especially the various commission and task force reports, seem to be written in the manner of manifestos—heavy on the polemic, strident warnings of impending crisis, and urgent pleas for immediate corrective action. In some cases, though not all, the propaganda value seems to outweigh the attention given to conventional standards of evidence and argument. Certainly such phrases as "a rising tide of mediocrity" and "an act of unthinking, unilateral educational disarmament"—some of the most familiar and dramatic rhetoric from *A Nation at Risk*[7]—seem designed to incite belief and action, if not reflection and research. In various ways, the documents appear primarily as efforts to capture the attention of both distracted citizens and undiscerning professionals with a single, dramatic message. Schools are drab, uninteresting, boring places at best; and, at worst, so dangerously ineffectual as to be a serious threat to "our national defense, our social stability, and our national prosperity."[8] American high schools in particular are portrayed as confused and confusing places. According to one author who actually visited and observed, "they seem unable to put it all together. The institution is adrift."[9]

The solutions put forth in the various reports also share some consistent features. Most call for some degree of return to a "traditional" curriculum emphasizing science, mathematics, English, and social studies; increased testing to improve overall academic achievement; and increased standards for teachers. Some reports note a need for improving the conditions of schools for both teachers and students, raising teacher salaries, and, in various ways, increasing the intellectual and academic rigor present in classrooms. The differences in specific recommendations are important, but the overall tenor of the reform agenda is shared: schooling can be improved only through rigorous, and frequent, enforcement of higher standards for both students and teachers.

It is not my purpose here to present an extensive review or critique of the various examples of reform reports. Others have done that often and well.[10] Having said that, I would like to digress briefly to consider one powerful theme of the reform discussion that may indeed be the basis of such little attention to reform with and within special education.

THE LIMITS OF EGALITARIANISM

Any reform effort seeks to redirect public opinion and action away from what is seen as the status quo. In part, the success of the effort rests on the ability of its proponents to elaborate a clear choice, to minimize complexity and exaggerate distinction, although some examples seem to have more of a political agenda than others.[11] These reports, like those from other eras of reform, seek an ideological shift from an emphasis on one long-standing explanation of the purpose of schooling to a competing one. What mandate should schools fill—the democratic ideals of equality, access, and opportunity, or the socioeconomic need for a differentiated but content and efficient workforce? The most dominant voices in the current discourse clearly adopt the latter choice, shifting away from a previous emphasis—in statement if not in practice—on achieving equality in public education.

In fact, some of the current educational reports charge 1960 egalitarian reform efforts with the current demise of excellence. *A Nation at Risk* argues that we have "squandered the gains in student achievement made in the wake of the Sputnik challenge," while *Making the Grade* boldly asserts that "the federal government's emphasis on promoting equality of opportunity in the public schools has meant a slighting of its commitment to educational quality." This indictment of equality reform generally takes one of two forms. One position argues that earlier reforms resulted in such substantial changes for such an increased array of students that available resources are now spread too thin, watering down excellence for everybody. Alternatively, some argue that the equality reforms failed to make any substantive difference for those students they were designed to serve, and so can be safely discontinued in the face of competing demands.[12]

There is, of course, some truth to these interpretations, particularly as articulated in the second version. The equality reforms have failed to have the dramatic impact that they promised. Although the egalitarian fervor which generated detailed public policies like the 1975 amendments to the Education of the Handicapped Act (P.L. 94-142) did possess the potential to challenge the fundamental structures and philosophy of public schooling, the process of reform implementation succeeded not in abolishing inequality, but in extending it. The regulatory language of the EHA revisions concerning requirements for "individualized education programs," placement in the "least restrictive environment," and evaluation by a "multidisciplinary team" provides one excellent example, which I will discuss later in more detail. More broadly, however, the limited success of egalitarian reform arises from both the structural arrangement of special education's relationship to regular education, and the unrelenting meritocracy which pervades the cultural belief system of schools.

Active efforts to eliminate, or at least reduce, inequalities in schooling instead generate explanations for continued inequality. This occurs directly through the emphasis on equality of opportunity rather than equality of outcome. Schools escape the need to resolve the essential conflict between egalitarian ideals and inequitable social realities by demonstrating that inequality is equal. Students and teachers, as well as most of society, learn through their own school careers to embrace unquestioningly the belief that "it is vital for a technologically advanced society to be organized along hierarchical lines with responsibility, pay, authority, respect, and other rewards granted to those who merit moves up an unequal, but equally accessible ladder."[13]

Adherence to the notion of equality of opportunity instead of outcome frees schools and school reformers from even considering any retreat from schooling's function as the appropriate mechanism for neutrally and fairly preparing individual students with the skills, attitudes, and technical knowledge they need to fill the adult role that best suits their individual potential. Differentiated educational content becomes not a critique, but a mandate—legitimized by a meritocracy which itself depends upon an inequality of outcome.[14] It is hardly surprising then that teachers can be heard to explain about their students from working class families that, "our goal is to get our students so that they can function adequately in blue collar society. . . . Our goal is to get these kids to be like their parents."[15]

This meritocratic nature of schooling also accounts for the structural relations between special and regular education. As the heterogeneity of students increased dramatically with compulsory schooling, the then influential tenets of Social Darwinism served to legitimate separation of students by type of curricular content. Thus, students receiving vocational rather than academic preparation could be afforded their equal opportunities, according to their inherently different abilities, in separate classes. Similarly, the earliest examples of special education—the "ungraded classes"—collected a variety of students judged not to "fit" the curricular content of regular class.[16] What began as a parallel track soon developed into a parallel system, attached to regular education but not integrally entwined with it. The structural segregation of regular and special education was reinforced, rather than diminished, during the 1960s. Disproportionate numbers of poor and minority students in the schools' lowest tracks (similar to the disproportionate numbers of poor, non-English-speaking immigrant children a half century earlier) this time were said to be in need of a different educational approach and setting, for environmental instead of biological reasons. Cultural disadvantage might now explain the inequality, but the solution did not differ substantially. Renewed demands for equalized opportunities resulted in a variety of federally supported compensatory programs designed to overcome cultural and racial barriers by helping students to "catch up" or receive a "head start." Not only did special programs remain "add-ons" to the regular system; the fundamental explanation for inequality continued to reside within the student. Both in the 1960s and again in the 1970s, when reform efforts directly focused on the full range of students with disabilities, the effort to equalize opportunity rather than outcome guaranteed that what changes did occur would be limited to those that would not challenge the basic structures of schooling. Special compensatory programs, as well as special education, became new, lower levels of the multi-tiered system, serving more to inflate earlier standards of school accomplishment than to alter the accomplishment of those newly included. One must now complete four additional years of general schooling at a college or university to achieve the educational status, and rewards, once acquired with a high school diploma. According to one recent analysis, "what was gained by a decade of social activism [during the 1960s] was essentially a shift from exclusive meritocracy to inclusive meritocracy. Inclusion is not nothing, but it is not enough—and now even formal access is eroding."[17]

Some of the current reform reports have been sensitive to the negative effects of tracking and have called for its abandonment. Boyer's *High School* is perhaps the strongest voice among the major national reports arguing against tracking, pointing out not only the stigmatizing effects on students, but on teachers as well. The principle itself, however, continues to be upheld through calls for renewed attention to individualizing instruction. Schooling content must still be matched to varying individual potentials. In the end, it is individual worth that determines educational achievement. Though all contain the same message, *A Nation at Risk* is particularly uncompromising.

In the end it is *your* work that determines how much and how well you learn. When you work to your full capacity, you can hope to attain the knowledge and skills that will enable you to create your future and control your destiny. If you do not, you will have your future thrust upon you by others. Take hold of your life, apply your gifts and talents, work with dedication and self-discipline. Have high expectations for yourself and convert every challenge into an opportunity.[18]

Taken together, the current retreat from past equity reforms, which themselves represented only a flawed attempt to achieve a genuine egalitarian restructuring of schools, seems to be resulting in a new elitism which continues to reward students differentially according to race, gender, class, cultural difference, and ability. As the operative meritocracy in schools narrows, it is difficult not to conclude that "there is a tacit assumption here that disadvantaged, handicapped, and minority students are less likely to be central to filling the educational needs associated with a high-technology economy."[19]

PROGRESSIVE RESPONSES

Although many of the more progressive voices in the current literature agree with some of the specific suggestions for rejuvenating schooling for both students and teachers, they also find much to be lacking. The central theme of the progressive reaction is that the reform reports fail to address adequately the fundamental ideological and structural features of schooling. The effect of adoption of higher standards, increased testing, more direct collaborations with industry, and reductions in curricular offerings, they argue, will result primarily in a substantial strengthening of schools' sorting functions.

This growing body of literature argues that while an appreciation of the sorting and tracking processes of schools, particularly as they relate to economic analyses, can challenge the most conservative reports' uncompromising emphasis on merit at the expense of equality, these "reproductive" explanations ultimately fail to lead to real change. Uncompromising meritocracy becomes replaced by an equally uncompromising determinism which results only in "political paralysis," "social cynicism," and "dead-end one-dimensionality."[20] In trying to resist such conceptual cul-de-sacs, these new critical analyses generate several alternative reform agenda themes. Some authors focus on acquiring a more complete understanding of exactly how tracking and sorting occur in the context of interactions between students and teachers.[21] Schools do not simply mechanistically impose ideology or differentiated content on students, forcing some into an elite group of high achievement and others into the ranks of the oppressed. Rather, these progressive theorists seek to understand and explicate how students may actually cooperate in accomplishing these differentiated outcomes. Understanding such a subtle process might generate reform efforts that could challenge existing schooling inequities in a more thorough fashion than ever before.

Another strand of critical inquiry focuses on an examination of the teaching profession and the way in which teacher work changes from one reform era to the next.[22] Much of this literature criticizes the extent to which teaching has become "deskilled." That is, increasingly teacher work is recast from creative pedagogy to management of students, procedures, and paper. Alternatively, these analyses recommend a reconceptualization of the teaching profession to one that requires "intellectual labor" rather than "public service." This perspective views teachers as key initiators of ideological and structural reform through a reconceived pedagogy that enables and empowers students to resist and overcome disabling and differentiating tracking.

A third theme among some critical theorists focuses on understanding schools in terms of their bureaucratic structures and the manner in which those structures can facilitate or impede change, no matter how well conceived that change may be ideologically.[23] According to these analyses, schools must negotiate a fundamental organizational paradox between the demands of the formal, bureaucratic, hierarchically arranged structure and that of the informal, more loosely arranged, professional bureaucracy needed to perform the complex, teacher/student-oriented work of teaching. One outcome of the negotiation of these competing organizational configurations is dependence upon some standardization of teachers' skills in order to achieve organizational stability. Teachers' professional skill repertoires simplify their work by freeing them from the need to make continuous decisions only as long as student need or demand can be matched with that repertoire. Thus, teacher work becomes dominated by a process of matching solutions to problems, fitting instructional strategies and curriculum content to student needs. The resulting process of categorization and "pigeonholing," of course, creates both the "solution" of special education and the problem that inhibits future systemic reform. A second important outcome of schools' unique organizational configuration is their inability to change fundamental operations in any substantive way in response to new rules, regulations, or other fiat. Instead, demands for fundamental changes, those that require teachers to do something different from what they are "standardized" to do, become transformed and adopted as incidental changes, requiring only that schools do something additional.

All the reform literature, including these newest critical themes, has relevance for the future of special education. Certainly the present dominance of conservative voices in the discussion has the potential to create serious problems for special education students. However, it is even more important to understand what relevance the entire reform discussion, including the various analyses of the major reports, and some of the progressive analyses, might have for reform within special education and for possible changes in the relationship between regular and special education.

Reform With and Within Special Education

I said earlier that the national reports fail to mention special education, either as part of the schooling that they wish to reform, or as affected by their recommendations. In a strict sense this is true, not only of the major national reports, but also of most of the literature since 1983 that discusses the reform movement generally. However, both the authors of the initial reports and the subsequent discussants do refer in various ways to "low-track," minority, poor, and otherwise nonconforming students. As discussed by Sapon-Shevin in this volume, it is exactly these poor and minority students who most frequently acquire labels as mildly handicapped. Special education for mildly handicapped students has long been public education's boundary category with a membership that varies from one reform era to the next. During periods when reform efforts stress equality, even only an equality of opportunity, many "mildly handicapped" students become more visible in regular classes. For example, in the period from 1969 to 1972 the public schools declassified somewhere between 11,000 and 18,000 students who had previously been labeled "educable mentally retarded."[24] The last fifteen years, however, have seen many of these same students reclassified as "mildly handicapped," although not necessarily with the same label.[25] These students are defined not so much by an immutable set of traits and abilities as their failure to meet the varying standards of reform. They are not so much ignored by the reports as ignored as a result of them. According to one observer, "It is painfully clear that the least promising students are expected to do least well. Staying in school, passing an eighth-grade proficiency test, getting a job, not being a criminal, and staying off welfare become 'success' indicators."[26]

REFORM WITHIN SPECIAL EDUCATION

If special education for mildly handicapped students is at least implicitly dealt with by the current reform, the topic of special education for students not mildly handicapped—students who are collectively described as severely handicapped—is totally absent. This omission occurs despite the fact that the most significant reform in all of special education's history involved the inclusion of these severely handicapped students into public special education as a matter of right and not permission.

Public Law 94-142 attempted widespread, emancipatory reform throughout both special and regular education. Detailed regulations explicating principles of zero reject, least restrictive environment, parent involvement, nondiscriminatory assessment, and due process hoped to achieve the integrated inclusion of students previously unserved, most of whom were severely handicapped. In addition, the same demands hoped to reduce the stigma and self-fulfilling aspects of existing, mostly segregated, public special education for less severely handicapped students by requiring regular education teachers to problem solve creatively rather than classify and exclude.

The implicit, and sometimes explicit, vision of P.L. 94-142 was of completeness and inclusion. Public education should include and "work" for all of America's school children. Unfortunately, complete realization of this vision cannot explain why the current national reform conversation rarely mentions students with special needs, because the news after twelve years of effort is not all good.[27] More students are being labeled than ever before, with an overall growth from a little more than 8 percent of the total student population to nearly 11 percent. Fewer students labeled "learning disabled" and "mentally retarded" are being educated in regular classes in 1986 than in 1976; and a small (3) percent of students labeled "mentally retarded" or "emotionally disturbed" are more likely to receive public education in residential facilities or at home. Thus, EHA's demand to move toward less restrictive environments resulted instead in general movement toward more restrictive educational locations and opportunities for more special education students.

Certainly there are exceptions. There has been an overall decrease in the number of students labeled "mentally retarded"; and students with severe handicaps have moved from separate special schools and residential settings (decreasing 7 and 4 percent respectively) to self-contained special classes. As a result, the presence of students with severe handicaps in regular public schools has increased 10 percent overall.

Still, according to one recent analysis, "EHA has not succeeded ... in providing a uniform entitlement for all handicapped children."[28] Minority children continue to receive differentiated educational experiences in both regular and special education. Parent participation falls far short of unanimous (in fact, below 50 percent), with even less participation among poor families.[29] Programmatic and fiscal resources also continue to vary widely across districts, states, and geographic regions. In addition to failing to realize expected benefits, one assessment summarized the additional unexpected outcomes of P.L. 94-142 this way:

> The empirical evidence suggests that, rather than leading to a new technology for special education equity, the implementation of P.L. 94-142 has resulted in a system that encourages categorization, stereotyping and exclusion; reduces equal rights; legitimates other forms of discrimination and subjugation; and permits school professionals to treat "handicapped" students like second-class citizens.[30]

The news is not all bad, of course. Twelve years of effort also produced examples of EHA's vision of excellence.[31] From Oregon to Maine, creative and assertive people have crafted examples of team teaching between special and regular educators that permit the integration of typical and regular students in the same classroom. Districts, and even states, have closed separate special education schools in favor of moving classrooms into age-appropriate regular schools. Students in some rural areas exchange long rides to larger towns and programs for integrated, individualized programs in their home communities and neighborhood schools. Teachers, parents, and administrators in these pockets of excellence forge new relationships that encourage the creative problem solving necessary to produce program plans that help students acquire competence, visibility, and participation in their local schools and communities.

These best practice examples exist not just for students long familiar to public special education. Some of the most creative examples have involved students with very severe, multiple handicaps. A similar range of best practice examples exists from early intervention programs to model high school programs that successfully help students' transition from school to work and community living, regardless of the type, number, or degree of their handicaps. Finally, these pockets of excellence are not geographically bound. Every state can point to examples. Even in areas where long-standing, "cradle to grave," segregated programs continue to flourish, there are examples of creative integration of students who need ventilators to breathe, or use of referral and assessment procedures that begin and end in the regular classroom.

Clearly the problem is not that the vision of EHA cannot be realized, but that it has not been realized more widely, even after twelve years of effort. Instead, the rules and regulations that some hoped would effect so much have been absorbed by the school bureaucracy, producing only relatively unconnected pockets of more substantive change. As wider educational reform progresses largely uninformed and unconcerned with the demands of reform within special education, a new counterreform agenda is emerging. Generalized failure of mainstreaming or integration for students with mild handicaps now shapes a new demand for access to a different mainstream. Reform conversations in special education call for change in regular education and between regular and special education in order to achieve greater access for handicapped students to a newly restructured mainstream.[32] As evidence of both the need and the solution, critics point to the "pockets of excellence" examples mentioned earlier, often arguing that demonstration is necessary and sufficient to generate both the commitment to and achievement of widespread change. Two problems remain, however.

First, this newest reform initiative within special education focuses primarily on students with mild handicaps.[33] Somewhat more fragile attempts to advance the same arguments and demands on behalf of students with severe handicaps seem rarely to capture the attention of these other special education reformers, much less the general education reform community. Even if successful access to a restructured regular education can be achieved for students currently labeled mildly handicapped, the continued existence of a separate structural track for students with severe handicaps assures the presence of a boundary category between access and discrimination. As reform zeal wanes and new pressures redirect the attention of schools to new problems, this boundary category can once again absorb more students judged not to fit.

Second, calls for merger based on the evidence of a few examples do not well explain, either theoretically or practically, how to move from these pockets of excellence to generalized systemic reform.[34] Yet vitally helpful theoretical explanations exist within the ideological, structural and organizational analyses of critical theory. It seems a situation reminiscent of the well-worn cliché: theory without fact is empty; fact without theory is blind. In the remaining sections of this chapter, I will outline the possibility for a more optimistic resolution of these reform dilemmas by exploring the contribution of the most progressive practices that have emerged for students with severe handicaps in light of a critical theory perspective. I will illustrate that some of the best practices for students with severe handicaps contain the practical examples of generalized structural change that the critical theorists seek.

Forging New Links

Thus far, I have briefly outlined two arguments. First, the dominant voices in current reform discussions ideologically support an analysis of schooling that erodes public schooling's commitment to any form of equality. Second, simultaneous reform within special education which hoped to challenge fundamental inequities, instead succeeded in generally reinforcing them. In this section I will describe some of the details of this limited achievement, as well as some promising developments by focusing on three special education reform themes: (a) integration, (b) individualized planning and instruction, and (c) professionalization and specialization.

SPECIAL EDUCATION'S NEWEST STUDENTS

The qualifier "severe" seems strong enough to generate high agreement; however, even the Association for Persons with Severe Handicaps (TASH) continues to debate who should and should not be included in the category. Chapter 3 of this volume discusses this particular definitional issue more completely, but generally this group includes students who have previously been assigned such labels as moderately, severely, or profoundly retarded, autistic, trainable retarded, multiply-handicapped, and deaf/blind.

These students' uniqueness in public schooling lies in the fundamental challenge they present to the meaning of education—a challenge that is only now beginning to be resolved. Special education's traditional strategy of accommodating "different" students in appropriately merited tracks falters in the face of overwhelming physiology. On the one hand, it is more difficult to attribute lack of achievement to lack of interest, motivation, or application if a student clearly has limbs that don't move properly, senses that fail to register stimuli, or lacks certain brain cells. On the other hand, it is much easier to state explicitly what is only an implicit assumption about mildly handicapped students: students with severe handicaps are unable to learn. The demand to include this last group of students challenged public special education as it has never been challenged before. The field's long-held belief that children with moderate and severe retardation are quite simply "irremediable and uneducable" offered no easy response. Even earlier efforts to include excluded students produced a reluctant accommodation based more on charitable than egalitarian reasons:

Public schools can organize custodial classes within the public school system for the care, training, and supervision of the trainable mentally deficient child. ... It would not be expected that such children could be educated to care for themselves at the adult level, but through training (not education as we usually conceive it) could be taught to function socially at a higher level around the home and neighborhood. ... The group that must [still] be excluded from such classes consists of those children, such as idiots, who cannot be trained in the simplest routines of life.[35]

It is not surprising, then, that special and regular educators alike wondered in 1975 just what education could possibly mean for these new *severely* and *profoundly* handicapped students. What would be the purpose of schooling, what could be taught, for what future end? After twelve years of effort, the same forces that generated limited generalized success for students with mild handicaps produced a similar result for students with severe handicaps. Yet the unique promise of the most progressive pockets of excellence for students with severe handicaps exists precisely because of the dramatic differences these students possess.

Some authors explain the failure of EHA to produce generalized fundamental changes in schooling for all students by arguing that schools simply could not change.[36] For example, analyses of the organizational nature of schools reveals that regulating change by establishing new standards of performance for both the system and its teachers necessarily results in schools redefining the change from a fundamental one to an incidental one. Thus, new students, new principles of program structure, and even new standards of curriculum planning and instruction can only be accommodated by adding on additional programs, placements, and professional specialties. These theoretical explanations, together with others that focus on student/teacher interaction and ideological forces, do perhaps explain the limits of special education reform; but they do not as clearly realize the promise of best practice examples. In the remainder of this section I will provide examples of both critiques and promising examples of integration, individualization, and professionalization.[37]

LRE AND INTEGRATION

Implementation of the LRE (least restrictive environment) principle in all of public special education takes two primary forms. The goal for the majority of students is to move from separate, unequal, classes into regular classes; or, alternatively, to provide the necessary supports to maintain students with relatively mild differences in learning style and rate in the regular classroom. Integration through application of the LRE principle hoped to reduce, and perhaps eliminate, the stigmatization and victimization of segregated schooling by substituting opportunities to develop a variety of meaningful interactions and relationships between handicapped and nonhandicapped students. Instead, for most labeled students, the LRE principle resulted in continued separation through tracking, homogeneous class grouping, and ability grouping. Special education students invariably found themselves shunted to programs of lowest educational status. Even use of resource rooms in an attempt to break the rigid stratification of school tracking failed to meet the egalitarian ideal. Students assigned to regular class/resource class combinations generally leave the regular class during high status, academic, instruction. The not very hidden message of these status of knowledge distinctions is powerful indeed, and assures that most special education students will be perceived as "nonacademic," "dull," "slow," and "less intelligent" by their nonhandicapped peers.

The regulatory language that defines LRE as a continuum of educational placements ironically allows the maintenance of the same segregated settings that the law's backers originally intended to make obsolete. As a result, when new national reform efforts (such as the current one) move away from a commitment to equality, a continued masquerade of adherence to equity goes largely unchallenged even when students are moved to more restrictive educational environments. The implicit demand of any continuum is that some criterion must be met for movement from one location to another. While students with handicaps might earn their way from exclusion to inclusion, the underlying demand that individual placement depends upon demonstrated educational worth permits them to slip back into exclusion when the criteria for movement change.

Initial efforts to apply the principle of LRE to students with severe handicaps most often adopted the "continuum of placement" notion.

After all, more important than *where* students were educated was *that* they were educated. By 1980, however, educators believed that most severely handicapped students were receiving some educational services, even if in segregated settings. The focus could then shift from providing basic educational services, to integrating these services into the mainstream of public education through a reinterpretation of the LRE principle. This reinterpretation challenges the continuum interpretation of LRE which serves to reinforce educational tracking on the basis of individual ability and merit.

For students with severe handicaps, the integrative end of the continuum model—full-time regular class—seemed unlikely. Because of their very real and dramatic differences in ability and learning needs, these students seemed to require a range of placements that assured that most of them would remain completely segregated, even within regular public school buildings. In addition, many educators thought that "mainstreaming"—in the straightforward sense of placement in regular classes—was simply instructionally inappropriate for those with the most severe disabilities. Students with such different needs, both in terms of content and instruction would only be ignored by a teacher with twenty or thirty other comparatively homogeneous students. So, rejecting a continuum of placements, each "less restrictive" than the last, educators also redefined mainstreaming to refer to integration of students with moderate and severe handicaps into the mainstream of public schooling. In this way, even very difficult students could pursue learning in the company of the general population of age peers that they would encounter in communities after graduation. Such physical proximity, proponents argued, would achieve the immediate twin goals of providing typical models of behavior from which students with severe handicaps could learn the wide variety of normative, adaptive skills they were not able to learn from each other while, at the same time, permitting nonhandicapped students to develop an increasing tolerance for and appreciation of human differences. As Brown and his colleagues argue in this volume, this physical proximity and familiarity, it was hoped, would eventually lead students to seize opportunities for interaction, building relationships, and, possibly, even friendships.

Instead, what many severely handicapped students experienced initially as "opportunities for interaction with nonhandicapped peers" was too often confined to special education. Many of the "typical" students who found their way to classes for severely handicapped students came from other self-contained and resource programs.

Gradually, peer advocate or tutoring programs developed that offered nonhandicapped students course credit or other incentives in exchange for spending part of their day helping to integrate severely handicapped students into the life and culture of school. While peer tutoring programs have helped attract a wider range of student involvement than previously existed, particularly from students of "higher" tracks and status, these programs are often criticized by some special educators as inappropriately perpetuating one-dimensional "helping" rather than genuine "peer" relationships.[38] Yet, understanding and facilitating complex, multi-dimensional relationships between nonhandicapped and severely handicapped students, especially adolescents, is not nearly well enough understood. For example, nonhandicapped "tutors" may actually define their relationships as friendships despite the label bestowed by professionals.

Even those teachers who do understand, and facilitate quality interactions and relationships between their severely handicapped students and other school peers, still face another barrier to realizing their commitment to integration, particularly at the secondary level. Curricular innovations for students with severe handicaps demand that teachers spend increasing amounts of school time instructing their students in those settings where performance will actually be demanded. While these nonschool settings offer many instructional advantages for severely handicapped students, unfortunately they offer no age peers at all. And extending "opportunities for integration" beyond the school day into extracurricular high school life seems too dramatically to exceed reasonable expectations of even very willing and progressive teachers.

TOWARD A BROADER INTEGRATION

Alternative examples for students with severe handicaps emerged early in EHA reform, though few locales managed to be comprehensive about their innovations. In one area, for example, all students with autism might be integrated into regular classes in both private and public schools and supported by regular/special education teacher teams; while students with mental retardation, physical disabilities, or sensory impairments continued to attend segregated schools and self-contained classes. In other locales, very multiply handicapped children might enjoy integration into regular classrooms and classes in regular schools, while students with mild handicaps populated segregated schools. In still other examples, all severely handicapped secondary students in a region or state spent much of their educational day in community-based instruction while elementary students in the same district spent their time failing to "catch up" in skill-based developmental curricula. Despite the unevenness of these best practice examples, twelve years of ongoing development within these exemplars have led to even more promising examples of a broader integration which explicate in practice some of the new recommendations advanced for regular education reform.

Emphasis on non-school-based instruction for severely handicapped students in order to increase the relevance of instruction (described in the next section more fully) also emerges as a recommendation for regular education students. Some reports specifically urge increased use of nonschool settings as learning sites, while others propose a new "service requirement" for all high school students. In both cases the recommendations hope to alleviate the boredom and generalized lack of involvement of high school students in their communities. The unchallenged notion that "education best takes place in classrooms in school buildings,"[39] too often limits any attempt to reform the relevance of curriculum to "add-ons" that primarily attract those students for whom the core curriculum seems inappropriate, once again reinforcing rather than minimizing students' differences. Boyer finds that most high school students, especially poor and minority students, do not participate in any out-of-class activities, either within school or in their communities. He concludes:

Today it is possible for American teenagers to finish high school yet never be asked to participate responsibly in life in or out of the school, never be encouraged to spend time with older people who may be lonely, to help a child who has not learned to read, to pick up the litter on the street, or even to do something meaningful at the school itself.[40]

The current practice of fostering "peer" relationships between severely handicapped and nonhandicapped students anticipates one direction of needed reform in regular education. When peer involvement involves "low status" students, the effort may succeed in involving the very disenfranchised, uninvolved students whom high schools now fail to engage. Instead of discouraging, the experience of helping or tutoring another when your own schooling experiences only succeed in making you feel helpless and ignorant might instead represent the best schooling offers. The often dramatic differences that characterize the abilities of severely handicapped students suggest that the qualities of meaningful relationships might be different from those experienced among other, more similarly abled peers. In fact, perhaps such relationships will provide an insight about the meaning of "responsible participation in life" that all might benefit from.

In another way, teachers' efforts to balance directly relevant, community-based learning experiences with increasingly varied meaningful peer relationships might also serve as an example for broader reform. A functional, community-referenced curriculum is an appropriate goal for all students, though the content of such experiences would clearly differ for students who are not severely handicapped. Nevertheless, at a time when secondary schooling for many students resembles a prohibition from rather than a preparation for adulthood, any opportunity to establish connections with the community outside schools should surely be seized and emulated. These two lessons can even be combined. In some locales, nonhandicapped high school students spend time with severely handicapped peers as they learn to negotiate and participate in the ordinary features of daily community life, from shopping at a grocery store or eating in a fast food restaurant to withdrawing money from their savings account in order to attend a sporting event or movie. Certainly this involvement benefits the nonhandicapped students' abilities to appreciate and support differences in people, and may also contribute to their own growth of self-esteem. The severely handicapped students benefit in several ways. Some can acquire a variety of social and adaptive skills in the context of these peer relationships that would be difficult, and perhaps impossible, for adults to teach directly. But even those few students whose particular constellation of impairments and disabilities make it unlikely or impossible for them to acquire new competence in this informal fashion benefit from the social support and care of their peers. No matter how dramatically disabled a student, frequent regular presence among nonhandicapped peers inevitably generates the special interest of someone. One or more students will, for some reason, find even the most severely handicapped student charming or interesting. Support thus generated can grow into the community support network that will assure the disabled student's continued presence in the community long into adulthood. Such mingling of the students, as well as the educational experiences for students in the bottom tracks, can then "bubble up" to capture the involvement of even the highest status students, offering one strong and visible challenge to the power and logic of ability tracks, while providing needed opportunities for nonhandicapped students to feel a part of their community's life.

The most recent integration initiatives on behalf of students with severe handicaps emulate those for students labeled mildly handicapped by urging placement of *all* students in regular class. Vermont's "homecoming" model and Canada's "kaleidoscope"[41] are only two examples. They claim to achieve in practice what has only been recommended and encouraged. Proponents argue that only when integration becomes the beginning point rather than the terminal objective can schools evolve into the nongraded, unified, harmonious, creatively changing communities of learning that both students and society require. No one would suggest, of course, that such efforts be attempted without the presence of necessary supports. Some special education teachers find that they both enjoy and prefer providing their severely handicapped students with supportive and functional educational experiences in "classrooms without walls." The experience of integrating special education's most difficult students into the life and curriculum of a regular classroom, while still providing them with the functional programming that will enhance their participation and competence within and outside of that classroom, can only result in the kind of collaborative problem solving, emancipating pedagogy, and intellectual labor described as necessary for reform by progressive theorists.

INDIVIDUALIZED INSTRUCTION

The IEP is the most central, and perhaps the most far-reaching, of the P.L. 94-142 reforms. In fact, the powerful appeal of individual attention has led some reform participants to recommend expanding the IEP mandate, or at least some version of an individualized "plan," to all students in education, regular and special alike.[42] When first proposed by EHA, the idea of producing a detailed educational plan for each special education student seemed unnecessary and unduly time-consuming to many special educators. Nevertheless, despite initial reluctance, these plans did change parent participation in the educational decision-making process. While this involvement continues to be flawed by logistical and procedural constraints, as well as inadequate understanding and communication between parents and professionals, the principle of some level of shared decision making with parents is now firmly established in the field. In addition to parent involvement, the specificity of IEP goals and objectives provides a measure of administrative and professional accountability previously lacking, while also promising to help most efficiently students who have widely differing learning needs achieve new skills.

Despite these positive features, however, IEPs have also served to further isolate and blame students for their inability. These negative effects can occur at a number of different levels. On the one hand, the idea of individualization suggests that teachers should possess the commitment and skills to flexibly design and implement varying ways of presenting, sequencing, and teaching educational content in order to help a wide variety of students achieve the same learning outcomes. In this way, all students acquire the same basic abilities, though in various ways, and perhaps even to varying degrees of fluency. Unfortunately, all teachers, including special educators, are prepared with a repertoire of "standard" programs or interventions, which can be applied to predetermined situations or problems. The creative problem solving demanded by the spirit of the IEP to help students acquire skills and build competence too often only succeeds in generating detailed plans for remediating inability rather than acquiring ability in different ways. Goals and objectives more often detail the skill deficits expected to be overcome, or at least diminished, by the end of the specified time, than serve as a blueprint for helping students achieve the same learning differently. As a result, students may spend their time trying to catch up and conform in order to earn the opportunity to learn.

This emphasis on conformity extends to teachers' pedagogical practices, which too often emphasize rote learning, control, and repetition rather than techniques which foster spontaneity, creative expression, and divergent thinking.[43] Like other "low track classrooms," special education classrooms rely heavily on such authoritarian pedagogic techniques. Teachers pride themselves on their ability to provide their students with "structured learning experiences," but frequently this translates into instructional isolation. Resource rooms, a primary mechanism for delivering specialized instructions to students with mild learning handicaps, are much more similar to individual tutoring models than to classroom teaching. One effect of this one-to-one instruction is that it too often promotes control and efficient management of students rather than an emphasis on helping them develop active involvement and autonomy. In addition, the strongly behavioral language of IEPs tends to reinforce a climate of technical management and authoritarian control: highly specific, minutely fragmented, quantifiable goals and objectives commit students and teachers alike to experiencing education as a process where students attempt to come as close as possible to teacher-anticipated outcomes. An important risk of this style of individualization is that the burden of failure to learn comes to rest squarely on the individual student in classic "blaming-the-victim" fashion.

At best, where some form of individualized instruction has been implemented it has resulted in a more flexible approach to the pace of work, criteria for grading, and instructional techniques. It infrequently, however, results in the development of new curricula that are oriented to the particular experience, concerns, or needs of a student.[44]

Programs for students with severe handicaps certainly share both the promise and the risks of individualization. Perhaps more than any other students with handicaps, severely handicapped students learn alone. Regardless of program model, whether regular class or segregated school, the legacy of regular education's lockstep, homogeneous grouping tradition creates for students and teachers many groups of one. Since teachers really only possess the standard skills required for homogeneous group instruction, the need for this one-to-one pattern of instruction becomes a function not of teacher capacity but student incapacity. The less able the student, teachers argue, the more they must receive one-to-one instruction. Consequently, in some classrooms students sit at separate tables, working on separate tasks, waiting for their turn for intensive, teacher-directed instruction. Even among teachers who use small-group instruction for some types of tasks, there is almost total reliance on one-to-one instruction for tasks which involve long chains of discrete behaviors as is required to perform many of the daily living, domestic, and work skills that constitute functional curricula. Thus, even if several students are present, teachers often teach making a sandwich, for example, in one-to-one style. While one student is being instructed through a learning chain, others wait for a turn, sometimes watching, sometimes not. In addition, there are some students, usually those whom teachers identify as least able or "very low functioning," who never even achieve presence in a group. Instead, those students teachers define as most difficult to teach receive only one-to-one instruction, sometimes remaining totally unconnected to their classmates.

In addition to instructional isolation physically, highly technical, precise, teacher-controlled instructional techniques can result in other kinds of unintended results. Some students become so dependent upon the instructional contingencies teachers provide that they cannot spontaneously engage in any behavior without another person's exact instructional guides. Certainly, some of these outcomes result from errors teachers make in practicing a complex, and easily mismanaged, technical pedagogy. For students who frequently begin their education with a very small repertoire of abilities, however, even small errors of teacher judgment can result in dramatic, and difficult to alter, student behavior.

In response to the instructional dependence and rigidity learned by many students with severe handicaps, some educators now encourage teachers systematically to teach students to make choices.[45] Without this instruction, some argue, our instructional practices might actually diminish students' sense of control and autonomy resulting in "learned helplessness," or the belief that nothing one does makes a difference.

MORE SUPPORTIVE INSTRUCTION

Despite the limits of individualization for helping all students with handicaps achieve flexible, creative engagement in building competence relevant to adult functioning, some features of current innovations for severely handicapped students contain some promising potential solutions. Use of cooperative learning strategies in the context of group instruction, either instead of or in addition to individual instruction of students with mild handicaps, promises to reduce the need for distinctions between students, whether labeled or not. The resulting "adaptive education" afforded all students more nearly resembles the progressive vision of restructured schooling than the piecemeal, add-on, remnants of previous reforms.[46]

One outcome of "functional curricula," which first emerged for students with severe handicaps, is a much greater appreciation for a student's own unique experiences, interests, settings, and educational history. Some teachers, then, can individualize curricula not just to remediate individual deficits, or to vary learning pace, but, more positively, to enhance students' abilities to interact appropriately and effectively in their own long-term environments. Such practices produce greater appreciation for the uniqueness of students while minimizing the differences between them. Potentially, teachers will find ways to teach students within their own local communities, not using just any grocery store, restaurant, or shopping center, but using the specific stores and restaurants that a student might actually patronize outside of school. All school curricula could be so locally referenced, providing all students with knowledge about and participation in their own communities as a legitimate outcome of instruction.

Functional curricula can also counter individualization critiques in one other way. Teachers who routinely teach functional content outside of school buildings find that this instruction is managed most effectively in small groups. When venturing into students' communities teachers try neither to violate natural proportions by bringing a large class nor prevent students from interacting with and learning from each other by exclusively working one-to-one. Two current developments support and expand this trend toward small-group instruction. First, academic educators increasingly urge adoption of an activity-oriented, rather than a skill-oriented, curriculum. Rather than teaching students the component skills required to perform some functional activity on the assumption that the student can apply the skill in the necessary content, most recent advice recommends teaching the skills within the context of the activity itself. The distinction depends on the notion that it is more important for students with severe handicaps to participate in normal, everyday activities than for them to perform these activities in a "normal" way. That is, it is important to do some of your own grocery shopping, even if you must pay using a large bill because you have not yet acquired the ability to count out money. Not only does an activity-oriented approach respond to a range of other curricular concerns (including eliminating any dependence on a notion of readiness), it also minimizes one form of instructional dependency by teaching students to respond to those natural cues and reinforcers that exist within both the activity and the community setting. Finally, eliminating any readiness requirements assures that students with all levels of abilities can participate in the activity. This provides teachers the opportunity to form small groups of students of complementary skill levels for activity-oriented instruction, which both discourages instructional isolation and encourages peer interaction and support.[47]

Another recent development has the potential to secure group instruction firmly by fundamentally challenging the epistemological basis of individualism that still tends to pervade the functional approach at a deeper level. Educators' innovative practices still retain a "clinical" outlook that has difficulty responding to other kinds of social reform efforts. As one critic explains the issue,

The danger of the behavioristic influence lies in its assumption of a one-way causal relationship between environmental contingencies and individual states.

... In order to begin to appreciate the responses of people to disablement you need to go beyond the aggregated, statistically standardized individual, simply molded by circumstances, to a perspective that treats individuals and social worlds as mutually constitutive.[48]

While the category of "severely handicapped learners" has become the most heterogeneous of any special education category, those who seemed particularly challenging remained in separate, frequently private, settings. Now some of these students are moving to public special education class. Teachers refer to this trend when they describe their students as "getting lower." Indeed, these newer students come with very serious and dramatic multiple impairments, including very severe retardation, physical disability, and, often, significant or total sensory impairment. The prevalence of these students in public school classrooms will continue to rise as a result both of continuing deinstitutionalization and advancing medical technology in neonatology and pediatric medicine. The challenge for teachers is that these new students truly have no ability peers. Individualization is put to its strongest test. If current programming reforms, including activity-oriented instruction in community settings, are to include such students, teachers must recast the meaning of individualized educational programs to instruction in groups of students with not just complementary, but totally disparate, abilities. When a student challenges the fundamentals of operant teaching and learning because they have few reliable responses to any kind of stimuli, teaching itself must acquire new meaning. It seems that such students will participate in activities not so much from their own agency as through the interactions which others in the environment create with them. Individualized instruction becomes a task of creatively noticing and nurturing a student's reliable and meaningful presence in the midst of the ongoing life of school and community. This stretching of both theory and practice in special education, occasioned by the presence of students with very severe handicaps and driven by a logic of social inclusion and civil rights, provides both the opportunity for and an example of structural change in education.

UNREMITTING PROFESSIONALIZATION

The established separateness of special education from regular education is powerfully reinforced by the processes of professionalization and specialization that have occurred within the field. Even more, in many respects the subareas within special education have become the route of professionalization and specialization for all of education. As special education grows in numbers and variety, regular education teachers function less as teachers than as managers. The very homogeneity of their students seems to require less and less creative problem-solving pedagogy. One recent case study of an elementary school, for example, found that as much as 80 percent of class time during the morning hours was taken up not with instruction, but with managerial tasks such as grading papers, recording scores, giving general instructions and answering logistical questions. For their part, students completed dittos and tests, followed instructions, and moved from class to class—each of which followed the same pattern.[49]

This homogeneity in regular education classes results primarily from the very existence of all of special education's levels into which nonconforming regular class students (or potential regular class students) can be sorted. From the beginning, special education responded to its charge to deal with regular education's rejected students by finding professional status in the stigma. Following the paths laid by other occupational groups seeking to transform work into profession, special educators developed a unique technical expertise, licensing procedures, professional organizations, and a separate lexicon with which to baffle consumers and nonspecial colleagues alike. This rise of professionalism within the field of education cannot be seen as an unreservedly positive development. While it does help special educators to establish their credibility within the larger clan of educators, it provides a way to monopolize knowledge about a field and control access to a population of students which assures a continuing market for the specialized professional service.[50]

With each influx into special education of increasingly different students, educators found the need for a new brand of teachers with different, more specialized skills, further delineating their professionalism by disability category. This process continues, despite a full panoply of categorical specialists, to produce specialists for different "levels" of disability (mild and severe), or for specific types of problems (interfering behavior). This process continues to be encouraged, perhaps unintentionally, by EHA's heavy reliance on a professional model of special expertise. Both the assessment/diagnostic process and program design depend upon the delivery of what typically becomes fragmented services delivered by designated professionals.

This kind of fine-grained specialization produces many curious effects for all students in special education, including those with severe handicaps. Initial access to services requires the specialized activity of a school psychologist to confirm the obvious: that the student is indeed mentally retarded. Too often what the process fails to produce is information that can genuinely aid program development and decisions. Similarly, the responsibility to provide a wide variety of ancillary and related services continues to be dispersed among a growing number of professional fiefdoms. Physical and occupational therapists, along with various itinerant consultants, behavior specialists, speech pathologists and vocational specialists (to name but a few) spend isolated blocks of time delivering special, technical services that produce little coherence in a student's educational life. Even when these various specialists try to communicate and coordinate their activities, they must steal the necessary time from either instruction or personal life. Such powerful negative contingencies contrive to extinguish even the most energetic and committed. As a result, parents as well as teachers and building administrators continue to rely on new, added technical expertise when generic solutions might better, and more quickly, serve students' needs.

If special education has found its identity in increasing specialization, regular educators are now pursuing reforms intended to raise the status of teaching to a profession.[51] Two key national reports, one by the Holmes Group and the other by the Carnegie Commission,[52] outline a series of recommendations aimed at improving teaching and schools by reforming teacher preparation. As with other reform reports, these too have generated a great deal of discussion and dissension.[53] Nevertheless, the major themes of teacher preparation reform outlined in these two reports seem to be weathering the storm. Teachers should build their professional competence on a foundation of strong liberal arts undergraduate education; the bulk of professional preparation should emulate that of other professions (such as law and medicine) and occur during a graduate degree program offered by professional development schools; teaching staff should be differentiated hierarchically according to their knowledge, and as reflected by their certification; and standards for entry and continuation in the profession should be stiffened, nationally articulated, and regulated. Some states, eager to respond to this reform subagenda, have already abolished undergraduate teacher preparation programs, instituted new testing requirements for both entry and exit to teacher education programs, and begun to revise the array of available certifications to resemble more closely emerging national standards, tests, and trends.

Unfortunately for special education, this new professionalization initiative in regular education threatens to undermine and even entirely thwart some of the current reform trends for students with handicaps. For example, one outcome of renewed emphasis on integration of students with handicaps into regular classes has been an effort to mirror that integration in the preparation of teachers. If universities postpone professional education for teachers to postbaccalaureate and graduate programs, however, these still fragile attempts to integrate or combine preparation of special and regular education teachers are likely to be abandoned under pressure of time and cost. Further, states (such as Oregon) that have previously required special education teachers first to complete certification in regular elementary or secondary education, may also be forced to abandon this kind of broader preparation in the face of teacher shortages. Few prospective teachers will be able to afford the time or money to complete up to six years of college preparation in order to accept a job paying less than that preparation cost them to work with those students least valued by public education.

The silence in discussion of reforms in teacher education on such issues seems to promise walls rather than bridges between regular and special education. The simple but powerful premise underlying the current reform activity that teacher candidates need more time to acquire necessary knowledge, skills, attitudes, and values, combined with schooling's tradition of labeling, sorting, fragmenting, and adding on specialized alternatives, offers thin hope for fundamental changes in how special and regular educators communicate and work together. Reinforcing specialization and standardization in teacher preparation also seems unlikely to result in the kind of reconceived teacher work outlined by some of the critical theorists. Liberal arts undergraduate preparation alone seems unlikely to undo the rigidity and deskilling frequently criticized as inhibiting teachers from the kind of creative, empowering pedagogy found missing in most of today's classrooms.

AN ALTERNATIVE

It should be clear that the preparation of teachers in special education escapes few of the critiques leveled at teacher preparation generally. As with the other themes addressed in this section, however, some alternative examples can be found in the pockets of exemplary programs for students with severe handicaps. There are two ways that preparing teachers for schooling's most different students can escape some of the professionalism pitfalls that plague the preparation of teachers for more able students.

First, the impressive variety of educational needs, impairments, constellations of multiple impairments, and learning requirements that severely handicapped students present prohibits any standardized approach to teacher preparation. It is simply impossible to predict the set of situations or contingencies that severely handicapped students present to teachers comprehensively enough to prepare teachers with a repertoire of standard responses or programs. Instead, the best teachers receive from the preparation programs several important kinds of knowledge which they will then apply as they create the practice of education for students with severe handicaps. They must be equipped with both a theoretical and practical grasp of specific content, instructional skill, the regular school context, the demands of the community, and the fundamental processes of research and inquiry, since it is only when so grounded that they can create the "solutions" to the problems students present. Even the most extensive list of prepared strategies and instructional tricks (assuming the teacher had the time to learn them and the capacity to remember them) could not support a teacher for long.

Second, the accumulated best practice examples provide teachers, parents, and teacher educators with a clear vision of what public special education can accomplish for even very different students. Using a process that reflects the principles of collaboration, fairness, substantive family involvement, and effectiveness, the field collectively has a very good idea of how to design and implement educational programs that include content guided by the principles of age-appropriateness, community-referencing, future orientation, comprehensiveness, and family referencing, and how to produce outcomes guided by the principles of community integration, supportive social networks, participation, and ordinariness and invisibility.

Also clear is that these best practice educational experiences cannot be created by a teacher alone. Only a very few very rare individuals possess the necessary excellence in curriculum and learning theory, instructional delivery, personnel management, education of adults, communication and negotiation, organizational theory, resource development and management, and research and systems change to support the full complement of best practices. Instead, most teachers must enter a setting and create the community of support that together can create exemplary programs. Teachers must seek out and use the resources of other educators, a variety of specialists, parents, local business people, neighbors, nonhandicapped students, as well as a variety of people without titles that they and their students encounter in the context of functional, community-based educational programming. The mantle of professionalism weighs less heavy when it must be so shared. Instead, creative problem solving, flexible and dynamic planning, and frequent revision and improvement can replace the often stultifying and isolating practice of specialized expertise.

Capturing the Optimism

Change is always easier when narrowly conceived. The ideological, organizational, and professional forces in schools overwhelmingly encourage a response to change that minimizes the accommodation necessary. Demands for fundamental structural reform become redefined, transformed, and adopted as much more manageable additions to the structure. Much about the current reform conversation seems to reflect this process of diminution.

I have argued, and tried to show, that in today's reform environment there is reason for more optimism. The pockets of excellence currently serving as exemplars to special education and, I expect, to regular education as well, succeed precisely because they fundamentally challenge previous explanations and values about education and schooling. Understood, protected, and nurtured, these voices of the future can succeed in resolving the current reform dissonance and ambiguity by supplying a new set of values and practices to guide all of American schooling.

FOOTNOTES

1. Seymour Sarason, *Schooling in America: Scapegoat and Salvation* (New York: Free Press, 1983).

2. The National Commission on Excellence in Education, *A Nation at Risk: The Imperative for Educational Reform* (Washington, D.C.: U.S. Department of Education, 1983). Other conservative examples include: Twentieth Century Fund Task Force on Federal Elementary and Secondary Education Policy, *Making the Grade* (New York: Twentieth Century Fund, 1983); National Science Board/National Science Foundation, *Today's Problems, Tomorrow's Crises* (Washington, D.C.: National Science Board, 1982); Business in Higher Education Forum, *America's Competitive Challenge: The Need for a National Response* (Washington, D.C.: Business in Higher Education Forum, 1983); Task Force on Education for Economic Growth, *Action for Excellence: A Comprehensive Plan to Improve our Nation's Schools* (Denver, CO: Education Commission of the States, 1983).

3. John Goodlad, *A Place Called School: Promise for the Future* (New York: McGraw-Hill, 1984); Ernest L. Boyer, *High School: A Report on American Secondary Education* (New York: Harper & Row, 1983). Also generally included in this group of reports, although some might not choose to label them "liberal," are Sarason, *Schooling in America*; Theodore Sizer, *Horace's Compromise: The Dilemma of the High School* (Boston: Houghton Mifflin, 1984); Mortimer J. Adler, *The Paideia Proposal: An Educational Manifesto* (New York: MacMillan, 1982); idem, *The Paideia Program: An Educational Syllabus* (New York: MacMillan, 1984).

4. Some of these include Lawrence C. Stedman and Marshall S. Smith, "Recent Reform Proposals for American Education," *Contemporary Education Review* 53, no. 2 (1983): 85-104; Walter Feinberg, "Fixing the Schools: The Ideological Turn," *Issues in Education* 3, no. 2 (1985): 113-38; H. Svi Shapiro, "Education, the Welfare State and Reaganomics: The Limits of Conservative Reform," *Urban Education* 20, no. 4 (1986): 443-71; Ann Bastian, Norm Fruchter, Marilyn Gittell, Colin Greer, and Kenneth Haskins, "Choosing Equality: The Case for Democratic Schooling," *Social Policy* 15, no. 4 (1985): 34-51; Jeannie Oakes, "Tracking, Inequality, and the Rhetoric of Reform: Why Schools Don't Change," *Journal of Education* 168, no. 1 (1986): 60-80; and Stanley A. Aronowitz and Henry A. Giroux, *Education Under Siege* (South Hadley, MA: Bergin and Garvey, 1985).

5. See, for example, Feinberg, "Fixing the Schools"; and Oakes, "Tracking, Inequality, and the Rhetoric of Reform"; Jeri J. Goldman, "Political and Legal Issues in Minimum Competency Testing," *Educational Forum* 48 (Winter 1984): 207-16; and Martha M. McCarthy, "Application of Competency Testing Mandates to Handicapped Children," *Harvard Educational Review* 53 (1983): 146-64.

6. Two very recent exceptions are Marleen Pugach and Mara Sapon-Shevin, "New Agendas for Special Education Policy: What the National Reports Haven't Said," *Exceptional Children* 53, no. 4 (1987): 295-99, and Mara Sapon-Shevin, "The National Education Reports and Special Education: Implications for Students," *Exceptional Children* 53, no. 4 (1987): 300-6.

7. National Commission on Excellence in Education, *A Nation at Risk*, p. 5.

8. Task Force on Education for Economic Growth, *Action for Excellence*, p. 4.

9. Boyer, *High School*, p. 63.

10. See citations listed under note 4.

11. Compare, for example, the report of the National Commission on Excellence in Education (*A Nation at Risk*) and of the Twentieth Century Fund (*Making the Grade*) with the more scholarly efforts of Goodlad, *A Place Called School* and Boyer, *High School*.

12. See also Bastian et al., "Choosing Equality," or Edward Berman, "The Improbability of Meaningful Educational Reform," *Issues in Education* 3, no. 2 (1985): 99-111.

13. George H. Wood, "Beyond Radical Educational Cynicism," *Educational Theory* 32, no. 2 (1982): 55-72.

14. See, for example, Samuel Bowles and Herbert Gintis, *Schooling in Capitalist America* (New York: Basic Books, 1976); Martin Carnoy and Henry M. Levin, *The Limits of Educational Reform* (New York: McKay, 1976); Michael W. Apple, *Cultural and Economic Reproduction in Education* (Boston, MA: Routledge and Kegan Paul, 1982); and Henry A. Giroux, *Theory and Resistance in Education* (South Hadley, MA: Bergin & Garvey, 1983).

15. Cited in Boyer, *High School*, p. 63.

16. Seymour B. Sarason and John Doris, *Educational Handicap, Public Policy, and Social History* (New York: Free Press, 1979).

17. Bastian et al., "Choosing Equality," p. 39.
18. National Commission on Excellence in Education, *A Nation at Risk*, pp. 35-36.
19. Carnoy and Levin, "Educational Reform and Class Conflict," pp. 43-44.
20. Wood, "Beyond Radical Educational Cynicism," p. 62. See also, Henry A. Giroux, "Thunder on the Right: Education and the Ideology of the Quick Fix," *Curriculum Inquiry* 15, no. 2 (1985): 57-62, and idem, "Critical Pedagogy, Cultural Politics and the Discourse of Experience, *Journal of Education* 167, no. 2 (1985): 22-41.
21. See, for example, Paul Willis, *Learning to Labour: How Working Class Kids Get Working Class Jobs* (Farnborough, England: Saxon House, 1977); idem, "Cultural Production Is Different from Cultural Reproduction, Is Different from Social Reproduction, Is Different from Production," *Interchange* 12 (1981): 48-67; Jean Anyon, "Social Class and School Knowledge," *Curriculum Inquiry* 11, no. 1 (1981): 3-42; Michael W. Apple and Lois Weis, "Seeing Education Relationally: The Stratification of Culture and People: The Sociology of School Knowledge," *Journal of Education* 168, no. 1 (1986): 7-34.
22. See Michael W. Apple, "Curriculum and the Labor Process: The Logic of Technical Control," *Social Text* 5 (1982): 108-25; Aronowitz and Giroux, *Education Under Siege*; Gary Sykes, "Contradictions, Ironies, and Promises Unfulfilled: A Contemporary Account of the Status of Teaching," *Phi Delta Kappan* 65, no. 2 (1983): 87-93; and Henry A. Giroux and Peter McLaren, "Teacher Education and the Politics of Engagement: The Case for Democratic Schooling," *Harvard Educational Review* 56, no. 3 (1986): 213-38.
23. See, for example, Thomas M. Skrtic, *An Organizational Analysis of Special Education Reform* (Lawrence, KS: University of Kansas, 1987); Karl E. Weick, "Sources of Order in Underorganized Systems," in Yvonna S. Lincoln, ed., *Organization Theory and Inquiry: The Paradigm Revolution* (Beverly Hills, CA: Sage Publications, 1985); John W. Meyer and Brian Rowan, "The Structure of Educational Organizations," in Marshall W. Meyer, ed., *Environments and Organizations* (San Francisco: Jossey-Bass, 1978).
24. Donald L. MacMillan, Reginald L. Jones, and C. Edward Meyers, "Mainstreaming the Mildly Retarded: Some Questions, Cautions, and Guidelines," *Mental Retardation* 14, no. 1 (1976): 3-10.
25. National Center for Educational Statistics, *The Condition of Education* (Washington, DC: U.S. Department of Education, 1985); and Office of Special Education and Rehabilitative Services, *Ninth Annual Report to Congress on the Implementation of the Education of the Handicapped Act* (Washington, DC: U.S. Department of Education, 1987). See also Christine Sleeter, "Learning Disabilities: The Social Construction of a Special Education Category," *Exceptional Children*, 53, no. 1 (1986): 45-54, for an analysis of the shift in use of "MR" to "LD" for this group of "delabeled" students.
26. Oakes, "Tracking, Inequality, and the Rhetoric of Reform," p. 75.
27. See, for example, Judith D. Singer and John A. Butler, "The Education for All Handicapped Children Act: Schools as Agents of Social Reform," *Harvard Educational Review* 57, no. 1 (1987): 125-52, as well as Office of Special Education and Rehabilitative Services, *Fifth Annual Report to Congress* and *Ninth Annual Report to Congress*.
28. Singer and Butler, "The Education of All Handicapped Children Act," p. 151.
29. Ibid.
30. Skrtic, *An Organizational Analysis of Special Education Reform*, pp. 37-38.
31. Douglas P. Biklen, *Achieving the Complete School: Strategies for Effective Mainstreaming* (New York: Teachers College Press, 1985); Steven J. Taylor and

Dianne L. Ferguson, "A Summary of Strategies Utilized in Model Programs and Resource Materials," in Susan Stainback and William Stainback, eds., *Integration of Students with Severe Handicaps into Regular Schools* (Reston, VA: Council for Exceptional Children, 1985), pp. 125-45; David W. Johnson and Roger T. Johnson, "Mainstreaming and Cooperative Learning Strategies," *Exceptional Children* 52 (1986): 553-61.

32. The following represent only a small sample of the conversation in one journal: Alan Gartner, "Disabling Help: Special Education at the Crossroads," *Exceptional Children* 53, no. 1 (1986): 72-76; Margaret C. Wang and Maynard C. Reynolds, "Catch 22 and Disabling Help: A Reply to Alan Gartner," *Exceptional Children* 53, no. 1 (1986): 77-79; Bob Algozzine and James E. Ysseldyke, "Learning Disabilities as a Subset of School Failure: The Oversophistication of a Concept," *Exceptional Children* 50, no. 3 (1983): 242-46; William Stainback and Susan Stainback, "The Merger of Special and Regular Education: Can It Be Done? A Response to Lieberman and Mesinger," *Exceptional Children* 51, no. 6 (1985): 517-21; William Stainback, Susan Stainback, Lee Courtnage, and Twila Jaben, "Facilitating Mainstreaming by Modifying the Mainstream," *Exceptional Children* 52, no. 2 (1985): 144-52.

33. See, for example, all of the above, and Skrtic, *An Organizational Analysis of Special Education Reform*; Madeleine Will, *Educating Students with Learning Problems* (Washington, D.C.: U.S. Department of Education, 1986); Donald L. MacMillan, Reginald L. Jones, and C. Edward Meyers, "Mainstreaming the Mildly Retarded: Some Questions, Cautions, and Guidelines," *Mental Retardation* 14, no. 1 (1976): 3-10; Bob Algozzine and Lori Korinek, "Where Is Special Education for Students with High Prevalence Handicaps Going?" *Exceptional Children* 51, no. 5 (1985): 388-94.

34. Skrtic, *An Organizational Analysis of Special Education Reform*.

35. Samuel Kirk and G. Orville Johnson, *Educating the Retarded Child* (Cambridge, MA: Houghton Mifflin, 1951), p. 8.

36. See citations listed in footnote 23.

37. This and the following section represent an extension of the analysis contained in Dianne L. Ferguson, *Curriculum Decision Making for Students with Severe Handicaps: Policy and Practice* (New York: Teachers College Press, 1987).

38. For example, Robert F. Johnson and Luanna Meyer, "Program Design and Research to Normalize Peer Interactions," in Michael P. Brady and Philip L. Gunter, eds., *Integrating Moderately and Severely Handicapped Learners: Strategies that Work* (Springfield, IL: Charles C Thomas, 1985), pp. 79-101.

39. Sarason, *Schooling in America*.

40. Boyer, *High School*, p. 209.

41. Marsha Forest, "Keys to Integration: Common Sense Ideas and Hard Work," *Entourage* 2, no. 1 (1987): 16-20.

42. Goodlad, *A Place Called School*.

43. Some writers find that the degree of passivity and obedience increases as one descends the levels of academic performance and status. See, for example, Bowles and Gintis, *Schooling in Capitalist America*; Boyer, *High School*; and Sizer, *Horace's Compromise*.

44. H. Svi Shapiro, "Society, Ideology and the Reform of Special Education: A Study in the Limits of Educational Change," *Educational Theory* 30, no. 3 (1980): 222.

45. Doug Guess and Ellin Siegel-Causey, "Behavioral Control and Education of Severely Handicapped Students: Who's Doing What to Whom? and Why?" in Diane Bricker and John Filler, eds., *Serving the Severely Retarded: From Research to Practice* (Reston, VA: Council for Exceptional Children, 1983), pp. 230-44; Doug Guess, Holly A. Benson, and Ellin Siegel-Causey, "Concepts and Issues Related to Choice-

Making and Autonomy among Persons with Severe Disabilities," *Journal of the Association for Persons with Severe Handicaps* 10, no. 2 (1985): 79-86; Martin Seligman, *Helplessness: On Depression, Development and Death* (San Francisco: W.H. Freeman, 1975); Mayer Shevin and Nancy K. Klein, "The Importance of Choice-Making Skills for Students with Severe Disabilities," *Journal of the Association for Persons with Severe Handicaps* 9, no. 3 (1984): 159-66.

46. David W. Johnson and Roger T. Johnson, "Mainstreaming and Cooperative Learning Strategies," *Exceptional Children* 52 (1986): 555-61; David W. Johnson, "Building Friendships Between Handicapped and Nonhandicapped Students: Effects of Cooperative and Individualistic Instruction," *American Educational Research Journal* 18, no. 4 (1981): 415-24. See also the chapter in this volume by Stainback and Stainback.

47. See, for example, Wayne Sailor and Doug Guess, *Severely Handicapped Students: An Instructional Design* (Boston: Houghton Mifflin, 1983): Barbara Wilcox and G. Thomas Bellamy, *Design of High School Programs for Severely Handicapped Students* (Baltimore, MD: Paul H. Brookes, 1982); idem, *The Activities Catalog; An Alternate Curriculum for Youth and Adults with Severe Disabilities* (Baltimore, MD: Paul H. Brookes, 1987); idem, *A Comprehensive Guide to the Activities Catalog; An Alternate Curriculum for Youth and Adults with Severe Disabilities* (Baltimore, MD: Paul H. Brookes, 1987).

48. Gareth H. Williams, "The Movement for Independent Living: An Evaluation and Critique," *Social Science and Medicine* 17, no. 15 (1983): 1009.

49. Robert V. Bullough, Jr. and Andres D. Gitlin, "Schooling and Change: A View from the Lower Rung," *Teachers College Record* 87, no. 2 (1985): 219-37. See also, Apple, "Curriculum and the Labor Process"; Boyer, *High School*; and Sizer, *Horace's Compromise*.

50. Stephen T. Kerr, "Teacher Specialization and the Growth of a Bureaucratic Profession," *Teachers College Record* 84, no. 3 (1983): 629-51; Magali Sarfatti Larson, *The Rise of Professionalism: A Sociological Analysis* (Berkeley, CA: University of California Press, 1977).

51. Amitai Etzioni, ed., *The Semi-professions and Their Organization* (New York: Free Press, 1969).

52. The Holmes Group, *Tomorrow's Teachers: A Report of the Holmes Group* (East Lansing, MI: Holmes Group, 1986); Carnegie Commission, *A Nation Prepared: Teachers for the 21st Century* (New York: Carnegie Forum, 1986).

53. For example, in just one issue of the journal *Educational Policy*, vol. 1, no. 1 (1987), the following articles appeared: Hugh G. Petrie, "Teacher Education, the Liberal Arts, and Extended Preparation Programs" (pp. 29-42), Alan R. Tom, "A Critique of the Rationale for Extended Teacher Preparation" (pp. 43-56), R. Jerrald Shive and Charles W. Case, "Differentiated Staffing as an Educational Reform Response" (pp. 57-66), Susan Moore Johnson and Niall C. W. Nelson, "Conflict and Compatibility in Visions of Reform" (pp. 67-80), Hendrick D. Gideonse, "The Holmes Group Proposals: Critical Reactions and Prospects" (pp. 81-92).

CHAPTER III

Characteristics of Educational Programs for Students with Severe Intellectual Disabilities

KATHY ZANELLA ALBRIGHT, LOU BROWN,
PAT VANDEVENTER, AND JACK JORGENSEN

Philosophically, the goals of public education for the highest intellectually functioning students in our school population are the same as those for the lowest. We expect *all* of our children to become productive members of society, to advance the culture, to be the best that they can be, to be responsible citizens, to give more than they take, and so forth.

Obviously, at some point these lofty and rhetorical goals must be converted to actual educational practices appropriate for the day-to-day activities of school. When amorphous goals are converted to specific expectations for the highest intellectually functioning students, we usually say that they should succeed in higher education, lead corporations, become powerful and influential political officials, and solve the major health and social problems of the day. We then design and implement educational programs that are preparatory for attaining such outcomes.

When the lowest intellectually functioning students in our society are addressed, the purpose of educational programs is to prepare them to function with maximal productivity, individuality, competence, freedom, and integrity in all environments and activities experienced by people without disabilities. That is, they should live and function as productively and efficiently as they possibly can in normalized homes; they should perform real work in real work places next to

---

This chapter was supported in part by Grant Nos. G008302977 and G008630388 to the University of Wisconsin and the Madison Metropolitan School District from the U.S. Department of Education, Office of Special Education and Rehabilitative Services, Division of Innovation and Development; and by Grant No. G008400669 to the University of Wisconsin from the U.S. Department of Education, Office of Special Education and Rehabilitative Services, Division of Personnel Preparation.

people without disabilities; they should enjoy the rich and varied recreational and leisure environments and activities experienced by all; and they should function effectively and appropriately in a wide variety of general community environments, such as stores, malls, buses, streets, hospitals, and restaurants.

The highest intellectually functioning students in any school system almost always attain the goals delineated for the lowest intellectually functioning students without the need for years of direct instruction provided by school personnel in actual domestic, vocational, general community, and recreational/leisure environments and activities. Unfortunately, students with severe intellectual disabilities do not. That is, many of the skills, attitudes, and values typically ascribed as responsibilities of parents or guardians, peers, churches, community organizations, and recreational and leisure agencies can and must be taught by school personnel or they will never be acquired. For example, few school personnel would consider spending time teaching students in the highest intellectually functioning 1 percent of our school population to walk from their house to a bus stop, to fold letters at an integrated work site, or to use their local Y.M.C.A. However, such skills are critical to the integrated life functioning of people with severe intellectual disabilities and must be taught using the resources, talents, and longitudinal commitments of school personnel. If they are not taught, these students will lead unduly constricted and nonproductive lives and billions of tax dollars will have been wasted.

The primary purpose of this paper is to delineate and justify eleven characteristics of educational services that are critical to the growth of students who are severely intellectually disabled. If school personnel fail to actualize at least these characteristics in direct educational services, they are remiss in their instructional responsibilities.

Before the eleven critical characteristics are addressed it seems appropriate to offer a definition of students who are severely intellectually disabled and to review several, but certainly not all, of their most relevant learning and performance characteristics.

Students with severe intellectual disabilities are those who function intellectually within approximately the lowest 1 percent of a naturally distributed general population. Traditionally, I.Q. scores below 50 and the labels "moderate," "severe," and "profound" mental retardation have been used to describe many of these students. In addition to functioning among the lowest 1 percent of the general population intellectually, these students often manifest a remarkably wide variety of related difficulties such as deafness, blindness, deafness and blindness, limited use of extremities, serious maladaptive behaviors, inability to communicate verbally, inability to walk unassisted, extremely low response rates, and severe medical problems.

Learning and Performance Characteristics of Students with Severe Intellectual Disabilities

The label "severely intellectually disabled" should mean differences both in degree and in kind from those not so labeled. When such students are compared to nondisabled chronological age peers, they manifest difficulties in relation to almost all generally acknowledged learning and performance phenomena. These difficulties must be addressed individually and constructively in educational programs. This is not to minimize the valid and extremely important reality that while different intellectually, they are the same as all other citizens when human dignity, constitutional rights, individual freedoms, educability, and other quality of life dimensions are considered. Six of the many relevant learning and performance characteristics that are of particular significance are addressed here and are similar to those discussed by Brown and his colleagues.[1]

Number of skills that can be acquired. From birth to age twenty-one students who are severely intellectually disabled will acquire fewer skills than approximately 99 percent of their chronological age peers. Thus, it is extremely important that those selected for instruction be the most important for functioning effectively in both current and subsequent integrated environments and activities. Conversely, instructional time should not be wasted teaching skills that are not sufficiently preparatory for a decent quality of life in integrated environments and activities. One strategy to determine the relative importance of a particular skill is to use the "Why Question," which asks the teacher to examine the relationship between a particular educational activity and the students' present and future needs.[2]

Number of instructional trials and amount of time needed. Generally, the more intellectually disabled a student, the greater the number of direct instructional trials needed to acquire skills at meaningful performance criteria. Thus, when providing direct instruction, individually and empirically determined increases in the number of trials must be arranged. Conversely, time-determined progressions through curricula should generally be rejected such as "Each Friday in

November we will go bowling" or "During February we will do a unit on shopping."

Forgetting-recoupment. Forgetting refers to decrements in the performance of an acquired skill after time passes during which the skill is not utilized or is utilized infrequently. Recoupment refers to the instructional time and effort necessary to relearn a skill at original performance criteria. In general, students who are severely intellectually disabled forget more and require substantially more time and instructional trials to return to original performance criteria than do all others. These forgetting-recoupment difficulties suggest four instructional principles:

1. Skills that are consistently required in the nonschool environments in which students currently function must be selected for instruction.

2. *Prior* to selection for instruction it must be verified that the skill of concern will actually be performed frequently if it is learned.

3. Direct instructional services throughout the calendar year must be available.

4. Meaningful communication and coordination between significant people in school and nonschool environments must be arranged.

Transfer-generalization. Performance of a skill under conditions different from those under which it was acquired is called transfer of training or generalization.[3] In general, the more intellectually disabled a student, the less confidence one can have that skills acquired under one set of circumstances will be performed acceptably under others. For example, it is doubtful that a student who is severely intellectually disabled and who has cerebral palsy will be able to transfer the skills necessary to remove twelve plastic eggs from a plastic egg container and put them into a plastic refrigerator egg box in a simulated school kitchen to his home where it is necessary to remove real eggs from a brittle styrofoam container and place them delicately in his refrigerator.

Skill complexity. There are thousands of complex skills that can be acquired by nondisabled students that either cannot be acquired by those who are severely intellectually disabled or that are extremely cost-inefficient when the return for educational investment is considered. Investing twelve years in the memorization of basic addition facts, or naming the letters of the alphabet, or the learning of the names of the presidents of the United States are but a few examples. Additionally, teaching complex skills that require disproportionate amounts of time and effort can result in severe curricular imbalances. Allocating two hours per day to teach categorizing foods into four groups at the expense of teaching skills required to prepare a simple meal, to purchase needed items at a grocery store, and to order food from a real restaurant menu is but one example. School personnel must provide cost-efficient instruction of individually relevant complex skills that are appropriately balanced in relation to the demands of a wide variety of integrated school and nonschool environments.

Synthesis skills. A nonintellectually disabled student may learn one skill as a result of mathematics instruction, another from reading instruction, and a third from language instruction. He or she is then capable of synthesizing and applying these different skills to make a purchase in a neighborhood grocery store. Rarely is a student with severe intellectual disabilities able to synthesize skills learned in three different contexts and apply them functionally in a fourth. These difficulties make it necessary to provide direct instruction in environments and activities that inherently require synthesis. In other words, the many social skills required to make purchases (e.g., reading and language skills, motor skills, skills related to mathematics and money, and skills related to street safety) must be taught in the process of making real purchases.

To summarize, envision someone who can learn, but not as much as 99 percent of his or her chronological age peers; who needs more time and instructional trials to learn and to relearn than all others; who forgets more than almost all others without consistent practice; who has difficulty transferring that learned in one environment to another; and who rarely synthesizes skills acquired from several different experiences in order to function effectively in a novel situation. Then, ask the question: What are the critical characteristics of an educational program that will allow this student to be as productive, as independent, and as efficient as possible in a wide variety of integrated environments and activities at the end of the school career?

Critical Characteristics of Educational Programs

Eleven critical characteristics of a minimally acceptable educational program for the lowest intellectually functioning 1 percent of our student population will be discussed here. In our judgment, the eleven critical characteristics are: integration, a life-space oriented curriculum, functional skills, chronological age appropriateness, skill transfer verification, practice, parent or guardian involvement, nonschool instruction, the principle of partial participation, individualized adaptations, and individualized transition plans.

INTEGRATION

For over 100 years we have spent billions of tax dollars serving people with severe intellectual disabilities in homogenized environments such as "institutions for the retarded," segregated schools, segregated classes in regular schools, and segregated art, music, and physical education classes. We now realize that the logic and economics of homogeneity and the associated segregated service systems that accrue from them are no longer acceptable. Heterogeneity or integration is now the rule of the day. We now know that students with and without disabilities must be physically next to each other as much as possible if both are to flourish.

If educational environments and activities are naturally proportioned and if students are in close physical proximity to their chronological age peers without disabilities, several extremely important outcomes are highly likely to occur. First, substantial parts of our society will become desensitized to and tolerant, understanding, and supportive of people with disabilities. Second, students without disabilities will learn how to help their peers who are disabled. Third, many people without disabilities who will ultimately become public service providers such as physicians, bus drivers, nurses, and restaurant workers will learn how to provide direct services to those who do not see, speak, hear, walk, and so forth. Fourth, many young people who are the future parents of children with disabilities will be better prepared for that role. Fifth, many people who presumably act on behalf of people with severe intellectual disabilities, such as law enforcement officers, legislators, supervisors, and public administrators, will be acting with the knowledge and experience that can only come from long-term personal involvement. Finally, in integrated environments and activities the likelihood is greatest that warm, stimulating, and mutually gratifying friendships with nondisabled others will be established.[4]

At least three phenomena must be realized before students who are severely intellectually disabled can be considered educationally integrated:

1. The students must use the same environments and participate in the same activities at the same times as their nondisabled chronological age peers.

2. The environments and activities must be naturally proportioned. No more than approximately 1 percent of any large group should consist of students who are severely intellectually disabled; and in any case no more than two students with disabilities should be present in any environment or activity.

3. Individual acknowledgements and accommodations to unique abilities and disabilities must be recognized and honored. All reasonable allowance must be made to arrange for the maximum involvement of all students in all environments and activities.

A LIFE-SPACE ORIENTED CURRICULUM

The phrase "life space" refers to factors and experiences that impinge upon the existence of a person 24 hours per day, 7 days per week, 365 days per year. A life-space oriented curriculum refers to delineating, organizing, analyzing, and addressing instructionally the significant phenomena that have an effect on the nature and quality of a life space. These phenomena include places, people, activities, materials, problems, dreams, attitudes, demands, and values.[5]

Unfortunately, students with severe intellectual disabilities almost always experience substantially fewer normalized community environments and activities per day, per week, and per year than do their nondisabled peers. Thus, one major purpose of an educational program must be to prepare for acceptable functioning in a dramatically increased quantity of rich and varied integrated community environments and activities. A second major purpose must be to enhance the degree of participation in each environment and activity.

When students do not function in reasonable accordance with capability in a tenable number of environments and activities, unduly constricted lives are too common, valuable human and economic resources are wasted, and specialized educational interventions are clearly in order. A life-space analysis must secure instructionally meaningful information about the number of environments and activities in which a student currently functions, the number in which he or she should function in the near future, and the nature and quality of involvement in each. Comprehensive and detailed life-space analyses are particularly important so that:

1. individually meaningful participation in a reasonable array of integrated environments and activities can be arranged;

2. as much instructionally useful information as is necessary to offer habilitative and cost-efficient instructional services can be secured;

3. home/school communication and cooperation can be maximized;

4. meaningful longitudinal educational and related service plans can be designed and implemented;

5. instruction that allows individually meaningful productivity and actualization in a variety of integrated nonschool environments can be provided;

6. reasonable and empirically acceptable inferences related to transfer of training from school to nonschool and postschool environments can be made; and

7. practice opportunities that minimize forgetting and recoupment problems can be engineered.

FUNCTIONAL SKILLS

A functional skill refers to an action that must be performed by someone else, if it is not performed by a student with severe intellectual disabilities. For example, Sue is responsible for washing her breakfast dishes. The skills necessary to do this are considered functional because if she does not wash her dishes, someone else must. A reasonable repertoire of functional skills is extremely important because the more one can do for oneself the more valued and respected one will be.

A nonfunctional or an other than functional skill refers to an action that will not be performed or is not required to be performed by someone else, if it is not performed by a student with severe intellectual disabilities.[6] For example, Jason is being taught to place pegs in the holes of a pegboard. In order to determine whether or not the necessary skills are nonfunctional, the question that must be asked is "If Jason does not put the pegs in the holes, must or might someone else?" If the answer is "No" those skills are considered nonfunctional in accordance with the definition offered.

Should skills that *do not* meet the definitional criterion of functionality offered here be selected for instructional purposes for students with severe intellectual disabilities? Definitely, Yes. It is extremely important that all students acquire and perform an individually meaningful variety of nonfunctional skills in that the quality of a life space will be substantially better. Recreational and leisure skills are good examples. Sam is fourteen years old. If he does not perform the skills necessary to look through a magazine while listening to audio tapes of his favorite music, must someone else? The answer is "No," so the skills in question are nonfunctional. Nevertheless, it is extremely important that they be in his repertoire for without them his quality of life would be diminished considerably. For Sam, these skills are valuable because they are appropriate to his chronological age; they can be used frequently; they can be used throughout his life; they can be performed at home, in school, at the public library, at work, or on a bus. And they are valuable *because they are subjectively enjoyable.*

At any point in an educational career a student with severe intellectual disabilities can be provided instruction in only a small proportion of a large population of functional skills. Thus, informed judgments about which should and should not be selected for instruction must be made. Janet is fifteen years old, nonambulatory, and attends a senior high school. Her parents, teachers, and therapists were at the point in an Individualized Education Program planning meeting at which they had to decide between teaching her to shop for clothes or for food. Both skill clusters were functional—if she did not buy her clothes or buy her food, someone else would. After considering many factors in addition to functionality, it was decided to teach her to buy food, but not to buy clothing for the following reasons: (a) buying food can be performed biweekly thereby allowing important practice opportunities; (b) buying food is something she can do for others in her home, as others do many things for her each day; (c) a grocery store is in her neighborhood and she can learn to wheel to and from it by herself; and (d) the grocery store manager will allow her to "charge" her purchases since she cannot count.

In sum, since a minimally acceptable educational program must contain the direct instruction of both functional and nonfunctional skills, some of the issues that must be addressed are:

1. Of all the possible functional skills that could be taught, which should be chosen for direct instruction and why?

2. Of all the possible nonfunctional skills that could be taught, which should be chosen for direct instruction and why?

3. Within an instructional week, what proportion of skills should be functional as opposed to nonfunctional and why?

CHRONOLOGICAL AGE APPROPRIATENESS

Chronological age appropriateness refers to utilizing environments, activities, skills, language, attitudes, and instructional materials that are associated in affirmative, culturally sanctioned, and respected ways with particular age groups.[7]

Students with severe intellectual disabilities will never be able to learn all the skills, attitudes, values, acquired by chronological age peers without disabilities. Nevertheless, one of the basic purposes of educational programs must be to minimize rather than maximize differences between them and their chronological age peers. Thus, the instructional responsibility of the educational community becomes that of delineating whatever learnings can be acquired of a chronological age appropriate nature and ensuring that the instructional services necessary for their development are arranged.

Historically, educators have used developmental age to determine educational curricula for students with severe intellectual disabilities. Tragically, this strategy has resulted in long-term instruction designed to teach chronologically evolving students to become more and more like normally developing infants. Over time, the differences between them and their nondisabled chronological age peers were maximized and at age twenty-one it was considered inconceivable that they could function effectively in integrated environments and activities with nondisabled adults. Thus, they were confined to segregated environments for the rest of their lives. It is highly recommended that after about chronological age five such concepts as developmental age, I.Q., mental age, social age, and language age be deleted from references to people with severe intellectual disabilities because they only result in devaluation, demeaning curricula, and educational experiences that do not prepare for reasonable functioning in the most habilitative environments and activities in adulthood.

SKILL TRANSFER VERIFICATION

Transfer refers to the acquisition and performance of skills under one cluster of conditions, and the extent to which they are performed under different conditions, without direct instruction, in the absence of school personnel, and within a relatively short period of time.[8] Neil is a fourteen year old student with severe intellectual disabilities who attends a junior high school. He was taught to make scrambled eggs at acceptable criteria in the kitchen of a teacher's house near his school. One Saturday morning shortly thereafter his father asked for scrambled eggs. His mother announced that she was too busy. His father jokingly asked Neil to make the scrambled eggs, even though he had never demonstrated the required skills in his home. Minutes later he served scrambled eggs to his extremely surprised Dad. This is an example of rare, yet remarkably good, skill transfer. Skills that were taught as part of a school program were performed acceptably under different conditions, without direct instruction, in the absence of school personnel, and within a relatively short period of time.

Because people with severe intellectual disabilities manifest extreme memory, generalization, and transfer difficulties, it is unacceptable to infer that if performance is expressed at criterion in instructional conditions, it will be manifested under different conditions at some point in the future. Therefore, it is extremely important that individualized and systematic arrangements for maximal skills transfer are arranged *prior* to the initiation of actual instruction. *Before* selecting an environment, activity, instructional materials or skill for instructional purposes, at least the following must be ensured:

1. that significant others will allow and encourage the performance of the skill. Joe received instruction several hours a week learning how to cook, but at home his parents kept him away from the hot stove. Opportunities for skill transfer were not available.

2. that the student has access to natural environments under noninstructional conditions. Allen receives instruction on how to use a bowling alley several times each week. Unfortunately, his parents hate to bowl and he never has an opportunity to use the alley under noninstructional conditions. Jane receives weekly instruction learning how to use a sit down restaurant, but her parents cannot afford to take her to such environments. In both cases opportunities are not available for skill transfer and valuable instructional resources are being wasted.

3. that natural materials are used during instruction; and

4. that the performance criteria required to function in the real world are realized.

PRACTICE

Two reasons for labeling people "severely intellectually disabled" are that they manifest more memory difficulties than 99 percent of the general population, and that once they forget that which has been learned, they are likely to take longer and to need more instructional trials in order to relearn than all others. The question thus becomes: If we know a student is highly likely to forget and that recoupment will require almost as many resources as original learning, why should we select a skill for instruction without a prior commitment for practice opportunities under noninstructional conditions?

Practice refers to the performance of a skill under noninstructional conditions once it has been acquired. In general, it is extremely difficult to justify the selection of a skill for instructional purposes without prior commitments from noninstructional personnel that opportunities for practice will be arranged consistently. Obviously, a priori practice commitments from noninstructional personnel also require the support and systematic involvement of parents, guardians, brothers, sisters, and significant others in the educational process.[9]

INVOLVEMENT OF PARENTS AND GUARDIANS

In the past when parents and guardians banded together and established educational services because public school personnel would not serve their children, many actually determined the nature of the entire educational experience. Teachers and other direct service personnel often were allowed limited professional input. Conversely, there have been professionals who have systematically and effectively excluded parents and guardians from even minimal involvement in the design and implementation of the educational and related services offered their children. Most now realize that parent and guardian involvement in the education process is critical and that a constructive balance between parents and guardians and professionals in decision making is educationally sound.

All reasonable attempts should be made to ensure the informed and consistent input of parents and guardians into the design and implementation of educational programs. The delicate professional issue seems to be that of balance and proportion. How much decision-making authority and what decisions should be ascribed to parents and guardians and to professionals? Decisions that should be rotated, compromised, or made jointly are matters that must be determined individually.[10]

If the effectiveness of the instruction provided is to be maximized, students must have opportunities to transfer and practice the skills that they are learning under noninstructional conditions. Parents and guardians must be involved to ensure that transfer will occur. The authors have observed a situation that illustrates the point:

When a life-space analysis of Matt was conducted with his family, it was determined that almost every day after school and during weekends he was alone, with family members, or with people paid to be with him. He had no friends. His family considered this unbearable and requested assistance from school personnel. An instructional program to engender friendships between Matt and chronological age peers with and without disabilities in his neighborhood was designed and implemented. After a few short months, Matt spent approximately 50 percent of his free time after school and on weekends with chronological age appropriate friends.

NONSCHOOL INSTRUCTION

Historically, educators have tried to teach students with severe intellectual disabilities many skills over long periods of time in relatively few environments. Specifically, almost all instruction was provided on school grounds. Unfortunately, this strategy has not resulted in an acceptable return for the investment of valuable educational resources. After years and years of instruction in relatively few environments students completed their school careers and, in an overwhelming majority of the cases, spent the rest of their lives in unduly costly segregated day activity centers and sheltered workshops.

It is more educationally prudent to teach relatively few skills in many environments than it is to teach many skills in a few environments. That is, individualized, systematic, longitudinal, and comprehensive direct instruction in a wide variety of nonschool environments must be provided during the educational career so that meaningful functioning in the widest possible variety of integrated environments in adulthood can be realized.

Nonschool instruction refers to providing direct instruction in appropriate nonschool environments in which students currently function, and in the most habilitative environments in which they are most likely to function in the near future.[11] It is critical that students with severe intellectual disabilities receive instruction in a variety of integrated nonschool environments starting no later than age four. Elementary school age students should receive instruction in a variety of nonschool recreational, domestic, and community environments. During the middle and high school years direct instruction in integrated community vocational environments should be added. Generally, as students get older the amount of integrated nonschool instruction provided should increase from approximately 30 percent in elementary school to at least 50 to 60 percent in middle and high schools. During ages eighteen to twenty-one, almost all instruction should be provided in normalized arrays of integrated nonschool environments.

Nonschool instruction is critical because students with severe intellectual disabilities always experience significant difficulties generalizing and transferring what they learned in a school building. Additionally, by providing nonschool instruction, individuals without disabilities can be desensitized to and learn to help, serve, and develop friendships with individuals with disabilities. Finally, respect, understanding, and cooperation can be enhanced substantially if taxpayers actually see these students being taught to perform meaningful skills in community environments.

THE PRINCIPLE OF PARTIAL PARTICIPATION

The principle of partial participation is an affirmation that all students with severe intellectual disabilities can acquire many skills that will allow them to function, at least in part, in a wide variety of integrated environments and activities. Specifically, the principle of partial participation affirms that:

1. partial participation in chronological age appropriate integrated environments and activities is educationally more advantageous than exclusion from such environments and activities;

2. students with severe intellectual disabilities, regardless of their degrees of dependence or levels of functioning, should be allowed to participate at least partially in a wide range of integrated school and nonschool environments and activities;

3. the kinds and degrees of partial participation in integrated school and nonschool environments and activities can and should be increased through direct and systematic instruction;

4. the kinds and degrees of partial participation in integrated school and nonschool environments and activities should result in a student being perceived by others as a more valuable, contributing, striving, and productive member of society; and

5. systematic, coordinated, and longitudinal efforts must be initiated at young ages in order to prepare for at least partial participation in as many integrated environments and activities as possible.[12]

These students will never be able to learn all of the chronological age appropriate and functional skills in the repertoires of people without disabilities. Nevertheless, it is important that educators use the principle of partial participation so that no one is excluded from integrated environments and activities because they are unable to perform, or are unlikely to learn *all* of the skills required. For example,

Jenny expresses a clear preference to function vocationally in an office. Unfortunately, due to her physical and intellectual disabilities, she is incapable of performing *all* the tasks typically required of an office worker without disabilities of her chronological age. Specifically, she cannot read mail, use a word processor, a dictaphone, or the telephone. If she were required to perform all that workers without disabilities do, she would be unable to work in an office. However, the principle of partial participation allows the educator to ask the question: "Is there anything Jenny can do to make a contribution to the functioning of an office?" In this case, the answer is clearly "Yes." Specifically, she can learn to stamp return addresses on mail, collate packets of information, staple papers, and open and seal envelopes. Even though she cannot perform *all* the skills required of nondisabled others, she can perform some. If allowed to participate partially, she has access to integrated vocational environments.

INDIVIDUALIZED ADAPTATIONS

Individualized adaptations are portable objects, materials, and other phenomena created for and used by individuals with severe intellectual disabilities so they can at least partially participate in integrated environments and activities.[13] These adaptations are specifically intended to compensate for a variety of behavioral, cognitive, sensory, and motoric difficulties. Pocket calculators and floppy disks, and head pointers and picture cookbooks are examples of adaptations created for and used by our highest and lowest intellectually functioning students respectively. For example,

Nancy is receiving her vocational instruction at a local travel agency where she is learning how to stamp return addresses on advertising brochures. She was unable to grasp the stamp, so an adaptation was developed by her teacher. This adaptation consisted of a mounted self-inking stamp on a sheet of plexiglas. By placing her hand on the top of the plexiglas and pressing down, she was able to stamp the brochures without having to grasp the stamper.

James is learning how to take a city bus to a shopping center in his neighborhood in order to purchase groceries for his family. Repeated efforts to teach him to choose the correct bus failed. Thus, he was reliant upon a person without disabilities getting him to and from the store. In an attempt to enhance his independence, an adaptation in the form of a picture of a bus with the appropriate name was taped to an index card. After receiving instruction on how to select his bus by matching the picture on the index card to the cues on an actual bus, he was able to go to and from the grocery store unassisted.

One extremely important attribute of individualized adaptations is that they allow students with severe intellectual disabilities to be perceived by others as striving, capable, and contributing members of society. These enhanced perceptions often lead to students with the most severe intellectual disabilities and the brightest students in our schools participating in the same environments and activities. In turn, this heterogeneous participation often leads to the development of extremely important and meaningful friendships.

Students with severe intellectual disabilities are simply not able to function in many important environments and activities without the aid of a wide variety of individually meaningful adaptations. All educators must be aware of how important adaptations are to the growth of these students, must ensure that all personnel secure the most up-to-date adaptation related information, and must participate as much as possible in their justification, design, and utilization. This is particularly important since many adaptations will require substantive changes in the way educators think, organize information, and allocate dollars, space, and other resources.

INDIVIDUALIZED TRANSITION PLANS

An Individualized Transition Plan is an instructional strategy offered as one attempt to minimize difficulties encountered when moving across environments and activities.[14] Individualized, longitudinal, and comprehensive transition plans must be designed and implemented in relation to moves from elementary to middle schools, from middle to high schools, and from high schools to post-school environments, activities, and services.

Typical transition plans developed for students without disabilities are episodic and superficial in nature. When students who are severely intellectually disabled are of concern, such plans must be intensified. Since students with severe intellectual disabilities have difficulties generalizing and transferring that learned in one environment to others, they require direct instruction in the actual environments for which they are being prepared to function. Thus, if students are moving from an elementary to a middle school, direct instruction in the actual middle school environments and activities they will experience must be provided no later than the last year of the elementary school career. Additionally, since they often have difficulties developing and maintaining friendships during transition periods, it is extremely important to ensure that close personal relationships are promoted and sustained. Finally, a well-designed transition plan will minimize the waste of instructional time and effort by ensuring that the actual skills needed in receiving environments and activities are taught by sending personnel.

Concluding Statement

Over the past forty years educational service models for students with severe intellectual disabilities have evolved from rejection and exclusion from public schools, to segregated private schools, to segregated public schools, to special classes in regular schools, and even to regular classes in regular schools. In the past, few regular educators went to public schools or received college-level instruction to prepare them for working with students with severe intellectual disabilities. Thus, thousands of regular educators are now being required to provide important services without having had any personal involvement with this significantly disabled population. Future generations of teachers, administrators, therapists, and other educational service personnel are now growing up with brothers, sisters, friends, and neighbors who are severely intellectually and physically disabled. Thus, future generations of educators will have a better understanding of and will be better prepared to honor their educational needs.

Footnotes

1. Lou Brown, Jan Nisbet, Alison Ford, Mark Sweet, Betsy Shiraga, Jennifer York, Ruth Loomis, "The Critical Need for Nonschool Instruction in Educational Programs for Severely Handicapped Students," *Journal of the Association for the Severely Handicapped* 8 (Fall 1983): 71-77.

2. Lou Brown, Betsy Shiraga, Patty Rogan, Jennifer York, Kathy Zanella Albright, Eileen McCarthy, Ruth Loomis, Pat VanDeventer, "The 'Why Question' in Educational Programs for Students Who Are Severely Intellectually Disabled," in *Communication Assessment and Intervention Strategies for Developmentally Disabled Adults*, ed. Jan Bedrosian and Steve Calculator (San Diego: College-Hill Press, in press).

3. Trevor F. Stokes and Donald M. Baer, "An Implicit Technology of Generalization," *Journal of Applied Behavior Analysis* 10 (Summer 1977): 349-67; Wes Williams, Lou Brown, Nick Certo, "Basic Components of Instructional Programs," *Theory Into Practice* 14 (April 1975): 123-36.

4. Lou Brown, Alison Ford, Jan Nisbet, Mark Sweet, Anne Donnellan, Lee Gruenewald, "Opportunities Available When Severely Handicapped Students Attend Chronological Age Appropriate Regular Schools in Accordance with Natural Proportion," *Journal of the Association for the Severely Handicapped* 8 (Spring 1983): 16-24.

5. Lou Brown, Betsy Shiraga, Jennifer York, Kathy Zanella, Patty Rogan, "A Life Space Analysis Strategy for Students with Severe Intellectual Disabilities," in *Educational Programs for Students with Severe Handicaps*, ed. Lou Brown, Mark Sweet, Betsy Shiraga, Jennifer York, Kathy Zanella, Patty Rogan, Ruth Loomis (Madison, WI: Madison Metropolitan School District, 1984), pp. 23-54.

6. Lou Brown, Mark Sweet, Betsy Shiraga, Jennifer York, Kathy Zanella, Patty Rogan, "Functional Skills in Programs for Students with Severe Intellectual Disabilities," *Educational Programs for Students with Severe Handicaps*, ed. Brown et al., pp. 55-59.

7. Brown et al., "The 'Why Question' in Educational Programs."

8. Lou Brown, Betsy Shiraga, Jennifer York, Kathy Zanella, Patty Rogan, "Skill Transfer in Programs for Students with Severe Intellectual Disabilities," in *Educational Programs for Students with Severe Handicaps*, ed. Brown et al., pp. 49-54.

9. Brown et al., "The 'Why Question' in Educational Programs."

10. Ibid.; H. Rutherford Turnbull, *Free Appropriate Public Education, the Law, and Children with Disabilities* (Denver: Love Publishing Co., 1986); Ann P. Turnbull, Bonnie B. Strickland, John C. Brantley, *Developing and Implementing Individualized Education Programs*, 2d ed. (Columbus, OH: Charles E. Merrill, 1982).

11. Brown et al., "The Critical Need for Nonschool Instruction in Educational Programs for Severely Handicapped Students."

12. Diane Baumgart, Lou Brown, Ian Pumpian, Jan Nisbet, Alison Ford, Mark Sweet, Rosalie Messina, Jack Schroeder, "Principle of Partial Participation and Individualized Adaptations in Educational Programs for Severely Handicapped Students," *Journal of the Association for the Severely Handicapped* 7 (Summer 1982): 17-27.

13. Ibid.

14. Lou Brown, Ian Pumpian, Diane Baumgart, Pat VanDeventer, Alison Ford, Jan Nisbet, Jack Schroeder, and Lee Gruenewald, "Longitudinal Transition Plans in Programs for Severely Handicapped Students," *Exceptional Children* 47 (May 1981): 624-31.

CHAPTER IV

Mild Disabilities: In and Out of Special Education

MARA SAPON-SHEVIN

If an outsider were asked to describe the American educational system, she might report that schools contain two kinds of classes: those identified by the grade level of the students (first and fourth grades), and those identified by the exceptionality of the students ("mentally retarded," "learning disabled" and "emotionally disturbed"). She would see that universities prepare teachers either according to the age of the students they will teach, the subject matter they will teach (History or English), or the type of exceptionality their students will have. For those of us "inside the system," these categorical ways of viewing and separating children and their teachers are so embedded that we rarely think about either how things got to be this way, or, alternatively, how things might be different. Are these categories real and educationally responsive? Could educational institutions respond differently to the students they now label as "mildly handicapped"? The purpose of this chapter is to examine the origins, growth, and development of the field of mild disabilities within a broad social and political context and to examine alternatives for describing and educating children now served within the categories of mild disability.

Calling a handicapping condition a "mild disability" differentiates it from those called severe disabilities. Although confusing variations among states and school districts are common, mild disabilities generally include the specific categories of "learning disabilities," "mild mental retardation," "emotional disturbance," and "speech handicaps."[1] These categories can be differentiated from "severe handicapping conditions" in several ways: (a) they occur with a much higher frequency (and are sometimes called "high incidence handicaps"); (b) their definition, identification, and eligibility criteria

---

I wish to thank Mayer Shevin for the significant contribution he made to this chapter through his conceptual clarity and thorough editing.

tend to be based primarily on psychometric results (rather than on, for example, physical characteristics); and (c) they are thought to be less disabling or handicapping than more severe handicaps.

In this chapter, the history of these categories is reviewed chronologically rather than categorically for two reasons: first, specific historical events and landmarks often affected the development of educational programs for students across categories, and second, the relationship *among* the categories has also been altered by time-bound events such as legislation and litigation.

A Brief Historical Review: How Did We Get Where We Are?

It is important to understand that the history of society's response to disabled people does not involve a discrete and stable group of people dealt with differentially over time. Rather, social realities and policies have altered both the size of, and the labels given to, the population we now refer to as "mildly handicapped."[2]

1875-1920

During this period, many children previously unschooled attended public schools for the first time. The passage of compulsory schooling and child labor laws, a growing belief in universal education, a large influx of immigrants, and tremendous urban growth all contributed to changing the size and diversity of the public schools. Prior to the enactment of compulsory schooling laws, many children whose needs could not be met in the regular classroom either did not go to school or dropped out when it seemed clear that the fit between child and school was poor. Once schools were forced to deal with this large influx of children previously believed disruptive to the education of the majority, the creation of special classes followed. This period also saw the development of the first public school programs for mentally retarded students while many other special education classes seemed reserved for children of foreign-born parents.[3] By the turn of the century, special education classes in many large schools included students identified as "slow learners, the mentally subnormal, epileptics, learning disabled, chronic truants, behavior problem children, physically handicapped or immigrant children suffering from language or cultural handicaps."[4]

With the development of special education came an increased use of standardized psychological assessment. In particular, Alfred Binet developed his first intelligence test, which was later modified by his student Theodore Simon. The Binet-Simon test allowed psychologists to classify retarded children into the three categories of idiots, imbeciles, and morons. The psychologist Henry Herbert Goddard, building on the educational measurement work of Binet, began his campaign to control and limit the population of feebleminded persons through the practice of eugenics or selective breeding. Goddard argued that the social evils of the time were a product of feeblemindedness and that the solution for prostitution, crime, and moral degeneracy required the elimination of their breeding potential.[5]

By 1922, 23,252 pupils were served in special education classes of all types. Goddard estimated that 2 percent of New York City's school-aged children were feebleminded (an estimate adopted by many educational planners).[6] The primary purpose of special programs for children identified as mentally retarded was to remove them from the regular classroom where they were seen as disruptive influences on the learning of others and to provide "way stations or clearing-houses for children who were en route to the prevailing treatment facilities (that is, institutions) for the physically, mentally, or morally 'deviant' members of our society."[7]

1920-1940

This period can be described as one of growth and proliferation in the provision of public school special education services. By the 1920s some schools became far more discriminating about the students considered acceptable for public school attendance, raising the minimum IQ required to 40 and then to 50.[8] Thus, classes for children with "mild disabilities" grew, while children with severe handicaps remained excluded.

The mental hygiene movement, initiated in 1909, resulted in the establishment of public school mental hygiene programs designed to serve children with behavior problems, as well as special rooms, schools, classes, and consultative help for disturbed children.[9] The work of Sigmund Freud began to have a profound effect on the way children's "disturbed behavior" was viewed and treated, and the American Orthopsychiatric Association was founded to encourage research on the education of behavior disordered children. At this time the Council for Exceptional Children was formed, marking an increasing recognition of the educational needs of mentally retarded and other exceptional children.

Research during this period generally confirmed the efficacy of special education programs, and many teacher training institutions began offering classes on exceptional children. By 1930, sixteen states had passed mandatory or permissive special education legislation, and by 1934, almost 85,000 students were enrolled in special classes across 427 cities.[10]

1940-1960

Special education for mentally retarded students continued to grow, with even more division of special classes according to age and disability level. National enrollment figures rose to 109,000 in 1940 and then to 361,000 in 1963.[11] Most students identified and served as mildly retarded were boys from families of low socioeconomic status. In the 1954 landmark case of *Brown v. Board of Education*, the Supreme Court ruled school segregation illegal, leading to racial integration of many previously segregated students and to an increased heterogeneity in the populations public schools were required to serve. Intelligence testing continued to expand with the addition of the Wechsler Intelligence Scale for Children and the first attempts at "culture-free" tests. The American Association on Mental Deficiency introduced five levels of mental retardation (borderline, mild, moderate, severe, and profound) along with the concept of adaptive behavior.[12]

While school-based programs for mildly retarded students continued to grow, the seeds of the categories of emotional disturbance and learning disabilities were sown by the work of Alfred Strauss and his colleague Heinz Werner. Their neurological theory attempted to explain unusual behavior of children with normal intelligence as a kind of "brain injury," distinguishing between "endogeneous" and "exogeneous" children, a discrimination later argued to be simply the difference between "retardation" and "learning disabilities."[13] Strauss's work also led to the creation of the category of "emotional disturbance" with his recognition that the learning problems of brain-injured children were often accompanied by emotional problems. Strauss advocated highly structured consistent environments for "brain-injured" children, laying the groundwork for later educators to stress environmental and behavioral control for children identified as "disturbed" or "behavior disordered."[14] By the mid-1950s, although there were few such classrooms, the field recognized a need for systematic procedures to identify disturbed children.

Debates about the advisability of segregating retarded students flourished, raising serious concerns about the stigma and isolation experienced by children educated in special classes. Although most of the research of the time supported the advantages of special classes, some studies questioned their efficacy.[15]

1960-PRESENT

The last quarter century of special education has seen tremendous growth in all of the categories of "mild disability." During the early 1960s efforts to structure appropriate classroom environments for children identified as "brain injured" continued. Hewett designed the "engineered classroom" for children with learning and behavior problems, while Haring and Phillips urged highly structured, predictable classroom environments for children with "behavior disorders."[16] Although labels vary, most schools now serve a category of children for whom behavioral and social problems are considered the primary difficulty.

"Born" officially in 1963 at the first Association for Children with Learning Disabilities conference, learning disabilities has since become the fastest growing special education category.[17] Although identification controversies abound and prevalence estimates vary tremendously, the category of learning disabilities is now firmly established.

This period was also marked by challenges to special education's orientation and desirability in the form of efficacy studies. Much of the efficacy debate centered on the wisdom of removing students from the regular classroom in order to provide them with differential education, and the extent to which this differential education actually improved academic and social performance.[18] Considerable attention was also given to potential negative effects of labeling, including loss of self-esteem, stigma, social isolation, and the self-fulfilling prophecy.[19]

Other major challenges to special education practice arose from litigation[20] which produced the following rulings:

1. Ability grouping (tracking) based on student performance on standardized tests is unconstitutional. (*Hansen v. Hobson*, 1967).

2. Children whose primary language is not English need to be tested in both their primary language and English. School districts discriminate against Mexican-American and Chinese students enrolled in EMR classes by using IQ tests which are linguistically and culturally biased. (*Diana v. State Board of Education*, 1970).

3. Any handicapped child has a right to a "constructive education," including appropriate specialized instruction. Schools must also follow due process rules regarding exclusion, termination,

or classification into a special program. (*Mills v. Board of Education*, 1972; *PARC v. Commonwealth of Pennsylvania*, 1972).

4. Schools must provide screening and follow-up evaluations which will locate and serve learning disabled students. (*Frederick L. v. Thomas*, 1976, 1977).

5. The rights of black and Hispanic students are violated as evidenced by their disproportionate placement in "special day schools" for emotionally disturbed students. (*Lora v. New York City Board of Education*, 1978).

6. The California state education department is enjoined from using intelligence tests to place black students in EMR classes, ordered to re-evaluate all black students currently enrolled in EMR classes and required to take steps to reduce their disproportionate placement in special education classes. (*Larry P. v. Riles*, 1979).

The cumulative effect of these court cases has been to alter significantly the proportions of students placed in various categories of special education. Increasing sensitivity to cultural bias and the inappropriateness of IQ testing for the evaluation and placement of minority students has led to a marked decrease in the number of minority students placed in classes for the mentally retarded. At the same time, the proportion of ethnically diverse students in classes for the learning disabled (originally a category populated almost entirely by white, middle-class students) increased.[21] Meanwhile a growing sensitivity to the stigma of labeling and need to protect individual rights led to a stabilization of the category "emotionally disturbed" even though professionals identify it as one in which children are underidentified.

Another powerful impact on the growth of special education has been the activity of consumer and advocacy groups, especially parents' groups. The Association for Children with Learning Disabilities and the Association for Retarded Citizens both played major roles in litigation against school systems which resulted in service requirements and the passage of P.L. 94-142. Passed in 1975 and effective in 1978, The Education for All Handicapped Children Act required that all handicapped children be provided with a free, appropriate public education in the least restrictive environment. While there is still tremendous variation in the extent to which states have committed themselves to this goal, parents, for the first time, had the law on their side in demanding school programming for their handicapped children, many of whom were still excluded from school prior to the passage of the law.

Current Definitions and Status of the Categories

MENTAL RETARDATION

In 1973, the American Association for Mental Deficiency defined mental retardation as "significantly subaverage general intellectual functioning existing concurrently with deficits in adaptive behavior and manifested during the developmental period."[22] This terminology represented a change from an earlier 1961 definition in several important ways and illustrates how definitional changes affect who does and does not fall within a category. First, "low" intellectual functioning can no longer be the sole defining criterion; there must also be deficiencies in adaptive behavior. Second, a person must attain a score of at least two standard deviations below the mean on standardized intelligence tests to be considered "retarded," instead of the previous criterion of one standard deviation.

Mildly retarded children, also referred to as "educably mentally retarded" or "EMR," are frequently not identified as retarded until they enter school. These mildly handicapped children have often been defined as those "unable to profit sufficiently from the regular program of the school," but still "educable" in the areas of academic, social adjustment, and occupational skills.[23] Such a definition, of course, is incompatible with any notion of mainstreaming or integration, since it declares a priori that they cannot be part of the regular program.

Prevalence estimates for children labeled "EMR" range from 1 to 3 percent of the school-age population. This wide variation can be attributed to differences in IQ cut-off scores used to determine intellectual subnormality, different ways of determining adaptive behavior, the strong correlation between social class and mental retardation (a majority of "EMR" children come from the lower socioeconomic classes), and the fact that the prevalence of mild mental retardation varies by age (low for preschool age, high during school-age, and declining in adolescence and adulthood).

The President's Committee on Mental Retardation, in a report entitled *The Six-Hour Retarded Child*, observed that some children are "retarded" only during the six hours they are in school, but not during their hours in family and neighborhood settings. They attribute this phenomenon to the activities, requirements, and expectations of the school and the ways in which these requirements differ from nonschool environments.[24]

Continuing controversies in the field of mental retardation, particularly critiques of IQ tests as culturally biased and discriminatory against members of ethnic and racial minority groups, together with litigation, substantially altered the definition and process of identification of mental retardation employed by schools. Current efforts seek to eliminate culturally biased testing instruments, create culture-fair tests (such as SOMPA), and include an increased emphasis on adaptive behavior for determining mental retardation.[25]

LEARNING DISABILITIES

The category of learning disabilities is the fastest growing of the categories officially designated as a handicapping condition by P.L. 94-142. A "specific learning disability" is defined there as:

a disorder in one or more of the basic psychological processes involved in understanding or in using language, spoken or written, which may manifest itself in an imperfect ability to listen, think, speak, read, write, spell, or to do mathematical calculations. The term includes such conditions as perceptual handicaps, brain injury, minimal brain dysfunction, dyslexia, and developmental aphasia. The term does not include children who have learning problems which are primarily the result of visual, hearing, or motor handicaps, of mental retardation, of emotional disturbance, or of environmental, cultural, or economic disadvantage.

Extensively revised and rewritten, most recently by a 1981 joint committee of professional organizations,[26] this definition is still highly controversial and not universally accepted. Nevertheless, most definitions of learning disabilities include three common themes: (a) the L.D. child must have a measured IQ that is average or above average, (b) there must be a significant discrepancy between potential (as measured by IQ) and achievement, and (c) the disability must *not* be due primarily to any other psychological, environmental, or physiological condition, although these may exist concurrently (often called the "exclusion clause").

Prevalence estimates for L.D. are extremely difficult to make because of ambiguities in definition, inconsistencies in identification and assessment procedures, and the tremendous growth rate of the category (approximately 3 percent per year). Still, estimates of the number of students with learning disabilities range from 1 to 30 percent of the school population. In 1983-84, 42 percent of those in special education programs (approximately 4.62 percent of the total school population) were classified as L.D.[27]

EMOTIONAL DISTURBANCE

Children in this category possess a variety of labels, including socially maladjusted, psychologically disordered, and emotionally handicapped. Definitions of emotional disturbance vary tremendously, and like definitions of learning disabilities, often have exclusionary clauses. P.L. 94-142 defines "seriously emotionally disturbed" as:

a condition exhibiting one or more of the following characteristics over a long period of time and to a marked degree, which adversely affects educational performance:

  a. An inability to learn which cannot be explained by intellectual, sensory, or health factors.

  b. An inability to build or maintain satisfactory interpersonal relationships with peers and teachers.

  c. Inappropriate types of behavior or feelings under normal circumstances.

  d. A general pervasive mode of unhappiness or depression.

  e. A tendency to develop physical symptoms or fears associated with personal or school problems.

The term does not include children who are socially maladjusted, unless it is determined that they are seriously emotionally disturbed.

Problems of measurement, a lack of agreement in what constitutes good mental health, and the wide variety of theories of emotional disturbance, each of which uses its own terminology and definitions, all contribute to a lack of common definition of emotional disturbance. Predictably, these problems of definition make prevalence estimates difficult. While the U.S. Department of Education uses the figure of 2 percent for estimating funding and personnel needs in this field, 1983 government reports indicated that only about 0.88 percent of the school-aged population was being served as seriously emotionally disturbed.[28]

THE CATEGORIES COMBINED

A 1985 report[29] of data from all fifty states shows consistent increases in numbers of learning disabled students, consistent decreases in numbers of mentally retarded students, and relatively constant numbers of students labeled "emotionally disturbed." Algozzine and Korinek document that more than 90 percent of children determined to require special education receive one of the four high prevalence labels of L.D., M.R., E.D., or S.I. (speech impaired). These figures, and the documented growth rate of special education (over 3 percent a year), constitute a "growing alternative educational system."[30] Special education is indeed a "big business," with over 4 million students and federal appropriations of over $800 million in 1979 (double that of the previous year).

Another Look at History: The Values That Guide Us

At one level the history of the education of students with mild disabilities appears to be one of increasing inclusiveness and beneficence. Having moved beyond viewing handicapped children as unworthy or incapable of education, schools now include more and more children within their educational purview. Schools see their role as not simply removing some children from the streets or from regular classrooms, or even preparing them for more segregated institutions, but rather as accepting the goal of educating children with disabilities to reach their full potential in the "least restrictive environment."

However, the growth of special education presents a darker side as well. Rather than viewing the growth of special education as evidence of an increasing willingness of the schools to attend to individual differences in children, the proliferation of new categories (particularly the mild disability categories) can be seen as equally reflecting an *unwillingness* of the regular public school system to assume responsibility (within regular classrooms) for children who are not succeeding. Several underlying assumptions established, and now maintain, schools' rigid system of classification. Consider, for example, the growth of the category of learning disabilities and the concomitant shrinkage of the category of mental retardation. It might be argued that the number of students identified as "learning disabled" increased because of improved diagnostic strategies, while the number of mentally retarded students decreased as a result of early intervention, parent programs, and improved technology. Alternatively, Algozzine and Korinek propose that the changing demographics of special education reflect an increasingly "ineffective system" in which decisions about categorization and placement are based largely on social, political, legal, and economic factors rather than on rational educational decision making.[31]

It can also be argued that there are no disabled students in any absolute sense; rather, we create disabilities by how we view students, the meanings we create, and the ways we think about people and their differences. Any historical analysis of the growth of special education for those labeled "mildly handicapped" then must include an examination of both explicit and unspoken motivations for practice and intended and unintended outcomes. Unfortunately, the unquestioned assumptions and principles which guided the growth of special education have also limited subsequent analyses and critiques; certain kinds of questions have been considered legitimate, while other more basic assumptions have never been challenged.

Gonzalves urges us to examine the social consequences of the theory presented by Goddard in the establishment of the category of "mild retardation." She argues that if the consequences include defining some people as having fewer rights, then the theory and facts are themselves unacceptable.[32] The entire history of the field of mental measurement can be seen as an effort to classify people according to a fixed hierarchy, and then to treat people differentially based on these categories. Some critics argue that intelligence testing was developed in order to facilitate the segregation of poor and ethnically different students into special classes; others argue that special classes were created as a practical solution for dealing with a rapidly expanding and diverse student population. Further, the subsequent focus on testing as a legitimating strategy serves to draw attention away from the critical role of teacher referral in determining who ends up in special education. Still others argue that intelligence testing neither constituted the reason for special class assignments nor established the need for special classes. In fact, these same authors suggest, intelligence testing did not become "mischievous" until later, when the combination of differential funding for special education and the need for a scientific basis to support segregation provided an incentive for classifying as many students as possible as "mentally retarded."[33]

Despite debates, it is undeniable that the development and expansion of intelligence testing facilitated and routinized the systematic placement of low-income and minority children into special education classes. Psychometric testing has played a powerful role in shaping our belief systems, our educational policies, and our practices. It was through intelligence testing that Goddard "discovered" the "feebleminded"—a population defined only psychometrically, not functionally. This process of psychometric identification was repeated fifty years later with the new category of learning disabled.

In both cases once the category was defined, schools found increasing numbers of students who fit and created the necessary mechanisms for dealing with them. Numerous critiques of the categories of mild mental retardation and learning disabilities focus on the need to define members of the category more clearly, as if precision in labeling is the key problem. We need more reliability and consistency of identification to determine *who* actually belongs in which category. Educators and researchers now attempt to discriminate, for example, between children who are *truly* learning disabled and those who are just low achievers, to clarify whether an identified child is actually learning disabled or mildly mentally retarded.[34]

Concerns about accuracy lead to concerted efforts to "tighten" the categories so that they admit only the "truly retarded" or "truly learning disabled." Sensitivity to the overrepresentation of minority group members in EMR classes,[35] and the development of multifactored assessment tools such as SOMPA, have significantly reduced the numbers of minority students served as "EMR." The "promotion" to EMR classes of children who were previously served in classes for the "trainably mentally retarded," and a decrease in the number of students with good adaptive behavior in EMR classes represent other important demographic shifts.[36]

We might applaud the decrease in numbers of students labeled "EMR" on the grounds that fewer students will be victimized by labels, educators will acquire more sensitivity to cultural differences, and assessments will be less biased. However, limiting eligibility for EMR classes is not necessarily in children's best interest if it deprives them of needed services or eliminates the perceived need to change the regular education classroom in which they originally failed. Even assessment instruments designed to be "culture-fair" or "culture-free" simply alter who gets identified as mentally retarded and do little to address what happens to the children who are still identified or those who struggle, only to fail, but remain without formal identification. Discrimination in assessment should be eliminated; learning problems (or, perhaps more accurately, learning differences), however, cannot be mandated, legislated, or measured away. "Continued efforts to eliminate pupils who demonstrate primarily school-based problems ignore the reality of why they were initially referred for services."[37] According to one report "even if truly nondiscriminatory assessment measures were developed, they would do little to reduce the systematic bias that has been documented to occur both prior to and following assessment."[38] Removing a Hispanic child from an EMR classroom and replacing him in a regular education classroom where he continues to fail can hardly be considered progress.

Despite a wide recognition of bias in the classification process and of the "socially constructed" nature of mental retardation,[39] students in this category are still largely poor and/or ethnic. A recent study found that almost 75 percent of the variance in EMR prevalence was predictable by socioeconomic indicators.[40] Others find that cultural/ linguistic variables are more influential in the probability of special education placements than are the often cited socioeconomic variables.[41]

One response to these critiques and to legislation which forbids the use of IQ tests for placement in EMR classrooms has been the reclassification of EMR children as LD, since this label is generally considered less stigmatizing to children and their parents. This reclassification in turn has prompted a tightening of entrance requirements and eligibility criteria for LD programs. However, shifting students between categories (from programs for the trainable mentally retarded to the educable mentally retarded, and from the EMR class to the LD class) does little to address the interface between regular and special education which initially forces children into the special education system. As in the game of musical chairs, our attention becomes focused on who belongs in what chair and what to do with the child who is left out, rather than on the conditions which initially established a "shortage" of chairs onto which children must be fit. The categorical labels themselves become embedded within broader structures of school administration and organization, funding, and teacher preparation, and begin to take on a life of their own. Although the motivations for identifying a population as "learning disabled" or "retarded" and the consequences of so doing may have differed substantially, we need to be very suspicious of the "reality" of any group that did not exist until we had a psychometric test to find its members.

The growth of special education categories reveals that every attempt by our society to move in the direction of more equality has been met by a countermove that is stratifying and hierarchical. Gonzalves argues that attempts to classify and segregate people can be seen as "the constant companion of attempts to share the social, political, and economic advantages of our society."[42] The first period of special education growth occurred after the legislation of compulsory schooling. The resulting influx of students constituted the generation of what Farber has labeled a "surplus population"— that "segment of the total population exceeding the number of individuals needed to fill the slots in a social organization."[43] In earlier times schools made no effort to teach all children. Since a substantial portion of school-age children never went to school, the differentiation and allocation of students effectively took place prior to school entry. With compulsory schooling, however, differentiation and allocation occurred after entry rather than before it.[44] The growth in special education after litigation (*Brown v. Board of Education* and *Hansen v. Hobson*) forced still greater school inclusion and serves as further evidence of this pattern. Once schools are required to serve broader populations, more differentiated programs result.

In the United States the ideology of equality of opportunity, coupled with the spread of schooling, fueled the growth of the field of mental measurement. The presumed scientific objectivity of mental measurement and the concepts of innate mental superiority and inferiority have been consonant with our notions of democratic schooling.[45] One social critic argues that "the movement to measure intelligence allowed for equality of opportunity and at the same time justified a hierarchical social structure, based on intelligence, in which all people were not equal."[46] In a land of "equal opportunity," the rhetoric insists that all people have an equal chance to be successful. The field of mental measurement provided us with a comfortable explanation of why some people were successful and others were not—an explanation that did not involve challenges to the basic economic and social structure of the country. Through the mechanism of differential education schools reflect, reproduce, and justify inequalities in social status,[47] while at the same time arguing that such allocation is neutral since it is based on scientific measurement. Under the guise of scientific neutrality, individualization and a philosophy of equal opportunity have resulted in extensive stratification and tracking in schools such that the quality and amount of education available to children varies tremendously according to race, social class, ethnic group, and handicapping condition.

Sleeter documents the manner and extent to which the category of learning disabilities succeeds in providing services to white, middle-class children while protecting them from the stigma of failure.[48] The racial discrimination inherent in the testing and placement used by special education led to low-achieving white students being placed in LD classes and low-achieving black students in classes for mentally retarded students. While fewer black students are now placed in EMR classes, they are increasingly overrepresented in classes for learning disabled students and thus overrepresented within special education programs generally. One analysis of the increase of minority children in learning disabilities classrooms indicates that "the LD category may represent the path of least resistance in obtaining special education service for such children" because "the vague definition of LD permits classifying students for special education almost independently of the reason for their lack of progress in the regular curriculum."[49]

More recent calls for rigid adherence to strict LD entrance requirements (e.g., that LD students have average or above average IQs with no evidence linking their learning problems to any cultural, environmental, or familial variables) may return us to programs that once more serve white, middle-class children and exclude children of color and lower-class backgrounds.[50] "Advantaged social groups will define failure in such a way as to protect their own children as well as possible from its painful consequence."[51] Special education's newest category, the "learning-disabled/gifted," seems to serve this function very neatly.[52] LD/Gifted is defined in such a way as to insure that its members are almost exclusively members of the dominant culture. They must obtain a high IQ and come from a home environment not characterized by educators as culturally, socially, or environmentally deprived. Children identified as "LD/Gifted" are provided with special services (by virtue of their learning disability) and with enrichment and high expectations on the basis of their gifted label. It appears that the category of learning disabilities serves important political functions within public schooling to the extent to which it insures specialized services for only a fraction of those children who are low-achievers.

The conceptualization of children's handicaps as primarily internal defects rather than outcomes of a social interaction process also serves to reify mild disability categories. Although the category of emotional disturbance is fraught with ambiguity, social judgment, and personal bias, the child is generally seen as the source of the problem. One critic argues that "it is time we faced the fact that disordered behavior is whatever we choose to make it; it is not an objective thing that exists outside our arbitrary sociocultural rules any more than mental retardation is."[53] Narrow, rigid standards and an overemphasis on power and control are conditions which encourage the identification and removal of "deviant" children from the mainstream of society lest they contaminate more "typical" children. Efforts to challenge the "overidentification" of children in this category are heartening, but again reveal an underlying concern for more precise identification of the "right" students without regard for those who *are* labeled as "ED" or those who are identified and then not labeled and served. As with other categories, the risks of "underidentification" (when this means underserved) are also real and disturbing.[54] Failure to provide services for children who are experiencing behavioral and social problems in schools and abandoning them to school failure, school discipline, or school withdrawal at age sixteen can hardly be cited as evidence that students experiencing behavioral problems have either vanished or been appropriately served.

As discussed in Ferguson's earlier chapter, the new political methods of the Right, which raise standards and requirements with little attention to the increasing numbers of children who fall by the wayside, can also encourage the abandonment (through *lack* of services) of children categorized as "emotionally disturbed" or "behavior disordered." As "surplus populations"[55] these children are sacrificed as part of an evolutionary process—a return to "survival of the fittest"— manifested by the school's willingness to invest only in the education of children likely to be most successful.[56] The "push for excellence" advocated by national reports may have devastating results for many students but especially for those with special educational needs.

The interaction between the regular education system and the labeled child must be closely considered, since the "failures" of regular education become the "students" of special education. Examining special education as a subsystem of regular education can help to illuminate the practices of regular education which are deviance-creating and which function as "organizational 'safety valves' diminishing school responsibility for individual failure."[57]

The response of schools to children who are ethnically or racially different illustrates both the use of psychometric testing as a mechanism for interpreting difference as deviance, and the propensity to see school failure as a problem of the child rather than the school. Schools defined appropriate school behavior so that cultural differences came to be perceived as academic and school liabilities. Children's failure to do well in schools dominated by white middle-class students and teachers could thus be taken as evidence of racial and ethnic inferiority.

Viewing children as deficient leads special education to direct its efforts toward forcing the child to change in order to fit in or be accepted. This approach legitimates behavioral and medical management techniques which attempt to "fix" the child:

Labeling is an integral part of medical and behavioral management, since, without the definitional act of diagnosis, further intervention or treatment would be impossible. Defining or treating a child as disabled or deviant directs attention away from the social and structural, since it takes the individual as its unit of concern.[58]

An adequate critique of the existing categories of mild disability needs to go beyond an analysis of the scientific validity of the categories. Concerns about bias-free assessment, reliable and consistent criteria for identification, and attempts to limit membership in special education to the "right" students, while all valid efforts, do not take us far enough. Even if the categories of "mental retardation," "learning disabilities," and "emotional disturbance" were scientifically rigorous and empirically defensible, they would still need to be challenged because of where they have taken us. One special education critic argues that "in social affairs one often lacks rational 'scientific' knowledge that is encompassing enough to guide the choice of action. The choice, therefore, has to be based also on values and assumptions."[59]

Toward a New Vision

A new vision of schools must emerge from an understanding of school functions and practices that incorporate historical, political, economic, and professional frames of reference about both education and disability. The underlying notions that have guided special education must now be replaced by a totally new way of viewing children and their differences. As some authors now suggest, only a paradigm shift can accomplish these necessary changes; piecemeal reform and surface changes will no longer suffice.[60] This section outlines the new assumptions that would emerge from such a fundamental reform. First, differences among children would be seen as both natural and enriching. It is not necessary or helpful to equate difference with deviance; rather, the ways in which we respond to differences reflect our own values about diversity. Second, the best interests of all people would be served by encouraging their interaction with a broad range of other people. Purposive, thoughtful heterogeneity enriches us all. Third, the primary responsibility for any lack of fit between the child and the school would rest with the school. It is the responsibility of professionals to create structures which can respond to children's differences while respecting their individuality, maintaining their full dignity, and keeping them connected to the broader school community.

In the remainder of this chapter, I will propose an alternative vision and discuss the changes which need to be made in order to support that vision. In particular I will focus on: (a) how schools will view difference in children, (b) how teachers will be prepared, (c) and how schools will be organized. I will conclude with some comments about our progress toward this alternative vision.

HOW SCHOOLS WILL VIEW DIFFERENCE IN CHILDREN

In recognition of the artificiality of special education categories and their negative effects, schools will abandon labels for children and will describe children in holistic and multidimensional ways. A child's failure to meet expected contingencies will be immediate cause for examining the reasonableness of expectations and/or for seeking ways to modify the environment so that success is more likely. Differences in human capabilities or characteristics will not be considered disabilities on which to base assignment to categorical groups. Individual characteristics might be used to assist educators in supplementing instruction, but they will not be used to "dictate differential placement and treatment according to a categorical affiliation which is often inherent in the disabilities approach to education."[61]

New ways of assessing children which emphasize dynamic assessment techniques will be implemented. Assessment findings will reveal how children learn best and how instruction can best be modified. Intelligence testing will be abandoned as a highly limited and limiting way of understanding children. Assessment will be multidimensional and broadly based, generating many ways of knowing students and describing their strengths and needs. Such assessment might replace testing with student observations, student interviews, criterion-referenced instruments, and curriculum-based assessment. Data drawn from formalized testing will not be considered more acccurate or helpful than information gathered through interview or observation.

Children who display large intraindividual differences will be viewed as good at some things and poor at others rather than as deviant. The use of criterion-referenced assessment and the abandonment of grade-level equivalents and discrepancies for describing children's repertoires will make it more comfortable for teachers to see variations in children's development as part of normal growth and development. Assessment will be closely linked to instruction providing both students and their parents with frequent feedback. Teachers will also emphasize teaching students self-assessment as a way of understanding their own needs, structuring their own learning, and monitoring their own progress.

HOW TEACHERS WILL BE PREPARED

The entire structure of schools of education will need to be altered. Departmental divisions, programs of study, course titles, and individual teaching responsibilities will all need to reflect a more generic approach to teacher education. The current separations between teacher preparation for "general education" and "special education" will be diminished and then eliminated. This will exceed cross-categorical teacher education programs that prepare teachers of the "mildly handicapped," since such continuing distinctions reify the reality and distinctiveness of the categories they newly combine.[62]

Most teachers will instead be trained as generic teachers, not as regular or special educators. Specialization will be in an academic area or in skill areas (communication skills, home/school relations, classroom management) and will likely occur at more advanced levels (perhaps at the Master's degree level). All teachers will receive extensive training in understanding and appreciating child variance and diversity, and will be trained to view differences as differences, not as deviance. Preparation will emphasize models of child study and observation which focus on curricular and instructional adaptations that will accommodate children's differences,[63] including such practices as multilevel teaching, cooperative learning, and social skills training. The focus of all teacher preparation programs will be on helping teachers learn how to create *inclusive* learning environments for students.

Because teacher training programs will foster teachers' tolerance for differences and broaden their perceptions of "what is normal," the pattern of referring children with special needs to an "expert" who works outside the regular classroom would change. Teachers will use models of consultation and team-work between specialists and generalists, or between pairs of regular education teachers that encourage problem solving.[64] Current "prereferral" models will not be *pre* anything, but will be standard operating procedure.

General education teachers, deskilled by special education in perpetuation of the myth that "it takes a special person to work with these kids," will become reskilled. Many of the instructional strategies now seen as the province of special education (task analysis, social skills training, adapted instruction) will become part of every teacher's preparation.

Teacher preparation programs will model the close communication and collaboration between regular and special education faculty members that we demand of public school teachers. The relationship between university training programs and state certifying agencies will change so that new certification standards reflect the eventual merger of regular and special education.

HOW SCHOOLS WILL BE ORGANIZED

The school will be a school for all children, with one teaching staff, sharing the same administrator, staff meetings, in-service programs and extracurricular activities. All children will participate in school-wide events (fund raising, assemblies, field trips, guest speakers, etc.). Signs on classroom doors will not identify students as being in a "special education class," yearbook pictures will picture students by last name in alphabetical order rather than by "EMR" class, and there will be a single PTA organization for all parents.

All school staff will receive orientation and training about students with differences. Custodians, cafeteria workers, school secretaries, and the like will all be familiar with the kinds of modifications and adaptations typically employed in the classroom. If there are children in the building who use sign language, training in sign language will be required of all school personnel and offered to all students. Heterogeneity will be structured, intentional, and highly desirable. An explicit goal of schooling will be teaching children to interact with people who are different while also acknowledging underlying similarities and connectedness.

Educational services for students will be linked to educational needs rather than to labels or categories. Parents, volunteers, classroom aides, and specialists will all be allowed to work with children who can benefit from their services or attention, without concern for the labels attached to either the providers or the recipients. Although there might be resource consultants or instructional specialists, they will be school-wide resources. Teachers will not be identified as "the third-grade teacher" or "the LD teacher," because each teacher would work with many groups of students in different contexts. Mr. Hernandez might be "the spelling teacher" *and* "the hockey teacher" *and* "the creative dramatics coach," thereby eliminating the stigma often associated with certain groups of students "having to go to that special teacher in that special room." The "reading expert" will provide reading services to all students who require such assistance, regardless of label or etiology. Schools will no longer support four separate remedial reading programs, distinctly funded and with individual eligibility requirements.

Collaboration and cooperative team-teaching will be emphasized. It will be common to find a class of fifty 10 to 12 year olds with three teachers, each having special expertise in a content area or methodology. Students previously labeled and separated will be part of the overall group, receiving whatever specialized services they require within the context of the regular class by one of the team of teachers. Teachers will be provided with elaborate support systems (release time, permanent district substitutes) to enable them to observe other teachers, to meet in small problem-solving groups, and to help one another support students who need help. Collaboration across age and grade levels will also be encouraged. Rigid, homogeneous age-grouping will be abandoned in favor of more flexible arrangements which respect children's needs to be with chronological peers, and to also interact comfortably with children older and younger than themselves. An eight-year-old who needs beginning reading instruction will receive that teaching without being placed "back" in a first-grade class or a remedial setting. Multi-age groupings for instruction will be common.

Collaboration between parents and teachers will be commonplace. Schools will provide support services (such as child care and transportation) so parents can be meaningfully involved in their child's education. Parents will be expected and encouraged to be active participants in setting goals for their children and in helping their own and other people's children meet these goals. Parents will understand the inclusive philosophy of the school and will be encouraged to engage in advocacy efforts to support that orientation.

Federal funding will be disassociated from categorical labels, thus encouraging innovation rather than categorical bounty hunting.[65] Money might be allocated according to numbers of students requiring a particular training option rather than numbers of students in a given category. Alternatively, districts or individual schools might be funded at specific levels and required to engage in district and school-wide planning to ensure the inclusion and education of all students within their boundaries.

Multiple kinds of instruction and many ways of mastering content will be typical. Individualization will be the order of the day, and not the exception. There will be increased emphasis on *cooperative learning*[66] and all students will be given multiple opportunities to work in heterogeneous groups. The alleged superiority of homogeneous or competitive and evaluative models grouping which result in the rank-ordering, separation, and labeling of students will be challenged. Heavy emphasis will be placed on peer collaboration and peer tutoring programs. Adaptive learning environments, such as the ALEM model described by Wang and Birch, will be used in all schools.[67] Emphasis would be on providing environments which fit children, rather than on fitting children into existing environments.

Teachers will create and adapt their own flexible, multilevel curricula rather than be asked to implement "teacher-proof curricula" which are an affront to teachers' intelligence and empowerment. Teachers will work together and receive release time and monetary support to write and disseminate new materials. By developing multilevel, flexible curricula, teachers will find it much easier to meet the needs of heterogeneous groups of learners.

The domain of essential school learning will expand. Teaching about differences and disabilities will be a significant and valid part of the general school curriculum, not limited to information about handicapping conditions, but including exploration of all kinds of diversity (racial, ethnic, religious, sexual, etc.). Social skills training, including friendship skills, sharing, and cooperation will be newly emphasized. Formal and informal instruction and assessment of social skills will be part of the "basics." Failing the lesson on "accepts others in the classroom" or the unit on "helping others with dignity" will be considered as significant as a failure to grasp binomial equations or geography.[68]

Students will view the highly diverse school population simply as "business as usual," or "ordinary." Students will comfortably accept people who use wheelchairs, who tape record lectures, who have their exams read to them, or who read at very different levels as part of their schools. National data might be reported on the extent to which any individual school successfully integrated students (an Integration Index, if you will), and published along with Iowa scores and percentages of students who attend higher education institutions. This kind of public valuing of integration might lead schools to look seriously at their programs and successes in this area.

THE MERGER OF REGULAR AND SPECIAL EDUCATION: BARRIERS AND HOPES

Within the last several years, several strong calls for regular and special education "merger" have been issued.[69] Proponents of merger urge a unified system arguing that the distinctions between regular and special education students and regular and special education instructional methods are arbitrary. Merger proponents cite the unnecessary time and expense of classifying students, the competition and duplication of services fostered by a dual system, the ambiguities of determining eligibility for services according to category, and the reduction of curricular options which occur as a result of classification. Madeleine Will, Assistant Secretary of Education, issued a call for "The Regular Education Initiative" (REI) which proposes collapsing the funding for many of the mild disability categories into more generic teacher improvement grants.[70] Similarly, the Office of Special Education is now funding grants which target improving regular education so it can accommodate more handicapped learners.

Reactions to these proposals have not been uniformly supportive,[71] generating instead a number of impediments to productive dialogue. First, the existence of a dual system fosters an atmosphere of suspicion and isolation between regular and special educators. Discussions of merger deteriorate into defensive posturing because the participants respond very differently to questions like: How badly is special education failing to do its job? If students in special education could/should be served in regular education, how willing is regular education to change? and Can special education divert and reform itself without a concomitant commitment on the part of regular education to reform? Many discussions of the feasibility of merger deteriorate into a chicken-or-egg debate concerning who should change first. Can special education students be returned to regular education before those teachers are prepared and ready, or will regular education teachers "get ready" only when students now served in special education return to their rooms and responsibility? Although there has been considerable discussion about the necessity for merger within the special education literature, there is no agreement amongst special educators, and little parallel discourse among regular educators.

Second, the dual system perpetuates concepts of professionalism that identify teachers with the students that they teach. Teachers of "emotionally disturbed" students subscribe to different journals, attend different professional meetings, and receive different in-service training than teachers of "third graders." Different job titles, funding mechanisms, and discrete administrative models all impede the possibility that teachers will see themselves as mergable. Efforts to revise special education funding so that it is tied to instruction and services (rather than to labeled children) are often met with resistance by special educators who are wary of the loss of their students' hard-earned educational rights. Special educators worry that services for students described as mildly handicapped will dissolve, and that students will be replaced in the same unresponsive mainstream from which they were originally excluded. The interrelationship between categorical training programs, state and federal funding models, and state certification requirements is so complex that each potential "player" is extremely cautious in instituting the kinds of massive redesign required. The time, funds, and energy already invested in establishing intricate assessment models, criteria for inclusion, and standards for placement and instruction are considerable, and serve to entrench firmly current models of service delivery.

Third, advocacy efforts are intimately linked to funding mechanisms and staffing patterns. Each disability group has its own advocacy group, and competition is often structured between groups. Current economic exigencies virtually insure that there is not enough money to "go around," and that parents' strong need to support their own child's program will take precedence over more global, far-reaching reform efforts. The worried, concerned reactions to the Regular Education Initiative from the Association for Children with Learning Disabilities and the Council for Exceptional Children provide good examples of the extent to which both parents and professionals are seriously challenged and frightened by the prospect of more generic funding and educational programs.

What can be done to overcome these barriers? One cannot mandate mutual respect among regular and special educators; it can only be accomplished through extensive dialogue at both school and university levels. Most importantly, this dialogue must be brought into the arena of regular education. Rather than having debates about the Regular Education Initiative at meetings of the Council for Exceptional Children, these debates should be taking place at meetings of the American Association for Colleges of Teacher Education and the American Teacher Education organization. If, in fact, the reform of special education lies within regular education, then regular educators must assume responsibility for continuing the dialogue. The "regular education initiative" should be renamed "the improvement of education initiative" or something more generic which does not reify the separation between regular and special education in its very title. A hopeful sign is exemplified by the recent focus of the Holmes Group on Teacher Education Reform on the interface between general and special education issues. Although the discussion of merger appears in this chapter following the analysis of other structures, the critical dialogue between regular and special education is actually a prerequisite to the achievement of all other "future visions."

Special educators must take responsibility for transforming notions of professionalism so that they cease to take pride in their distinctiveness and instead pride themselves on collaboration and cooperation. Funding mechanisms must be altered so that educators are encouraged to work together across traditional program areas, perhaps, for example, by funding only special education research which is based in the reform of regular education. Individual advocacy efforts must also be abandoned in favor of more general reform movements. As long as parents of children considered "learning disabled" are asking for changes in school programs independently of parents of children labeled "retarded," and in isolation from parents in the whole school PTA, there is little hope that school-wide reform will become a reality.

Movements toward merger must be made so that special educators feel that they have little to lose and much to gain. Schools might, for example, guarantee that no special educator will be dismissed; these teachers might be retrained (at district expense) or work in different roles (as members of an elementary team, for example), but they would be guaranteed continued employment. Schools must also be assured that they will not lose any federal funding by moving toward more generic, inclusive programming. Similarly, parents of children now receiving special education services must be guaranteed that their child's due process rights will continue to be held as paramount in program development and planning. Teachers and parents must both be guaranteed that school districts will not simply "dump" students into regular classrooms without making the kinds of provisions necessary for their continued success.

IN CONCLUSION—A FUTURE VISION

The analysis of an alternative vision presented in this last section has included a number of principles which would guide the revised educational system:

Children would be viewed in *holistic, multidimensional* ways with a focus on *functional* (rather than categorical) *assessment*. Teacher education would be far more *generic*, and schools of education that prepare teachers would model the *integration of faculty* which we ask schools to demonstrate.

Schools would be characterized by *inclusiveness*, the *integration of educational services, flexible teacher assignments and responsibilities, flexibility of instruction, collaboration between teachers,* and the acceptance of *child differences as "ordinary."*

And lastly, we would move toward the reform of education with *mutual respect and support* between special and general educators, *creative funding patterns, joint advocacy, altered notions of professionalism,* and a *continuing (or heightened) respect for due process and parent involvement.*

In an article entitled "Inventing a Future for Special Education: A Cautionary Tale,"[72] Mary Moran envisions two possible futures. In State A, special education continues to grow. Stricter eligibility guidelines are established for special education services, more funds are expended, and quality of education is judged by its effectiveness in preparing the handicapped for employment. As programs grow, however, so does the isolation and segregation of students with handicaps. When economic hard times develop, handicapped students become bitterly resented for their drain on state and local budgets and become targets of discrimination. Soon, programs are cut, advocacy groups battle each other into oblivion, and handicapped students are once more underserved and isolated in society.

In State B, the school population is viewed as an interdependent system and schools are freed from the constraint of having to identify special populations in order to provide services. Schools utilize the dropping birth rate as the occasion to reduce class size instead of reducing teaching staff. People with handicaps are not negatively differentiated from other students or citizens. Schooling and work are integrated and life-long, and all residents (including handicapped citizens) have the opportunity to engage in integrated rotations of schooling, work, and leisure.

Moran concludes that "alternative futures can be imagined if we free ourselves to question assumptions."[73] Although the extent and nature of the changes proposed in this chapter may seem overwhelming, fundamental changes must occur at many levels in order for schools to alter their perception and treatment of students with disabilities. Because the reform of the categories of mild disabilities is tied so intrinsically to general school reform, the kinds of changes called for here are broader and perhaps more challenging than changes which might be necessary in meeting the needs of other, much smaller groups of students with disabilities (visually impaired, hearing impaired, severely handicapped).

The most significant challenge to the implementation of the guiding principles identified in this chapter will be our societal history of failing to value diversity and the assumptions which keep us from envisioning the future differently. Our propensity for labeling and sorting, coupled with economic and social policies which often work actively against the poor, minority groups, and handicapped students, have left us with a society conspicuously stratified by race, class, gender, and handicap.[74]

As a society, we suffer the ill effects of losing the possible contributions of a substantial portion of our population: those assigned to special education who often become segregated from the rest of society, and those who slip through the educational cracks, becoming unemployed dropouts and otherwise marginalized individuals. This is a future we can ill afford. True success will be achieved when diversity is considered "typical" or "ordinary," and any efforts to separate children are perceived as "unnatural" and uncalled for. When schools take seriously their responsibilities to all students, and their responsibility to provide for those students in integrated settings, we will have true cause for celebration.

FOOTNOTES

1. Although speech handicaps are often included in district level counts of students receiving special education, they fall outside the domain of this chapter because such services are typically provided either to students who are served within regular education or to students who are served primarily within another special education program. As such, there are rarely special, segregated programs for these students, there is minimal stigma attached to receiving speech services, and there is little conflict or controversy surrounding the assignment of students to this category.

2. For a detailed history of mental retardation, see Richard C. Scheerenberger, *A History of Mental Retardation* (Baltimore: Paul Brookes Publishing, 1983). For a more general history of special education, see Steven J. Taylor and Stanford J. Searl, Jr., "The Disabled in America: History, Policy and Trends," in *Understanding Exceptional Children and Youth*, ed. Peter Knoblock (Boston: Little, Brown, 1987), pp. 5-64.

3. Irving Hendrick and Donald MacMillan, "Coping with Diversity in City School Systems: The Role of Mental Testing in Shaping Special Classes for Mentally Retarded Children in Los Angeles, 1900-1930," *Education and Training in Mental Retardation* 22, no. 1 (1987): 10-17; E. Anne Bennison, "Before the Learning Disabled There Were Feebleminded Children," in *Learning Disability: Dissenting Essays*, ed. Barry Franklin (New York: Falmer Press, 1987), pp. 13-28.

4. Seymour B. Sarason and John Doris, *Educational Handicap: Public Policy and Social History* (New York: Free Press, 1979): 267.

5. Linda Gonzalves, "Henry Herbert Goddard and the Politics of Mental Measurement (1910-1920)" (Paper presented at the Annual Meeting of the American Educational Research Association, April, 1983).

6. Scheerenberger, *A History of Mental Retardation*, pp. 166-67.

7. James Ysseldyke and Bob Algozzine, *Introduction to Special Education* (Boston: Houghton Mifflin, 1984), p. 84.

8. Scheerenberger, *A History of Mental Retardation*, p. 169.

9. James M. Kauffman, *Characteristics of Children's Behavior Disorders*, 3d ed. (Columbus: Charles E. Merrill, 1985), pp. 38-62.

10. Scheerenberger, *A History of Mental Retardation*, p. 201.

11. Ibid., p. 233.

12. Herbert Grossman, ed., *Manual on Terminology and Classification in Mental Retardation* (Washington, D.C.: American Association of Mental Deficiency, 1977).

13. Barry Franklin, "From Brain Injury to Learning Disability: Alfred Strauss, Heinz Werner, and the Historical Development of the Learning Disabilities Field," in *Learning Disability: Dissenting Essays*, ed. Barry Franklin (New York: Falmer Press, 1987), pp. 29-46.

14. Kauffman, *Characteristics of Children's Behavior Disorders*, pp. 52-54.

15. Scheerenberger, *A History of Mental Retardation*, pp. 236-40.

16. Kauffman, *Characteristics of Children's Behavior Disorders*, pp. 57-59.

17. Douglas Biklen and Nancy Zollers, "The Focus of Advocacy in the LD Field," *Journal of Learning Disabilities* 19, no. 10 (1986): 579-86.

18. Lloyd M. Dunn, "Special Education for the Mildly Retarded: Is Much of It Justifiable?" *Exceptional Children* 35 (September 1968): 5-22; G. Orville Johnson, "Special Education for the Mentally Handicapped: A Paradox," *Exceptional Children* 29 (October 1962): 62-69.

19. Nicholas Hobbs, *Issues in the Classification of Children*, Vols. I and II (San Francisco: Jossey-Bass, 1975).

20. *Hansen v. Hobson*, 269 F. Supp. 960 (E.D. Pa. 1976), aff'd, 57 F. 2a 373 (3d Cir. 1977); *Diana v. State Board of Education*, C.A. No. c-70-37 R.F.P. (N.D. Cal., filed Feb. 3, 1970); *Larry P. v. Riles*, 343 F. Supp. 1306 (N.D. Cal. 1972), aff'd. 502 F. 2d 963 (9th Cir. 1974); *Mills v. The Board of Education*, Civil Action No. 1939-71, U.S. District Court of the District of Columbia (1972); *Pennsylvania Association for Retarded Children v. Commonwealth of Pennsylvania*, 334 F. Supp. 1257 (E.D. Pa. 1971), 343 F. Supp. 279 (E.D. Pa., 1972); *Frederick L. v. Thomas*, 419 F. Supp. 960 (E.D. Pa. 1976), aff'd, 57 F. 2a 373 (3d. Cir. 1977); *Lora v. New York City Board of Education*, 456 F. Supp., 1211, 1275 (E.D. N.Y. 1978).

21. Christine Sleeter, "Learning Disabilities: The Social Construction of a Special Education Category," *Exceptional Children* 53, no. 1 (1986): 46-54.

22. Grossman, ed., *Manual on Terminology and Classification in Mental Retardation*, p. xii.

23. Samuel A. Kirk and James J. Gallagher, *Educating Exceptional Children*, 4th ed. (Boston: Houghton Mifflin, 1983), pp. 123-24.

24. Presidents' Committee on Mental Retardation, *The Six-Hour Retarded Child* (Washington, D.C.: U.S. Department of Health, Education, and Welfare, 1969). This study was highly significant in illuminating the extent to which mild retardation could be seen as a social construct, in this case the product of rigid and narrow behavioral expectations within public schools.

25. See, for example, Jane R. Mercer and Jane F. Lewis, *System of Multicultural Pluralistic Assessment (SOMPA)* (New York: Psychological Corporation, 1978).

26. Donald D. Hammill, James E. Leigh, Gaye McNutt, and Stephen C. Larsen, "A New Definition of Learning Disabilities," *Learning Disability Quarterly* 4 (Fall 1981): 336-42.

27. Biklen and Zollers, "The Focus of Advocacy," p. 579.

28. Kauffman, *Characteristics of Children's Behavior Disorders*, pp. 27-29.

29. Bob Algozzine and Lori Korinek, "Where Is Special Education for Students with High Prevalence Handicaps Going?" *Exceptional Children* 51, no. 5 (1985): 388-94.

30. Bob Algozzine, James E. Ysseldyke, and Sandra Christenson, "An Analysis of the Incidence of Special Class Placement: The Masses Are Burgeoning," *Journal of Special Education* 17, no. 2 (1983): 141-47.

31. Algozzine and Korinek, "Where Is Special Education for Students with High Prevalence Handicaps Going?" p. 392.

32. Gonzalves, "Henry Herbert Goddard and the Politics of Measurement," p. 37.

33. Hendrick and MacMillan, "Coping with Diversity in City School Systems."

34. See, for example, James Ysseldyke, Bob Algozzine, Mark R. Shinn, and Matthew McGue, "Similarities and Differences between Low Achievers and Students Labeled Learning Disabled," *Journal of Special Education* 16 (Spring 1982): 73-85; and James Ysseldyke, Bob Algozzine, and Susan Epps, "A Logical and Empirical Analysis of Current Practice in Classifying Students as Handicapped," *Exceptional Children* 50, no. 2 (1983): 161.

35. For an exploration of the continuing cultural and language biases which result in the overrepresentation of children of color and other minority groups in special education, see Ed. N. Argulewicz, "Effects of Ethnic Membership, Socioeconomic Status, and Home Language on LD, EMR, and EH Placements," *Learning Disabilities Quarterly* 6 (1983): 195-200; James A. Tucker, "Ethnic Proportions in Classes for the Learning Disabled: Issues in Nonbiased Assessment," *Journal of Special Education* 14, no. 1 (1980): 93-105; Larry Maheady, Richard Towne, Bob Algozzine, Jane Mercer, and James Ysseldyke, "Minority Overrepresentation: A Case for Alternative Practices Prior to Referral," *Learning Disabilities Quarterly* 6 (1983): 448-56; and Christine E. Sleeter, "Learning Disabilities: The Social Construction of a Special Education Category."

36. Edward Alloway and J. David Smith, "Changes in Mild Mental Retardation: Population, Programs, and Perspectives," *Exceptional Children* 50, no. 2 (1983): 149-59.

37. Ibid., p. 156.

38. Maheady et al., "Minority Overrepresentation," p. 449.

39. Deborah S. Bart, "The Differential Diagnosis of Special Education: Managing Social Pathology as Individual Disability," in *Special Education and Social Interests*, ed. Len Barton and Sally Tomlinson (New York: Nichols Publishing, 1984), pp. 81-121; Robert Bogdan and Judy Kugelmass, "Case Studies of Mainstreaming: A Symbolic Interactionist Approach to Special Schooling," in *Special Education and Social Interests*, ed. Barton and Tomlinson, pp. 173-91.

40. Steven A. Gelb, "From Moral Imbecility to Maladaptive Behavior: The Social Construction of Educable Mental Retardation" (Paper presented at the Annual Meeting of the American Educational Research Association, San Francisco, 1986).

41. Argulewicz, "Effects of Ethnic Membership," 195-200.

42. Gonzalves, "Henry Herbert Goddard and the Politics of Mental Measurement," p. 3.

43. Bernard Farber, *Mental Retardation: Its Social Context and Social Consequences* (Boston: Houghton Mifflin, 1968), p. 19.

44. James Carrier, "The Politics of Early Learning Disability Theory," in *Learning Disability: Dissenting Essays*, ed. Barry Franklin (New York: Falmer Press, 1987): 47-66.

45. Gelb, "From Moral Imbecility to Maladaptive Behavior."

46. Joel Spring, *American Education: An Introduction to Social and Political Aspects* (New York: Longman, 1985), p. 63.

47. See, for example, Michael W. Apple, *Education and Power* (Boston: Routledge and Kegan Paul, 1982); and Christine Sleeter, "Literacy, Definitions of Learning

Disabilities, and Social Control" in *Learning Disability: Dissenting Essays*, ed. Barry Franklin (New York: Falmer Press, 1987): 67-87.

48. Sleeter, "Learning Disabilities."

49. Tucker, "Ethnic Proportions in Classes for the Learning Disabled," p. 104.

50. For a good summary of this debate, see Sleeter, "Literacy, Definitions of Learning Disabilities, and Social Control."

51. Sleeter, "Learning Disabilities," p. 20.

52. For a critique of the formulation of the category of "learning-disabled/gifted," see Mara Sapon-Shevin, "The Learning Disabled/Gifted: The Politics of Paradox" in *Learning Disability: Dissenting Essays*, ed. Barry M. Franklin (New York: Falmer Press, 1987), pp. 178-203.

53. James M. Kauffman, "Where Special Education for Disturbed Children Is Going: A Personal View," *Exceptional Children* 46, no. 7 (1980): 524.

54. See James M. Kauffman, "Saving Children in the Age of Big Brother: Moral and Ethical Issues in the Identification of Deviance," *Behavioral Disorders* 10 (November 1984): 60-70; and James L. Paul, "Behavioral Disorders in the 1980s: Ethical and Ideological Issues," *Behavioral Disorders* 11 (November 1985): 66-72.

55. Marleen Pugach and Mara Sapon-Shevin, "New Agendas for Special Education Policy: What the National Reports Haven't Said," *Exceptional Children* 53, no. 4 (1987): 295-99; Mara Sapon-Shevin, "The National Education Reports and Special Education: Implications for Students," *Exceptional Children* 53, no. 4 (1987): 300-6; Michael W. Apple, "National Reports and the Construction of Inequality," *British Journal of Sociology of Education* 7, no. 2 (1986): 171-90.

56. Paul, "Behavioral Disorders in the 1980s," p. 69.

57. Deborah S. Bart, "The Differential Diagnosis of Special Education," p. 88.

58. Ibid., p. 111.

59. Marten Soder, "The Mentally Retarded: Ideologies of Care and Surplus Population" in *Special Education and Social Interests*, ed. Len Barton and Sally Tomlinson (New York: Nichols Publishing, 1984), p. 15.

60. See Lous Heshusius, "Paradigm Shifts and Special Education: A Response to Ulman and Rosenberg," *Exceptional Children* 52, no. 5 (1986): 461-65.

61. William Stainback and Susan Stainback, "A Rationale for the Merger of Regular and Special Education," *Exceptional Children* 51 (October 1984): 109.

62. Marleen Pugach and M. Elizabeth Whitten, "The Methodological Content of Teacher Education Programs in Learning Disabilities: A Problem of Duplication," *Learning Disability Quarterly* 10, no. 4 (1987): 291-300.

63. Maynard Reynolds and Margaret Wang, "Restructuring Special School Programs: A Position Paper," *Policy Studies Review* 2 (January 1983): 189-212.

64. Marleen Pugach, "Special Education Categories as Constraints on the Reform of Teacher Education" (Paper presented at the Annual Meeting of the American Educational Research Association (San Francisco, 1986); idem, "The National Education Reports and Special Education: Implications for Teacher Preparation," *Exceptional Children* 53, no. 4 (1987): 308-314.

65. Margaret C. Wang and Maynard C. Reynolds, "Catch 22 and Disabling Help: A Reply to Alan Gartner," *Exceptional Children* 53, no. 1 (1986): 77-79.

66. David Johnson and Roger Johnson, "Mainstreaming and Cooperative Learning Strategies," *Exceptional Children* 52 (April 1986): 553-61; idem, *Learning Together and Alone: Cooperative, Competitive, and Individualistic Learning*, 2d ed. (Englewood Cliffs, N.J.: Prentice-Hall, 1987); Mara Sapon-Shevin, "Who Says Somebody's Gotta Lose:

Competition as an Obstacle to Mainstreaming," *Education Unlimited* 2, no. 4 (1980): 48-50; Nancy Madden and Robert Slavin, "Mainstreaming Students with Mild Handicaps: Academic and Social Outcomes," *Review of Educational Research* 53 (Winter 1983): 519-69.

67. Margaret Wang and James Birch, "Effective Special Education in Regular Classes," *Exceptional Children* 50, no. 5 (1984): 391-99.

68. For examples of how all these social skills might be incorporated into regular class instruction, see Gwendolyn Carledge and Joanne Fellows Milburn, eds., *Teaching Social Skills to Children: Innovative Approaches*, 2d ed. (New York: Pergamon Press, 1986).

69. Stainback and Stainback, "A Rationale for the Merger of Regular and Special Education"; M. Stephen Lilly, "Divestiture in Special Education: A Personal Perspective" (Paper prepared for the President's Roundtable, International CEC Convention, Houston, Texas, 1982), p. 13.

70. Madeleine C. Will, "Educating Children with Learning Problems: A Shared Responsibility," *Exceptional Children* 52, no. 5 (1986): 411-15.

71. See, for example, "The Regular Education Initiative: A Statement by the Teacher Education Division, Council for Exceptional Children, October, 1987," *Journal of Learning Disabilities* 20, no. 5 (1987): 289-93; "The CLD Position Statements, The Board of Trustees of the Council for Learning Disabilities," *Journal of Learning Disabilities Quarterly* 20, no. 6 (1987): 349-50; and an entire issue of the *Journal of Learning Disabilities* (January, 1988) devoted to a rebuttal of the REI.

72. Mary Moran, "Inventing a Future for Special Education: A Cautionary Tale," *Journal for Special Educators* 19, no. 4 (1983): 28-36.

73. Ibid., 36.

74. Carl Grant and Christine Sleeter, "Excellence, Equality, and Equity: A Critique" in *Excellence in Education*, ed. Phillip Altbach, Gail Kelly, and Lois Weiss (Buffalo, NY: Prometheus Press, 1985), pp. 139-59.

CHAPTER V

Lessons from Life: Personal and Parental Perspectives on School, Childhood, and Disability

PHILIP M. FERGUSON AND ADRIENNE ASCH

The most important thing that happens when a child is born with disabilities is that a child is born. The most important thing that happens when a couple becomes parents of a child with disabilities is that a couple becomes parents. These two statements seem almost tautologous. Yet, the history of professional approaches to the personal experience of disability by parents and children creates an unfortunate but enduring need to reaffirm their truth. Whether in medicine, education, psychology, or social work, the professional approach to people living with a disability has repeatedly seemed to want to reverse biology. Thus, parents often became a curious trait usually associated with the disability under investigation, whether mental retardation, blindness, autism, or perhaps just handicaps in general. A full understanding of cerebral palsy required examination of prevalence, etiology, behavioral characteristics, and, oh yes, the personal aspects. Parents and children became the adjectives, disability the noun.

The situation is improving. Along with the moves to integrate the schools has been a parallel move to integrate the disability back into the context of the child's life as a whole and the family situation in general.[1] The contributions of "labeling theory" in sociology,[2] the principle of "normalization" in the human services,[3] and the disability rights movement of the last fifteen years or so[4] all have increasingly

---

I, Adrienne, thank my parents for all they have done and are as people. I add my voice to the many who have praised and thanked Josephine L. Taylor, the pioneer of the program in New Jersey of which I write here. Without her, my portion of this chapter and my entire philosophy would not be what it is. New Jersey's blind children, their parents, and people with disabilities throughout the nation owe her our deepest gratitude.

attacked the process of objectification or "reification" by which society obscures its discrimination behind a facade of misused physiology. Recognition of the largely social nature of disability and the "blaming the victim" style of past practices in special education, rehabilitation, and the medical professions is no longer novel. Other analysts have extended this perception to parents by showing how they have been made to share in their children's labels.[5]

Despite this progress, there is still a scholarly neglect of the direct, personal accounts of disabled individuals and their parents as a legitimate source of information for policy analysis and service reform. As we will use the term here, "personal narrative" refers to a published account of life with a disability written by a disabled individual or the parent of such an individual. If cited at all, these works by people unavoidably involved in the disabled community are used, at best, as poignant illustrations of what "serious" or "objective" research into personal adaptation to disability has already supposedly established. It is revealing that the most often cited personal narratives of recent years in special education have been two books written and edited by professionals in the fields of education or human services who also happened to be parents of disabled children.[6] The point is not that these books do not deserve this recognition. Both have much to recommend them. It is, rather, the exclusivity of scholarly attention (or, at least, the attention of scholars) that raises the question of whether the apparent credibility of these two books for other professionals has less to do with the content of the writing than the credentials of the writers. It is our contention that personal narratives constitute a large and neglected source of data for understanding how society in general, and schools in particular, could better support disabled children and their families. More specifically, since these narratives are situationally rather than conceptually based, they can reveal the personal perspectives in words chosen by the authors, rather than the predetermined categories of the researcher's survey questionnaire. This chapter will discuss what these perspectives—combined with some of our own views—suggest as being most supportive of the families with disabled children. Our overall purpose in this chapter is more descriptive than prescriptive. A deeper understanding of the complexity of living with a disability must precede—or at least accompany—our society's efforts to improve the educational experience of disabled students and their families. Parents and adults with disabilities are a singularly valuable resource for achieving that understanding. They have learned of the complexity not from books on curricular reform or theories of psychological adjustment, but through involuntary, firsthand encounters. They learned their lessons from life itself.

The Use of Personal Narratives

Personal narratives are certainly not created equal. The books and articles vary from the maudlin to the moving, the insightful to the superficial. Fortunately, few try for the often stilted tone and language of most professional literature. On the other hand, many of these accounts are written with the kind of heavy-handed piety or inspirational overkill that can make one yearn for the pedestrian prose of an academic treatise. It is simply a reality of putting experience into words that felicity of phrase is not a requirement of parents or professionals.

At least with personal narratives, there is almost always the push and tug of personality behind the words: the life after the clinic has closed; the home away from school. These authors are individuals, not cautiously striving to summarize expertise in academic argot, but showing their lives from the experience of having lived them, not studied them. These narratives, then, examine the same issues discussed in other chapters of this book. However, they examine those issues one family—one person—at a time, instead of one concept at a time.

It is also true that, regardless of the quality of the writing, the people who write these personal narratives are not typical of the disabled community as a whole. Most people living with a handicap do not write books or articles. Indeed, the very act of writing, with its implicit elements of reflection and recollection, requires certain amounts of steadiness and accommodation in one's life that are simply not available to many parents and disabled individuals still struggling with inadequate community resources.

There are at least two responses to this issue of generalizability. First, we do not claim that the examination of personal narratives is the *only* method of accurately discovering what it is like to live with a disability. It is, however, a neglected source of what some of those individuals want to say in a public format. Second, historians and other students of culture have long faced this problem of the reliability of published sources. The benefits usually outweigh the risks. What has been said of personal documents in historical research applies to our use of narratives as well:

A person speaks to the historical record in his or her own idiom. Impressions are not shaped and channeled by response categories on a questionnaire or an interview schedule. Of course, this eliminates the possibility of pursuing a line of questioning or probing the depths of a subject's level of meaning, but it also eliminates the influence of the researcher upon the perspective of the respondent.[7]

A final point: Just as personal narratives make no pretense of scholarly dispassion, neither do we in this chapter. Our examination of this literature is forged in the crucible of our own experiences. One of us (Asch) is disabled and the other (Ferguson) is the parent of a disabled son. We have liberally supplemented what we found in the narratives of others with our own personal accounts, experiences, and perspectives. Nor are our two perspectives always the same. Those differences, too, are reflected in the way we have organized our comments. What we share is an impatience with incomplete reform and a resistance to professional paternalism no matter how well-intentioned.

Our elaboration of themes common to both the personal narratives we reviewed and to our own personal experiences will alternate between our two perspectives. The perspective of parents is notoriously different from that of their children regardless of whether the children are disabled or not. Not surprisingly, then, the narratives of parents of disabled children sometimes emphasize different aspects of events than do the accounts of disabled adults recalling their childhood. Even more common is a difference in the events that each of the two subgenres considers. The perspective of an adult on his or her friendships as a child includes events that occurred without the presence of parents. Parents, too, encounter a world of friends and professionals physically, as well as emotionally, separated from their disabled child. Finally, the list of disabilities represented in the parent narratives is different from that represented in the individual autobiographies. Most mentally retarded children, for example, do not write books or articles when they grow up. Many parents, however, have written about mental retardation. On the other hand, comparatively few parent narratives exist describing life with a child who is blind, although there is a significant group of narratives written by blind adults.

For all of these reasons, our elaboration of the four themes that emerged from our consideration of the narratives seems to fit best within a dialogic format. One of us (Ferguson) will discuss a theme as it applies to parents. Then the other one (Asch) will consider the same theme from the perspective of the disabled individual as both response and supplement to the parent viewpoint. Finally, after this discussion, we will jointly summarize our recommendations for educational reform from the shared experience of family life as the various representatives of families have described them.

Parent and Child Relationships

THE PARENT PERSPECTIVE

My wife and I know what makes our son, Ian, laugh. After living with him for almost eighteen years, we should. However, the difference is that Ian happens to be severely retarded and physically handicapped. Some of what he finds hilarious would not be funny to a typical seventeen year old. It goes beyond that, though. Despite the "eternal child" stereotype, Ian's sense of humor is not somehow stuck at the level of a toddler. Rather, Ian's sense of humor is, for me, part of what makes him Ian, not part of what makes him retarded, even though his cognitive limitations have helped shape that humor. Furthermore, my knowledge of his particular sense of humor is part of what defines my relationship with Ian. I know what little movements mean within a chain of behavior that is meaningless to others, but a routine between him and his mother or me. Occasionally, I will watch Ian use these motions outside of the home (e.g., snapping his fingers in school in response to some overheard clicking), in isolation, and then he cracks up laughing for what must seem like no reason to other observers. I usually crack up, too, on such occasions. It is as though he is repeating a sort of nonverbal punchline to some of the physical "jokes" only he and I know.

This theme emerges repeatedly in parental accounts of their relationships with their children. It goes beyond a tolerance of difference in their children to an appreciation of a child's individuality that incorporates the aspects of disability. In some narratives, this relationship emerges as a parent's counterpoint to a perceived cultural message that a child's uniqueness is somehow swallowed up in a label of a specific disability. Clara Claiborne Park describes the dilemma this can create for parents in a discussion of her daughter's continuing odd, "autistic" behavior and conversations:

Jessy can keep her reactions under control. Yet we have not wished completely to bid farewell to these strange products of the imagination, especially as in their absence her conversation is flatly factual, limited, and uninteresting. One does not wish to encourage "bizarre thinking," yet to discourage it entirely is to sacrifice much of the individuality and charm which are among her greatest assets. In the adolescent years, however, it had to be discouraged since it led so often to behavior too bizarre to be tolerated in the social world she was increasingly able to enter.[8]

A second aspect of parent relationships that repeatedly emerges from the narratives is the positive contribution that a disabled child can make to some families. This, too, is a delicate matter to explain. Parent narratives written in the 1940s and 1950s, for example, often express a strong sense of religious growth as a result of this "special blessing from heaven."[9] Other parents just as strongly reject this divine justification of a natural tragedy,[10] yet still describe a family life of increased tolerance of differences, and a heightened awareness of the daily injustices needlessly dealt out by our society to people in one minority group or another. One parent ends her account of her struggles on behalf of her son, Jeff, born with spina bifida, with just this sense of personal growth.

I am profoundly glad to know Jeff. Once I heard Ramsey Clark, former Attorney General, say that his retarded daughter taught him greater truths than all of his travel and any of the great and famous people he had known. I understand that.

Jeff is neither my burden nor my chastisement, although his care requires more than I want to give at times. He is not an angel sent for my personal growth or my future glory; he is not a punishment for my past sins. He is a son.[11]

The "message" of this section is not that parents rejoice in the disabilities of their children. I certainly regret that my son's legs do not work right. No parent narrative expresses pleasure about the opportunity to deal with a child's physiological limitations. Nor is the message that many parents eventually reach some golden stage of adjustment called "acceptance" by some social workers and psychologists. The limitations of any disability are too much embedded in the biases of the culture to allow some simple acquiescence to the latest professional version of "biology is destiny." The narratives repeatedly express anger, frustration, and resentment not at fate, but at the unnecessary burdens they and their children face because of social attitudes and behavior toward disabilities.

The essential message of parent-child relationships from the parental perspective is that a mother's or father's love of a son or daughter does not become more abstract just because that child does not fit society's notions of normalcy. As a father, I do not love my son *in spite* of his handicaps, as some abstracted, idealized version of reality. The object of my affection is the flesh and blood Ian whom I dress every day, put in a wheelchair, and struggle to talk to in words he can understand. Disability complicates the relationship but does not necessarily damage it. Being retarded is part of who Ian is, but I hate the barriers it creates for him. My wife and I are constantly balancing our comfort with Ian as he is, with a sense of inward urgency that he change. The relationship of any parent and child is always a process, not an outcome. Nonetheless, the process can be described at any given time. The narratives suggest that, if lucky, parents include a kind of "uneasy satisfaction" as part of the description:

Cara has enriched my life with her outgoing, sweet, generous self. She has a spunky style that I find amusing and, occasionally, trying. She has proven, and I am sure will continue to prove, that low expectations about retarded people are outdated bunk. That is particularly satisfying to me as parent.[12]

THE PERSONAL PERSPECTIVE

The complexity of emotion and behavior with which parents react to their disabled children can be as difficult for the children to comprehend fully as it is for parents to explain fully. This makes it even more difficult to summarize the disabled child's perception of the parent-child relationship. The difficulty reflects the fact that parent-child relationships are rarely symmetrical. Parents have the authority, size, knowledge, and one hopes, the judgment to govern the child's life in the earlier years and gradually to relinquish that control as the child matures. It is not surprising, then, that descriptions of that relationship reflect that same asymmetry. Parents naturally describe their reactions to their children. Children, just as naturally, do the same thing. That is, children do not simply reverse the direction of parent narratives and describe their reactions to their parents. Instead, children's narratives will also describe the parent's reaction to the child (as seen from the child's perspective), and only then give the child's reaction to the parent's reaction. Some of our strongest memories of childhood are often not of something we did, but of the pride or displeasure our parents showed toward that deed. We remember reactions more than actions. Part of understanding ourselves involves understanding our parents.

This added complexity would make it surprising if children's accounts of relationships with their parents did not show some departures, some shifts in emphasis, from the experiences of parents. Unfortunately for educators, the difficulty in understanding the different perspectives on parent-child relationships is matched only by the importance of the effort. Parents are crucial to the personality formation of their children, and for giving them the tools to begin to cope with and enjoy life. In a world intolerant of difference, this parental influence is even more important to the life of the child who has a disability. A good relationship between parent and child means the school receives a child optimally able to use the experiences it offers. If that relationship is less than good, then the school has an additional job to do and can possibly make a difference. It is the difficult job of educators to be able to judge effectively the quality of that relationship from both the parent's and the child's perspective.

Even the most complicated relationships have some basic requirements and responsibilities. One well-known advocate for disability rights has composed a minimum set of opportunities that all disabled children need from their parents. Disabled children have:

1. the right to be helped to become fully developed persons;
2. the right to be granted as much freedom and independence as other children in the family;
3. the right to have one's abilities, and not disabilities, treated as the critical factors in success;
4. the right to have one's disability perceived as an obstacle to be overcome and not as a complete liability;
5. the right to have environmental barriers removed from the home and from home life.[13]

However, the successful realization of these basic rights of childhood is where the child's perspective can differ dramatically from that of the parent. Unanimously, adults disabled in childhood attribute much of their success and many of their problems to how parents treated them and in particular to how their parents handled their disabilities. Four themes emerge consistently in the literature: parents sheltered children from the world because something was wrong; parents pretended, through silence or denial, that nothing was wrong; parents sought ways to "fix" the actual disabilities or to minimize the difference of what could not be fixed; or parents minimized the impact of disability while working to ensure that the child had a full life.

Not surprisingly, adults with the most overprotective parents are underrepresented in personal narratives. Without the sense of possibility and entitlement that parents can instill, it is extraordinarily difficult for disabled children to battle the obstacles confronting them in school and society. Yet the moving stories of Frances Lynn as she struggles to attain her own sense that she is entitled to her own life and to her own decisions gives us the opportunity to watch someone move out from the smothering of concerned parents.[14] Supported by contact with others who have disabilities and by the disability rights and independent living movements, Lynn is going forward.

The other three categories of parent-child relationships may at first appear synonymous, but they seem to differ in the moods they convey and in the results they attain. The silence of some parents can be devastating for the children. Edwina Franchild and Naomi Woronov, both women who grew up with usable but very limited vision and definitely as legally blind, report being expected to act as though they did not differ in any way from others around them.[15] For Franchild, the disturbed family environment resulted in hospitalization for psychiatric disability, her mother's suicide, and an ongoing struggle to discern what her blindness means in her life. Her education, work, and social life have been profoundly impaired by her parents' silence. Woronov describes how, by refusing to discuss her vision with her, her parents communicated expectations that she would achieve in spite of any problems. She definitely got the message to succeed rather than a defeatist message that success was unlikely. However, at the same time she also reports her parents' failure to get her the information about alternatives to use. For Woronov, the consequence was that she lived without her family's emotional support as she struggled with academics and social life when she could not see well enough to use her eyes but knew of no other way to function. All too many narratives report that parents, in striving to instill a sense of competence and entitlement to the best, ignored their children's need for honest conversation about what was different, what was hard, what seemed beyond them.

There is a third category of parental response perceived by children where the parents do not so much deny through silence the reality of a disability as make that reality a constant focus of rehabilitative attention. Instead of denying the disability, these parents praise normalcy, and make an unintended obsession of the gap between the two.

Sondra Diamond and Harilyn Rousso, both talented therapists committed to promoting fulfillment for disabled people, have poignantly described gifts and pain in their parents' messages about disability.[16] Both were fortunate in having parents who believed that their daughters' physical limitations did not preclude academic and social life with nondisabled people, and both sets of parents worked to give them services and support to promote their independence. Yet Rousso describes what seemed like an endless round of lessons in walking in front of the mirror at her mother's insistence. Rousso's account echoes one of the themes found in the parent narratives about the incorporation of difference into identity. The echo is ironic, however, because in Rousso's case, her mother lacked that parental appreciation of a child's total identity, disability and all.

She made numerous attempts over the years of my childhood to have me go for physical therapy and to practice walking more "normally" at home. I vehemently refused all her efforts. She could not understand why I would not walk straight. Now, I realize why. My disability, with my different walk and talk and my involuntary movements, having been with me all of my life, was part of me, part of my identity. With these disability features, I felt complete and whole. My mother's attempt to change my walk, strange as it may seem, felt like an assault on myself, an incomplete acceptance of all of me, an attempt to make me over.[17]

Diamond vividly recounts how, at the age of ten, her father scolded her for not eating potato chips in the way that "normal" people ate them. Fortunately, she had gained a sufficient sense of her own worth to retort that she was getting them into her mouth and having a good time and wanted to be left alone. She herself, Diamond says, did not think about her disability all the time as did her parents.[18]

The last parental category finds some sort of balance between acceptance and improvement in the socialization of the child. The disability is neither denied nor emphasized, at least not as a pattern of the parent-child relationship. In the frustration of Rousso and Diamond, as well as the parents' perplexity, we find a deeply troubling, urgent question: At what point is it all right, even essential, to cease working on eliminating those differences disability can cause in appearance and behavior? My parents confronted the same dilemma and responded differently at different times. Repeatedly, but usually with patience and tact, my father pointed out that sitting with my head down and putting my finger in my eyes jarred people and interfered with their getting to know me. Generally he managed to explain without my feeling ashamed or humiliated. As a result, by the age of ten or so, I had learned to sit up straight and now, in fact, must work to slouch in informal gatherings when my friends are disconcerted by my too straight back and shoulders. Eating skills were different. Something about teaching me to use a knife and fork properly and keep my fingers from touching my food frustrated my parents and made them impatient. They gave up, ensuring family peace and my self-consciousness at formal meals to this day. Yet, since they could not be patient, they were wise to let it go. I did things differently, yes, but not grossly so, and there was no point in trying to get me to do everything in life as a person with sight would do it. Now, as an adult, I can get advice from each of my parents, sister, and brother about the proper way to serve, cut up, and eat cantaloupe only to discover that each one is convinced that a different method is best.

In thinking about the writings of disabled adults and reflecting on my own life, I can give my parents high marks. They did not deny that I was blind, and did not ask me to pretend that everything about my life was fine. They rarely sheltered. They worked to help me behave and look the way others did without giving me a sense that to be blind—"different"—was shameful. They fought for me, and then with me, to ensure that I lived as full and rich a life as I could. For them, and consequently for me, my blindness was a fact, not a tragedy. It affected them but did not dominate their lives. Nor did it dominate mine.

My own experience resembles the narratives of people whose parents encouraged them to believe in themselves, expected a lot of them, and helped them get the tools they needed for successful living. As did many others, my parents determined that I should go to my neighborhood public school. They moved to New Jersey, one of the first states where, as early as the 1940s, blind children were regularly in schools alongside sighted children and given the assistance to make integration work. Had they not believed in my inherent normality and potential, and had they not had the good fortune to meet professionals who also believed in the inherent normality of blind children, our relationship, my view of myself as a person who is, among other things, blind, and my life would be totally different. In general, my parents exemplifed that fourth theme of minimizing what Wright has termed the "spread" of disability:[19] I was blind, which meant that I used different methods to do some things and was precluded from doing others. I was not fundamentally different from other people, and they viewed their lives as not very different from the lives of parents with other children, disabled or not. Ordinariness for them and me meant that I had my share of chores to do, including raking leaves and picking apples (which I hated) and babysitting for my six-year-old sister and two-year-old brother starting when I was twelve, giving the chance for some knock-down-drag-out fights as they tried to see what they could get away with and I rose to the challenge to stop them. At first my mother tried to keep furniture in the same places, but there were too many people and too many activities in our house for that. Ultimately, she figured that I would have to live in a world not tailor-made for me and gave up trying to make the house unnaturally ordered.

Whether with classroom teachers, special agencies, or their friends and relatives, my parents fought for me to be allowed to do what I wanted to and thought I could do and sometimes went out of their way to arrange for me to participate in some activity. As soon as I began reading, my father made sure that I had a plentiful supply of braille books from the library for the blind. Because both she and my father liked Scrabble and wanted me to play it with them, my mother convinced the manufacturers to produce a braille version. From the fourth grade on I typed all of my own work. Once, also in the fourth grade, when I complained that a television program on blind children in which I was to appear was sentimental and embarrassing, my mother insisted that the script be changed.

Sometimes the battles were small and funny. During seventh grade I started getting poor grades in arithmetic because I could not complete all the problems in the time allotted the class. My problem, I suggested, was at least partly caused by having to juggle a braille writer, typewriter, and braille books on a small desk, my lap, and the floor rather than having them easily available at all times. I asked for a table and was refused. My mother urged that a table be placed beside my desk during tests; at first the teacher again refused. Suddenly the school relented, only to provide me with tables in all my classes. We then had to explain that I did not need a table everywhere and did not want to be separated from my friends by unnecessary furniture.

On another occasion, my parents compromised, promising not to sue the school or the New Jersey State Chorus if I got hurt during the annual three-day trip. They should not have had to, since the school and chorus were as obliged to cover me with their insurance as any other student, but compromise enabled me to participate whereas a refusal might have closed me out of something I loved and counted on continuing.

Actually, that particular episode stands out because it occurred at a point where my parents and I were otherwise in stormy and protracted adolescent conflict over how much time I would spend on music rather than on reading, and whether I was spending too much time with my boyfriend rather than with my other friends or with my family. To their credit, they did not let our differences interfere when the school or the outside world would discriminate because of disability and stop me from doing what we all thought I had a right to do.

Unfortunately, when I was too young to fight for myself and my parents would not fight for me, I sometimes missed out on opportunities I should have had, physical education being a prominent example. I had done the typical things: swim and dive, ice skate, ride a tandem bike, and climb trees, but my parents did not care about physical activity for themselves, their younger children, or me. So when the school refused to let me participate in any kind of physical education, my parents did not argue and I was deprived. Even then, and certainly now, what a disabled child learns in school should not depend upon how much of an argument parents are prepared to make. Whether or not they or I liked it, gym glass was expected of everyone else and could have been expected, at least in part, of me.

Children need to feel loved, appreciated, and enjoyed by their parents. For my parents none of their children was only, or even largely, a project. In my case disability was not a project. It was something that had to be thought about and contended with; sometimes it got them and me into humorous situations, and at other times it provoked serious struggle, but it was not what our relationship was about. In those instances where parents have turned minimizing their child's disabilities and differences into a project and have lost sight of the rest of the child, the school can help remind parents of what is unique, interesting, and fun about their child having nothing to do with disability. Every child must have that to flourish, yet some narratives of disabled adults are haunted by the pain and anguish of its absence.

Relationships with Professionals

THE PARENT PERSPECTIVE

The Education of All Handicapped Children Act (P.L. 94-142) has dramatically affected the lives of parents. Despite a continuing gap between programs promised and programs delivered, the basic procedural guarantees of parent participation and mandated responsibility of the public school system have made a crucial difference in the lives of many families whose needs would probably have been brushed aside a decade earlier. However, the full effects of this landmark legislation on families with disabled children are not yet reflected in many parent narratives. There are more such accounts in magazine and journal articles, but few of book length.

Parent narratives written in earlier decades can serve, however, as reminders that amidst our continued impatience with the pace of reform there should be room to acknowledge the improvements built on the years of incredible struggles of those preceding generations. One winces now to read of a mother's years of pleading with education professionals from the principal to the state commissioner simply to gain the services of a "home tutor" for her daughter for two hours a week. The daughter was excluded without question from attending any public school. She had cerebral palsy and walked with braces and crutches. She had no other problems and was far above average intelligence.[20] These narratives from the 1950s, 1960s, and even 1970s report the hardships of dealing with professionals who offered little more than labels. They also report the amazing efforts of many parents to teach their children when others would not try.

The powerful personal diaries of Josh Greenfeld's life with an autistic son named Noah detail the turmoil of life when a constant search for services yielded little but rejection. After being turned down by a famous program in Chicago because of Noah's age, and rejected from a similar school because Noah did not talk, a father's anger boils to the surface:

Beautiful. Like *Catch-22*. On the one hand, I'm always told that it's important a child like Noah get treatment early, while he still can be reached and before he's withdrawn completely. On the other hand, the treatment institutions say he is too far gone for treatment.[21]

Even after finding a program, Greenfeld's efforts make clear the insidious process by which professionals can impress upon the parents the fragility and "good fortune" of having any program at all. In different forms, and over different issues, it is a process commonly faced by parents.

Noah's school called: the school would be closed, the roof is leaking. I called the local school board: Could they furnish facilities, if we furnish the teachers? They told me it was out of their hands legally and not a good idea educationally. They would offer no substitute site during the period in which we lacked a school structure.

I don't mind accepting the conditions of life. It's just that I resent like hell the disadvantages that are heaped upon the already disadvantaged and then described as "conditions."[22]

Despite the improvements in services over the years, several problematic features of parent-professional relationships seem to persist. One of these is that educators are only one of many types of professionals with whom parents must deal. Just as teachers and school administrators generalize about the types of individual students they encounter, if only to put some order and classification to their jobs, so do parents inevitably merge the educators they encounter into the blur of professionals parading through their families' lives. Each therapist, each new teacher, each new social worker, is "merely" the last in a legacy of experts asking for a parent's trust, enthusiasm, patience, and consent. The history of experiences with those professionals inevitably governs the way each new professional is regarded, at least initially. Unfortunately, educators usually come to parents after the doctors do. If there is any one dominant rhythm to most parents' narratives, it must be the constant drumbeat of dissatisfaction with the medical profession's handling of, or approaches to, families with disabled children.

One version of this is that type of professional haughtiness that demands repeated acts of deference by parents whose time and comfort are "obviously" less important than that of medical experts. An eloquent account of this occurs in the Massies' book about raising their son who had hemophilia. The frequent clinic visits were always ordeals. The following description aptly illustrates the experience of too many parents, in too many clinics, whatever the disability.

> In the main waiting room, there were long lines of wooden benches. We sat there, as if we were in court, waiting. It was obligatory to be there at 8 A.M., when the clinic opened. No appointments were made. You waited....
>
> We all waited there, mothers of every race, tense and worried, with restless, bored children, reassuring in the same words: "It will be all right, dear; only a little while longer, dear. Try to be patient, dear...."
>
> Mothers were afraid even to ask "When will the doctor see us?" for fear that "Doctor" would get angry.
>
> Whole days slipped away in this manner. But we went on waiting, for there was no other place to go. That was the problem. How well I came to know the sullen anger, the mutinous rage, that grows in the helpless. They say nothing. What can they say? But angry thoughts boiled in me.[23]

The medical community, however, is not alone in its subtle lessons to parents of acquiescence and dependence. A "cult of expertise" seems to gather devotees equally from among the ranks of educators, doctors, therapists, and professionals of all levels and degrees. Parent narratives repeatedly describe the power struggles around that most valuable cultural commodity: specialized knowledge. The negative version of this is to devalue the worth of knowledge that parents have about their own children. Concerns are dismissed. Requests are patronized. Reports of home behavior are distrusted. Certainly, this is not true of all parent-professional relationships, but it seems endemic to special education with its historic association with a clinical model that has little room for "amateurs." The positive version of this is to overvalue the knowledge of experts. This leads to educators and others persistently defining problems of children and parents so as to require "specialists" for their comprehension, not to mention their solution. Unfortunately, the benefits of P.L. 94-142 have also brought an increased reliance on brigades of therapists and specialists when often a commitment to the common sense of generic service providers would more than suffice. Parents are taught from the first diagnosis that "more is better" when it comes to the involvement of experts.

In my own experience, I vividly recall a meeting to discuss my son's annual IEP (individualized education program) for the coming school year. When my wife and I entered the room we found ten professionals of various species arrayed around the table, each convinced that his or her information was the most essential to Ian's progress and his parents' edification. By the time introductions had been completed the time allotted for the conference was half gone. My vow then, as yet unfulfilled, was to attend at least one IEP conference for Ian before he left school accompanied by a phalanx of ten or twelve solemn-faced parents. Then, the professionals and parents could trade introductions, shake hands all around, and like some pregame football ritual decide with a coin toss which side would speak first. Of course, I would wear the striped shirt.

One final aspect of parent-professional relationships that the parents' narratives illustrate is an unfortunate tendency of some professionals to view parents mainly as potential infantry recruits to fight on the battlefront of some particular war over method or ideology. Often each disability field has its raging disputes. Families with deaf children hear shouts from both sides of the oral/total communication argument.[24] Physically handicapped children are said to make miraculous strides forward through a controversial technique called "patterning," if only the parents are willing to make the requisite sacrifices of time and energy.[25] With autism, parents face a bewildering set of conflicting approaches from the parent-blaming, psychoanalytic perspective, to programs that advocate the use of extremely aversive punishers, to the increasingly accepted methods of nonaversive, applied behavior analysis.[26]

Parents and professionals can certainly be powerful allies. Unfortunately, too many professionals—both traditional and progressive—seem to believe that the phrase "parents' rights" means only the right to listen and agree, not to consider and decide.

PERSONAL PERSPECTIVE

Parents rightfully categorize their reactions to special education professionals as before or after the Education of All Handicapped Children Act, P.L. 94-142. However, it is also proper for disabled adults to remind both younger parents and newer special educators that good things did occasionally happen in some public school systems before that landmark legislation. Without public school and the guidance and intervention of remarkable professionals, my school life would have been limited to segregated classes or residential segregated schools. Unfortunately, for most of today's disabled adults such an integrated education was not a possibility during their childhood. Even when autobiographies of disabled people praise teachers in segregated programs and acknowledge skills they learned, virtually all reflect on the negative psychological and social significance of having been isolated from "normal," "regular" kids. Messages of difference, inferiority, unworthiness abound.[27] In its 1982 report of a study on the education of disabled women, the Disability Rights Education and Defense Fund found that regardless of race, class, gender, type of disability or age at its onset, the more time spent in integrated public school classes as children, the more people achieved educationally and occupationally as adults.[28]

The personal narrative literature of disabled adults does not concentrate on educational experiences. When they mention them at all, the authors attest to the value and problems of studying alongside children without disabilities. Most praise their parents for fighting to put them in neighborhood schools or regret the consequences of segregated programs or being tutored at home and having no contact with children or teachers of any sort.[29] What they valued was the chance to compete with nondisabled children, to discover how they measured up, to get into the world beyond their parents. What they regretted was feeling "like an outsider," not being able to break through the children's fear or rejection of them. No personal narrative that I know of remarks on especially positive or negative treatment from public school teachers, whereas many contend that special educators, therapists, and physicians served only to heighten their feelings of shame, differentness, and limitations.

Yet, reflecting on why public school worked for me, I can vouch for the ways professionals either helped or hindered. First, my parents were not alone in our belief that I belonged in public school. The New Jersey Commission for the Blind aided them in calming anxious school administrators before I began public school and sometimes intervened with skeptical teachers during my years there. And unlike students caught in cynical versions of mainstreaming, I was not dumped without services: my braille or recorded books were generally there on schedule (except for the times when we started with a unit at the back of the book that would not be ready until Spring); a teacher knowledgeable in braille and various other specifics usually checked in with me and the school once a week to help keep things running smoothly. My parents had people they could call if they thought I was missing out on things or having problems related to my blindness or to people's attitudes about my blindness. Best of all from my standpoint, the contact with "The Commission" was minimal, intruding relatively little on my school day, rarely taking me out of classes for more than two hours a week. More contact and more special help would have heightened my sense of differentness when what I wanted was to be a member of the fourth-grade class and fit in. That experience of overzealous specialists, often mentioned by parents, was fortunately rare for me.

Some classroom teachers emphasized my differentness, overpraising me for ordinary things, not disciplining me when I deserved it, or vainly protecting me from problems with my peers. Others scolded me for knitting in class or for not turning in a homework assignment on time. From my standpoint such disciplining gave the message to me and my classmates that the teachers thought I was subject to the same treatment as everyone else. Some teachers too readily intervened when I was teased, whereas others recognized I would have to fight the battle of acceptance myself and would not get too far if authorities scolded my tormentors. In our homogeneous, white, middle-class community, where even being Jewish was a bit odd, the school probably could have used some general discussion of all sorts of differences. All those picked-on "creeps" and "weirdos" might have benefitted from more outward teacher support. In general, I recognized that I had to win acceptance on my own. What seemed to work best was knowing that the teachers knew what was wrong without openly intervening.

Friendships and Community Support

PARENT PERSPECTIVE

My wife and I have what sociologists would call a dense social network. Many of our dearest friends are, or have been parents, of disabled children and know each other as well as the two of us. These friends are the ones who we trust implicitly will be there to help, to understand, when we need them. Some of them live across the country, yet seem the closest to us. A reciprocity of interest and support in each other's lives exists with these other parents that goes without saying. Their presence is a comfort, secure without the pity or sentiment so frustratingly common in dealings with the community in general. They seem to us to give voice through their actions to the words of Emily Dickinson about that type of friend who is quietly supportive:

They might not need me—yet they might—
I'll let my Heart be just in sight.

Other friends of ours are certainly supportive, even though they have no disabled children themselves; my point is not to preach homogeneity of acquaintances. There is, however, a special bond of survived calamity and common struggle that I have noticed in parent advocacy groups or other gatherings. The parent narratives testify that my experience is not unique.

Many of the parent narratives revolve around an initial effort to start a parent group or else devote a lot of attention to the work done in such groups.[30] Others report the discovery that they were not the only family in town to face a particular problem.

There are, of course, wonderful stories of the responsiveness of friends who did not have handicapped children. What is striking is how often these stories are couched in terms of the parents' surprise at how supportive their neighbors and community acquaintances actually were. Certainly, there are also the painful accounts of rejection and bigotry that happen to most minority families. The stories of community support dominate the narratives. The Massies, for example, describe their gratefulness to their neighbors for turning out for a blood drive for their child with hemophilia:

> When the blood drive took place . . . most of our neighbors came—the Feidens, the Martinis, the Borgoses, the Deutsches, Janet Johnson, Julie Davidson . . . and many of them brought *their* friends, so that, in all, forty-five people came to the White Plains Armory to give blood for Bobby. We thought that this was wonderful; we never knew that there were forty-five people who cared that much.[31]

Friendships do not vanish merely because a parent has a child with special problems. New friendships, though, can be more difficult because there is no history of personality within which to frame one's explanations. As one mother explained the process of adjustment after discovering their child was mentally retarded, the family "had no difficulty with acceptance. Our neighbors learned about mental retardation right along with us. They helped with our door-to-door campaigns and our projects to get services for Robin."[32]

The acceptance of the community, however, is often complicated by the terms of that acceptance. All too often, a charity model emerges that cheerfully accepts the "duty" to help those "less fortunate than we." Bake sales and telethons are fine, but passing bond issues, or fully integrating the local high school, or demanding that the local McDonald's make its bathrooms accessible, all exceed the relationship of relying on handouts. On many occasions the local bureaucracies will pressure families into playing this "pitiful parent" role. The same blood drive that left the Massies sincerely grateful for the generosity of their friends and neighbors, infuriated and humiliated them with the public begging they felt forced to perform at the behest of the blood drive coordinators. Their comments about that even illustrate how pity and friendship are not merely very different bases for a relationship, but are to some extent mutually exclusive.

Beyond this, we were expected to cooperate in the effort to reach out beyond our friends and neighbors, and try to attract donors from the general public—in a word, to create, or at least submit to publicity. Dramatize the need for blood, put a face on it—if possible, the face of a stricken child. It's easier for people to give if they know where their blood is going. Pity is a powerful motivation. Try your local newspapers. Don't neglect the local radio stations. Tell them how tough it is. Forget your dignity, your privacy, your pride.[33]

The Massies' experience with blood drives also illustrates another dilemma closely related to the pity-friendship tension faced by many parents. How does one graciously accept an appropriate level of altruistic activity by community members without endorsing the systemic inequities that evoke the altruism in the first place? What is the proper balance between acknowledging acts of individual mercy while demanding correction of social injustice? We live in a decade of increasingly narrow definitions of appropriate social responsibility. It is as though parents are forced to play a "zero-sum" game whereby a specified quota of support is deserved. In such a game, then, parents who accept (much less actively seek) some amount of informal community support are implicitly portrayed as simultaneously excusing the service system from any responsibility for a similar amount of formal service. The natural evolution of community support within a context of appropriate formal services can never get very far as long as parents see themselves as part of some social equation that must always add up to zero.

Gender adds yet another factor to this equation that makes the addition even more problematic. A traditional role of women in our society has been the unpaid volunteer working untold hours for worthy causes. When a mother has a disabled child, the expectation often becomes a duty. Mothers can face not only the struggles of daily management of raising a disabled child without adequate services, but also the social burden of fundraising and free labor as the culturally accepted way of informally compensating for those formal inadequacies. In the name of parent involvement, schools and other service systems can sometimes justify parent exploitation with the implicit threat: "If you don't do it, Mrs. Jones, it just won't get done." No parent should have to face such bureaucratic blackmail in the absence of formal support.

PERSONAL PERSPECTIVE

Parents' social life and their circle of friends usually extend beyond their children's schools. For the children, however, the school is not only the center of their involvement with professionals, it is also the social center of their lives. Unfortunately, the personal narratives do not contain many examples of both educational and social integration. Regardless of how they fared academically, disabled adults have almost nothing but painful stories of social exclusion, teasing, and rejection. Often they could not play games requiring coordination, speed, strength, or sight. They could not hear all the whispered gossip. During adolescence they were rejected as dates. There is little point to spending time with nondisabled students if one cannot manage to make friends with them. And here the school can be crucial.

Despite a certain degree of academic success throughout my school years, what I always wanted most was friends. In the first years, when I discovered that being teased was painful but being ignored was worse, I looked for ways to make friends with my classmates. My parents aided me immeasurably. First, they welcomed my classmates to our house and transported them and me to and from activities. Second, my father advised that as a blind child I would "have to go more than halfway to make friends," and as a rule-follower, I would have to "go up the down staircase a few times" to let people know I would get into a little trouble and not always placate the authorities. (Never mind that I had gotten permission to disobey from the ultimate authority—hardly permission to disobey at all.) If people I liked did not invite me to do things with them, I made the invitations myself. After a while, the strategy worked though, and by the end of seventh grade I had made my first group of real friends. My parents' hospitality, a teacher who encouraged all her students to work on group projects, initiating interactions myself if others did not, and discovering activities in which I could participate had all paid off.

For me, participating meant joining chorus, the drama club, writing and debating groups. It meant not being excluded from after-school activities and class trips by teachers, club leaders, or the transportation system. If transportation arrangements for disabled students compel them to leave the minute the class day ends, their whole school experience can be undermined. Especially in a large school, a disabled student can be ignored. The institution, parents, and students themselves must create opportunities for socializing. After-school clubs and organized activities may be the disabled student's first chance to show others about talents and interests and to reveal a personality and not just a set of deficits and differences.

The class itself can aid or hamper. The move to mainstreaming, for instance, often places enormous reliance on paraprofessionals. However, the role of classroom aides for individual disabled students can be immensely harmful to social interactions if not properly circumscribed. An aide is not (or, at least, should not be) a chaperone, an administrative spy, a surrogate parent, or a personal servant. Any such role turns the aide into a shield or barrier between the disabled student and his or her nondisabled peers. Certainly aides can be friendly with the disabled students whom they assist; friends should never be *expected* to be unofficial "aides." I have always made it a point, for example, never to use my friends as readers. I never want that function to be a burden of friendship with me. By the same token, I do not want some artificial prohibition of mine to interfere with the natural acts of spontaneous assistance that friends normally provide to each other. Admittedly, it gets hard to know where to draw the line sometimes. That difficulty makes it even more critical for aides, teachers, and administrators to recognize the importance that the line needs to be drawn.

There are specific things that the classroom teacher can do in this regard. If students must sit at the front to hear, lipread, or see the teacher, they should not always sit with the same group of students. Those who need coats held or objects manipulated for them should get occasional help from fellow students as well as a designated aide. Disabled students can be assisted in finding ways to reciprocate. They and their classmates must discover how they can make a contribution to others as well as receive the help of others. Group projects where each student has a particular task to perform that is essential to the successful achievement of the goal will foster the inclusion of the disabled student and can generate mutual respect and appreciation. We can learn from the analogous work fostering interracial friendship and cooperation through group projects.[34]

In the world we wish to create, school administrators and faculty might not need to think any more about helping their disabled students make friends than they would think about the social life of the rest of the student body. We are far from such a world, and teachers may need to structure classroom and other activities to foster extended, equal status contact between disabled and nondisabled students to break the barriers of strangeness and fear that may beset everyone.

Some strategies strike me as doomed to failure: school assemblies and class discussions of disability with outsiders, complete with puppets and gimmicks, are likely to highlight difference rather than communicate commonality; having students simulate life in a wheelchair, blindness, or deafness generally serves only to increase pity and fear, not respect and discovery of mutual interests. Parents of one youngster with spina bifida wrote the parents of all the other children in the first-grade class in an attempt to answer their questions so that these parents, in turn, could help their own children to get used to their new classmate. I can think of nothing worse than the thought of my parents writing to my classmates' parents to tell them about me. All it does is highlight difference, warn parents, apologize, or communicate that there is some type of problem about which to be concerned. The time to deal with parents and children around particular disability problems is as they occur, not before. Give everyone a chance to see how the natural give and take of school life works, and intervene only if something really is amiss.

A Sense of Identity

There is a final theme that emerges from both the literature and our personal reflections. Perhaps a better way to describe it is that this theme seems to underlie all of the others. It is a theme that cuts through much of what we have already said, yet is important and controversial enough to deserve separate attention. We call this theme the sense of identity: How do disabled people come to think of themselves in ways that incorporate their disability as an important part of their personal and social identity?[35] It is a theme that complicates the call for educational integration. In both the literature and our personal reflections we find an undeniable recognition that a well-developed sense of identity as a disabled adult needs some significant involvement as a child with other people (children and adults) who have similar disabilities. As might be anticipated, this theme gains more prominence in the personal memories of disabled adults than in the parent narratives. A sense of self-identity is something best described, if only because uniquely perceived, by the individuals who have that sense, not by their parents, their friends, their teachers, nor their therapists. For that reason, we have reversed the order of our comments in discussing this final theme. Adrienne will summarize how the notion of disabled people as a minority group implies the need to nurture an identity that incorporates disabilities—including a sense of pride and commonality with other disabled people. Phil will then comment on how parents have discussed this issue and the differences that emerge between types of disability.

THE PERSONAL PERSPECTIVE

Growing up with a disability will never be without complications. New and unforeseen problems will accompany every step forward. Certainly educational integration has yielded its own set of concerns to go along with a tremendous potential for social reform and instructional improvement. I have addressed some of those problems as they involve the social integration of disabled and nondisabled students in natural friendships. An additional dimension of this problem of integration is the more neglected issue of lost opportunities for friendships between two disabled children. As we have seen, parent narratives often revolve around the sense of support and common purpose found within groups of parents of disabled children. The same potential benefit would seem to exist for the disabled children themselves, yet can also seem to run counter to the spirit of social acceptance and integration. The question needs to be asked: What about friendships among students with disabilities? Are such relationships important, and what should the role of the school be in integrating comfort with disability into identity?

Literature on integrating black and white students advocates a critical mass approach; a single black student or one of a very small number is likely to have increased social difficulty, but when the number of black students in school reaches more than 30 or 40 percent the "white flight" phenomenon often begins.[36] Given that disability, unlike race, does not lead to massive housing segregation, conscious integration programs will rarely contend with more than 10 percent of any student group having disabilities, many of whom will be invisible and unknown to other students and many teachers most of the time.

Nonetheless, whether students' differences are less readily apparent (learning disabilities, epilepsy, or chronic health problems such as diabetes, asthma, and heart conditions), or fairly observable (mental retardation, blindness, deafness, mobility or speech impairments, burns, or other cosmetic differences), they may be equally conscious of not being like more typical students. They may experience greater than average struggles with social acceptance, academic performance, and self-appreciation. They may feel that the key to success is beyond them because of their differentness. Some disability rights activists now echo what black activists have been saying since the late 1960s: going to school with whites is not in itself the prize, the be-all and end-all; rather, getting a good education and feeling good about oneself and one's possibilities in the world is what is important. Especially since disabled children, unlike blacks, do not grow up in families or neighborhoods where they will meet others with their disability, is it necessary for schools to promote a sense that disabled children can be as diverse and interesting, as talented or average, as those without disabilities? Can this be done without resegregating or without promoting that worst of all possible ghettos, the special homeroom and resource room for disabled students?

In my case, first through third grade were spent in such a braille class, and although I might have gained good braille and mathematics skills, and liked my teacher and some of the students I met, three years of that class were three years too many. I was always conscious of being *in* the second grade but not *of* it: knowing that I could not have lunch or recess with the second grade but had to have it with the braille class, being subjected to embarrassing special Lions Club parties the rest of the second grade did not have—all because I was blind. I was not always comfortable in those first years in my neighborhood school, but I knew it was better than the special class.

Yet having contact with other blind children my age was invaluable. At the camp run by the New Jersey Commission for the

Blind, kids from throughout the state met for a few weeks each summer. In addition to typical camp activities of swimming, hiking, and playing tricks on counselors, we talked about how our parents, teachers, and the kids in our schools treated us because we were blind. Sometimes someone who had solved a problem told the rest of us what she or he had figured out. Sometimes we complained together about those problems none of us had managed to solve. It was important to compare notes, have solid friendships where sight or the lack of it did not affect the terms of the interaction, and just in general not feel alone. As an adult, discovering that I needed to work with other disabled people to combat discrimination, I had a base to build on of knowing that I had had important friendships with some other disabled people.

We do not want the point of integration to be a message such as that one young woman expressed about living with her family and being the only disabled student in her school: "I knew that I was all right because I was their daughter and they loved me, but my parents feel that blindness has icky consequences and don't like other blind people or want me to know them." And another young disabled man recently commented on how critical it was to meet other adults with his disability that he could like and respect. We do not want to create a new generation of students who repeat the mistakes of all too many disabled people who see themselves as "exceptions," who see disability as embarrassing, shameful, pitiable, but see themselves as unusually talented because they have achieved social or professional status within the nondisabled world.[37]

The schools must inculcate within their staff and students an appreciation of how a person's disability is more than some bothersome hangnail, to be clipped off and forgotten as quickly as possible. The sentiments of Harilyn Rousso about her conflict with her parents and their constant efforts at rehabilitation are worth repeating here. Her words capture the complexity of how disability must be integrated within the person as well as within the society: "My disability, with my different walk and talk and my involuntary movements, having been with me all of my life, was part of me, part of my identity. With these disability features, I felt complete and whole."[38]

In its rush to remediate, the school must also appreciate a uniqueness of the student that not only includes that child's disability, but in some cases relies upon it. In its efforts to integrate, the school must not ignore the social heritage and fellowship that should be available to all disabled students as part of their membership in the disabled community.

THE PARENT PERSPECTIVE

Perhaps the main point to add from the parental perspective, is that the type of disability seems to make a difference in how some parents perceive the role of other disabled people in the lives of their children. In many cases, parents seem uncertain of their answer. Or perhaps it is more accurate to say that many parents seem certain of their ambivalence about the matter. It is surely not a topic with which parents are unfamiliar. If parents sometimes share what the sociologist Goffman called the "courtesy stigma" that comes with close association with devalued people such as those with disabilities, then, perhaps they also deserve a "courtesy status" as members in the disability community, its pride and identity. As I mentioned myself, in the section on friendship and community support, it is that common bond, that participation in a disability community if you will, that best explains our closest friendship with other parents of disabled children. Recognizing its importance in our own lives and our own parental identity, we parents should not be surprised that such a consciousness can be even more crucial to disabled children themselves. The dilemma remains, however. How do I nurture my disabled child's sense of identity without simultaneously reinforcing the segregative tendencies of a society so intolerant of differences?

A particular group of parents that has written a lot about this question is one whose children are deaf or hearing impaired. One parent writes of the struggle that he and his wife (not to mention their child) went through before realizing that their deaf daughter needed to have deaf friends and role models. They came to see the importance that their daughter Lynn meet others who were, as the title of the book says, "deaf like me."[39] It was not an easy insight.

We knew that Lynn would need more than our words and love. At first we found it painful to admit that we could not give Lynn all she needed to live in a hearing world. She needed the example of people like herself who had faced the same problems she would and solved them. Even at the age of six, Lynn had begun to see the world from the distinct perspective of her deafness. We could not entirely share that perspective. Bill and Bunny and other deaf friends could. Slowly we accepted the fact that only deaf people could provide some things Lynn would need, helping her through some of the important stages of childhood, pointing the way to a meaningful life.[40]

At least one national disability advocacy group has realized the need to bring parents of disabled students into more regular contact with adults who have similar disabilities. The National Federation of the Blind, therefore, has established a "Parents of Blind Children Division" to help reach parents, especially those with young blind children. The parents are encouraged to come to national conferences to learn the concerns and triumphs that the current generation of blind adults experiences, and how they, as parents, might better foster that sense of strength and identity in their own blind children. Indeed, the organization has even started a newsletter for the division called "Future Reflections." The efforts could well serve as a model for other advocacy groups and local service agencies.

The issue, then, seems fairly clear if not fully accomplished for parents of children who are blind, deaf, and perhaps physically handicapped. For other parents, however, encouraging their disabled children to have disabled friends and to participate in social events for disabled people just perpetuates the well-intentioned segregation of years past.[41] A sense of identity becomes transformed to "they enjoy being with their own kind," which, in turn, becomes the implicit rationalization, "we can keep their kind apart from our kind, and not feel bad about it." The fact that my son enjoys bowling but does not do it very well is, thus, used to try and convince us that he should attend a "retarded bowling" event every month with all the other retarded people within a fifty-mile radius. The "Special Olympics" program is a more organized and heavily financed version of the same arrangement. Through such opportunities, Ian can supposedly feel proud of himself, and enjoy an event without the competitive expectations of the real world that always place him at the bottom of the list.

For us this logic crumbles when we see Ian enjoying a film with a nondisabled classmate, when we notice how much he likes to go swimming at the "Y" even though it is not the designated "special recreation" night, or when we share his excitement upon completing a 5K race in his wheelchair along with a few hundred other people (mostly nondisabled) who run, jog, or walk their way across the finish line. There are segregated versions of all those events that Ian would probably also enjoy, but for us the struggle has always been to break down the segregation, not seek it out. It seems very risky to reinforce such tendencies without a very clear notion of what people like Ian would be gaining.

At the same time Ian also enjoys the company of his friend Matt, who is also labeled as mentally retarded. We certainly would not deprive Ian of Matt's friendship. For us, the approach is to begin with the natural setting and make sure Ian is included. Within that setting, it is not only appropriate, but beneficial, for Ian to have both disabled and nondisabled friends. I am not sure what Ian's sense of identity is, but I hope it includes an awareness at some level that his way of interacting with the world is not only acceptable, it is also *not* unique. There are other people in wheelchairs; there are other people who do not talk well; there are other people who need a lot of help from others; there are, in short, other people like himself.

Adrienne's discussion of how other minority groups handle this issue suggests a key distinction to me. The key difference between perpetuating segregation and preserving self-identity has something to do with who initiates the separation and how total it is meant to be. Forced separation can never be equal, and equal separation can never be forced. For my child, integration—both educational and social—is the only context within which a distinct identity as part of a disabled community can ever be clearly drawn.

Conclusion

It is difficult to summarize this review of parent and child experiences without risking the imposition of an artificial unity to what is a varied set of broad perspectives and specific opinions. Parents of disabled children and disabled adults sometimes disagree, both with each other and among themselves. This is as it should be; part of what educational integration is all about is the supportive recognition of individual differences as normal and valuable. Nonetheless, a comparison of the personal and parent narratives, and of our own personal experiences, convinces us that beneath all of the differences in specific opinions there is within the disability community a common set of concerns about how society in general, and educators in particular, respond to children labeled as handicapped. These common concerns lead us to a short list of suggestions for those involved in public schooling. The list is not exhaustive, but it does reflect some of the main points already discussed.

1. Schools should avoid the type of professional hubris that automatically assumes specialization and "expertise" are the solutions to problems related to a child's disability. Excessive reliance on formal, specialized approaches promotes the stigma of deficiency,

discourages natural socialization, fosters a kind of learned helplessness by both regular teachers and parents, and often does not solve the original problem anyway. In large part, this strikes us as a question of creating an atmosphere of acceptance within a school. Within such an atmosphere, the natural associations and informal solutions that the rest of us develop can also apply to the lives of disabled students. One begins with the assumption that integration is not an experiment to be tested, but a value to be followed, and then solutions arise. The principle seems to be: keep it simple, keep it small, and keep it bureaucratically "thin."

2. Looking for informal solutions and natural associations does not mean sitting back and taking a laissez-faire approach to educational integration. Schools must also insure a bedrock level of support and a basic commitment to integrative services that does not leave parents and children floundering in the mainstream. An increased reliance on generic approaches within natural settings must not be distorted into an administrative excuse to avoid giving parents and children access to the special skills and technology that can undeniably improve a child's functional skills and social participation.

3. Schools should provide opportunities for both disabled children and their parents to come together for informal discussions, social relationships, and advocacy. The sense of identity and mutual support available through such continued associations should not be lost in the name of integration. After-school activities, weekend and summer programs, parent groups as subcommittees of the PTA, all of these could be examples of how to incorporate such opportunities within the context of general educational integration.

4. Schools must make parental involvement worthwhile to the parents. This means actually expecting parents to help create educational program plans, not just ratify plans drawn up in advance for the parents' signatures. Such involvement cannot happen overnight if preceded by a parental history of meaningless meetings and demeaning professional encounters. So long as our professional services—medical, social, and educational—are often inadequate and unresponsive, then teachers and administrators will have to earn the trust of parents, not assume it.

5. Schools must listen to disabled children as well as to their parents when making program decisions. This assumes, of course, that schools are, in fact, also listening to parents.

6. Schools should seek out the expertise of adults with disabilities who can help guide teachers and administrators—as well as parents—

about the best ways to create supportive but unobtrusive educational environments for disabled children. Disability rights activists, just as much as parents, are appropriate advocates and models for disabled children. The schools and parents should approach representatives of such groups as allies rather than adversaries. As mentioned before, some national disability groups, such as the National Federation of the Blind, are providing excellent examples of how parents of disabled children can gain valuable insight into the lives of their sons and daughters through coming to know personally a number of adults with similar disabilities.

At its best, education gives us options, and the tools for choosing among those options. For disabled and nondisabled students, that means the opportunity to know, enjoy, cooperate with, learn from, disagree with, and care for people with and without the differences of disability. We close this chapter, then, with a call to schools to look to parents and to disabled adults to help our disabled students discover their own strengths, talents, and capacities for friendships with disabled and nondisabled people. In the past few years the nation has begun to acknowledge how much more we need to do to educate all our students; parents of disabled children and disabled adults themselves must be part of the team to improve what we provide to our disabled and nondisabled students as we reevaluate our entire educational program.

FOOTNOTES

1. John Gliedman and William Roth, *The Unexpected Minority: Handicapped Children in America* (New York: Harcourt Brace Jovanovich, 1980); Ann P. Turnbull and H. Rutherford Turnbull III, *Families, Professionals, and Exceptionality: A Special Partnership* (Columbus, OH: Charles C. Merrill, 1986).

2. Howard S. Becker, *Outsiders: Studies in the Sociology of Deviance* (New York: Free Press, 1963); Robert A. Scott, *The Making of Blind Men* (New York: Russell Sage, 1969).

3. Wolf Wolfensberger, *The Principle of Normalization in Human Services* (Toronto: National Institute on Mental Retardation, 1972).

4. Adrienne Asch, "Will Populism Empower Disabled People?" in *The New Populism: The Politics of Empowerment*, ed. Harry C. Boyte and Frank Riessman (Philadelphia: Temple University Press, 1986), pp. 213-28; Frank Bowe, *Rehabilitating America: Toward Independence for Disabled and Elderly People* (New York: Harper & Row, 1980).

5. Philip M. Ferguson and Dianne L. Ferguson, "Parents and Professionals," in *Introduction to Special Education*, ed. Peter Knoblock (Boston: Little, Brown, 1987), pp. 346-91; Seymour B. Sarason and John Doris, *Educational Handicap, Public Policy, and Social History* (New York: Free Press, 1979).

6. Helen Featherstone, *A Difference in the Family: Life with a Disabled Child* (New York: Basic Books, 1980); H. Rutherford Turnbull III and Ann P. Turnbull, eds., *Parents Speak Out; Then and Now*, 2d ed. (Columbus, OH: Charles C. Merrill, 1985).

7. Hyman Mariampolski and Dana C. Hughes, "The Use of Personal Documents in Historical Sociology," *American Sociologist* 13 (May 1978): 107.

8. Clara Claiborne Park, "Growing Out of Autism," in *Autism in Adolescents and Adults*, ed. Eric Schopler and Gary B. Mesibov (New York: Plenum Press, 1983), p. 286.

9. Marie Killilea, *Karen* (Englewood Cliffs, NJ: Prentice-Hall, 1952); Dale Evans Rogers, *Angel Unaware* (Westwood, NJ: Fleming H. Revell, 1953).

10. Philip M. Ferguson, "I Have These Boxing Matches with God," *Arise* 1 (June 1978): 15-16.

11. Elizabeth Pieper, *Sticks and Stones: The Story of Loving a Child* (Syracuse, NY: Human Policy Press, n.d.), p. 88.

12. Martha M. Jablow, *Cara: Growing with a Retarded Child* (Philadelphia: Temple University Press, 1982), p. 171.

13. Frank Bowe, *Comeback: Six Remarkable People Who Triumphed Over Disability* (New York: Harper & Row, 1981), pp. 154-56.

14. Frances Lynn, "Waiting Again," in *With the Power of Each Breath*, ed. Suzanne Browne, Deborah Conners, and Nanci Stern (Pittsburgh: Cleis Preis, 1985), pp. 133-35.

15. Edwina Franchild, "Untangling the Web of Denial," and Naomi Woronov, "A See-By-Logic Life," in *With the Power of Each Breath*, ed. Browne, Conners, and Stern, pp. 36-44, 159-72.

16. Harilyn Rousso, "Fostering Healthy Self-Esteem," *Exceptional Parent* 14 (December 1984): 9-14; Sondra Diamond, "Growing Up with Parents of a Handicapped Child: A Handicapped Person's Perspective," in *Understanding and Working with Parents of Children with Specific Needs*, ed. James L. Paul (New York: Holt, Rinehart and Winston, 1981), pp. 23-50.

17. Rousso, "Fostering Healthy Self-Esteem," p. 9.

18. Diamond, "Growing Up with Parents of a Handicapped Child," p. 30.

19. Beatrice Wright, *Physical Disability: A Psycho-Social Approach* (New York: Harper & Row, 1983).

20. Killilea, *Karen*; Marie Killilea, *With Love from Karen* (Englewood Cliffs, NJ: Prentice-Hall, 1963).

21. Josh Greenfeld, *A Child Called Noah* (New York: Holt, Rinehart and Winston, 1973), p. 89.

22. Josh Greenfeld, *A Place for Noah* (New York: Holt, Rinehart and Winston, 1978), p. 93.

23. Robert Massie and Suzanne Massie, *Journey* (New York: Knopf, 1975), p. 75.

24. Thomas S. Spradley and James P. Spradley, *Deaf Like Me* (New York: Random House, 1978).

25. David Melton, *Todd* (Englewood Cliffs, NJ: Prentice-Hall, 1968); Pieper, *Sticks and Stones*.

26. Greenfeld, *A Child Called Noah*; idem, *A Place for Noah*; Frank Warren, "Call Them Liars Who Would Say 'All is Well'," in *Parents Speak Out*, ed. Turnbull and Turnbull, pp. 221-29.

27. Jacob Twersky, *The Sound of the Walls* (Garden City, NY: Doubleday, 1959); Robert Russell, *To Catch an Angel* (New York: Vanguard, 1962); Don Zimmerman, "The Way I See Myself," in *Ordinary Moments: The Disabled Experience*, ed. Alan J.

Brightman (Baltimore: University Park Press, 1984), pp. 33-49; Nancy Kaye, "Nancy Kaye," in William Roth, *The Handicapped Speak* (Jefferson, NC: McFarland, 1981), pp. 49-69.

28. Disability Rights, Education, and Defense Fund, *The Disabled Women's Education Project: Report of Survey Results: Executive Summary* (Berkeley, CA: Disability Rights, Education, and Defense Fund, 1983).

29. Richard Moore, "Richard Moore," in *Experiments in Survival*, ed. Edith Heinrich and Leonard Kriegel (New York: Association for the Aid of Crippled Children, 1961), pp. 134-40; Brightman, *Ordinary Moments*; Roth, *The Handicapped Speak*.

30. Featherstone, *A Difference in the Family*; Killilea, *Karen*; idem, *With Love From Karen*; Pieper, *Sticks and Stones*; Spradley and Spradley, *Deaf Like Me*; Nicola Schaefer, *Does She Know She's There?*, updated ed. (Toronto: Fitzhenry & Whiteside, 1982).

31. Massie and Massie, *Journey*, p. 63.

32. Elsie Helsel, "The Helsels' Story of Robin," in *Parents Speak Out*, ed. Turnbull and Turnbull, p. 84.

33. Massie and Massie, *Journey*, pp. 62-63.

34. Janet W. Scofield and H. Andrew Sagar, "Desegregation, School Practices, and Students Race Relations," in *Consequences of School Desegregation*, ed. Christine H. Rossell and Willis D. Hawley (Philadelphia: Temple University Press, 1983), pp. 58-103.

35. Mary Johnson, "Emotion and Pride," *The Disability Rag* (January/February 1987): 3-10.

36. Christine H. Rossell, "Desegregation Plans, Racial Isolation, White Flight, and Community Response," in *Consequences of School Desegregation*, ed. Rossell and Hawley, pp. 13-57.

37. Harlan Hahn, " 'The Good Parts': Interpersonal Relationships in the Autobiographies of Physical Disabled Persons," *Wenner-Gren Foundation Working Papers in Anthropology* (New York: Wenner-Gren Foundation, 1983), pp. 1-38; Adrienne Asch and Lawrence Sachs, "Lives Without, Lives Within: The Autobiographies of Blind Women and Men," *Journal of Visual Impairment and Blindness* 77 (June 1983): 242-47.

38. Rousso, "Fostering Healthy Self-Esteem," p. 9. In the psychoanalytical tradition the connection between one's body image and one's ego formation makes this point even more strongly for people with physical disabilities. Andre Lussier uses the language of the analyst to summarize this perspective: "[T]he body one cathects from birth on, as it is and consequently as it is gradually perceived by the child, and not the body as it could or should be, is what matters psychologically." Andre Lussier, "The Physical Handicap and the Body Ego," *International Journal of Psycho-Analysis* 61 (1980): 181.

39. Spradley and Spradley, *Deaf Like Me*.

40. Ibid., p. 258.

41. Jeff Strully and Cindy Strully, "Friendship and Our Children," *Journal of the Association for Persons with Severe Handicaps* 10 (Winter 1985): 224-227.

Section Three
PRACTICE

CHAPTER VI

The Community-Referenced Curriculum for Students with Moderate and Severe Disabilities

ALISON FORD AND JAMES BLACK

Ms. Rogan's seventh-grade classroom was arranged quite differently than the surrounding classrooms in Jefferson Junior High. One large desk was the teacher's and another was shared by two instructional assistants. The furniture consisted of four small round tables rather than rows of student desks. In one corner of the room was a carpeted area with a bean bag chair and a bolster. Nearby shelves were lined with a tape player, magazines and books, electronic games, and an Apple IIe computer. Another area of the room contained instructional materials used to teach restaurant and grocery store skills. The small pictures of grocery items attached to the bulletin board and the restaurant menus displayed on large pieces of poster board provided a marked contrast to the bulletin boards in adjacent classrooms.

Ms. Rogan was in the hallway with two students who were getting their coats from their lockers. Jeremy, who uses a wheelchair, was being taught how to open his locker door and remove his coat while Sarah was learning to zip up her jacket. These students were preparing for a lesson that would take place at Nick's grocery store, a short distance from school. Every Tuesday morning, Ms. Rogan teaches Jeremy and Sarah the skills necessary to purchase the food items to be used in an afternoon home economics class. While Ms. Rogan is at the store with two students, her teaching assistants carry out the instruction she has planned for the remaining four students on her class list. On this particular day, one teaching assistant was providing vocational instruction to two students at Webb's Greenhouse where they were learning to mix soil, repot plants, store materials, and other greenhouse routines. The second assistant was in the gym helping the physical education teacher. Two students with severe disabilities were part of this seventh grade class.

The students on Ms. Rogan's class list are members of the growing number of students described as having moderate and severe disabilities who have gained entrance to regular public schools during the past decade. With their entry into regular public schools, they bring a new type of curriculum, one that is community-referenced. As illustrated in the example above, some components of the curriculum overlap with the curricular content traditionally offered in regular education. Physical education, home economics, and perhaps vocational education are examples of overlapping content areas, whereas restaurant use and grocery shopping appear to represent a significant departure from typical seventh-grade curricula. Unlike their nonhandicapped peers, the students on Ms. Rogan's class list rely heavily on *direct* instruction in order to acquire many community-living skills. For them, a community-referenced curriculum is an essential component of their school program, leading toward desired graduation competencies.

What is meant by a community-referenced curriculum? What conditions have surrounded its emergence in education? Furthermore, what lessons have we learned from implementing it, and what future directions do we foresee? The purpose of this chapter is to reflect on these questions, while simultaneously exploring the relationship between community-referenced curricula and what is generally referred to as "regular" education.

Defining a Community-Referenced Curriculum

A community-referenced curriculum, sometimes referred to as a "community-based," "functional," or "ecologically oriented" curriculum, can be described as follows:

1. Its guiding principles and goals are developed on the premise that every student, no matter how severe his or her disabilities, is capable of becoming an active participant and contributing member of an integrated society. In order for students with severe disabilities to accomplish this goal, the curriculum should be designed in accordance with the following principles:

   a. *Direct preparation for life.* The curriculum is one that *directly* prepares students to lead active, integrated adult lives in the community. The content is individualized, functional, and appropriate for the student's chronological age.

   b. *Social integration.* Students with severe disabilities are

integrated in regular school settings. Becoming a part of the school life is viewed as an essential step toward becoming a part of community life.
  c. *Interdependence.* Students are not excluded from an activity because they will not be able to do it independently. Partial participation or "interdependence" may also be a valued outcome of education.
  d. *Home-school collaboration.* Parental involvement is vital to the success of the educational program. Sincere efforts to establish home-school collaboration are required.
  e. *Experiential learning in a variety of settings.* Meaningful instruction is not limited to classroom settings: it takes place in the surrounding community where students can learn critical skills in real-life settings.

2. The core of a community-referenced curriculum is devoted to content that directly prepares a student to function in the real world. In an early effort to organize a community-referenced curriculum for students with severe disabilities, Brown and his colleagues identified four major content areas: vocational, recreation/leisure, domestic functioning, and general community functioning.[1] Others have suggested slightly different organizational schemes under such headings as "vocational," "leisure," and "independent living."[2] Despite these minor organizational differences, a common approach has been suggested for generating curricular content in the community living areas. This approach, often termed an "ecological" approach, is based on the notion that the performance demands occurring in real-life environments should provide the basis for curricular organization. Therefore, educators must first identify the environments and activities in which a student might be expected to function, both now and in the future. For example, these might include riding a public bus, shopping for grocery items, and receiving vocational training in a local business. Once these environments and activities have been identified, an on-site analysis is conducted to determine the specific skills and concepts to be taught to a particular student. The approach is a generative one that leads to highly individualized determinations about "what to teach," not one that leads to a fixed set of knowledge and skills to be taught to all students belonging to a particular educational classification.

3. Among the many instructional practices associated with a community-referenced curriculum are: an active, experiential learning

structure; small heterogeneous instructional groups; a reliance on instructional assistants; an emphasis on using natural materials, cues, and corrections; and systematic instruction in actual community settings. This experiential teaching format is considered a good match to the learning strengths of many students with moderate and severe disabilities.

4. To date, most available community-referenced curriculum guides contain extensive listings of activities. While these listings provide some help to teachers, they fall short of addressing basic decision-making requirements such as determining which of the many activities on the list are essential to learn, and at what age a particular activity should be introduced. The authors, along with others from Syracuse University and the Syracuse City School District, have been developing a community-referenced curriculum guide that incorporates decision-making processes.[3] Figure 1, which displays a sample scope and sequence chart from this guide, depicts activities in the area of "General Community Functioning," one of the four community-living domains included in the guide. In its present form, the chart contains activities considered to be *essential* or *negotiable*. Essential activities are those which everyone should be expected to engage in because of their survival value or prominence in everyday life (e.g., buying groceries). Negotiable activities are those which some but not all students may be expected to master since they are typically performed by someone in the environment but not necessarily by everyone (e.g., mowing the lawn). If students have not yet demonstrated a sufficient degree of mastery on an essential activity for their particular age, instruction would begin. If an elementary school student with moderate or severe disabilities has not yet learned how to buy a snack at a grocery store, this activity would become an instructional objective. Although a chart of this nature begins to offer a framework for decision making, it is still based on the "best guesses" of educators rather than empirically validated determinations. These modest beginnings are offered merely as an illustration of how much further development is needed before gaining a full understanding of what a progression of community-living content might look like.

Through a rapidly expanding body of literature and the widespread demonstration efforts occurring in today's schools, we now have a glimpse at how the concept of community-referenced curriculum is being interpreted and translated into practice. There seems to be a consensus among professionals and parents that community-referenced curricula have an established place in educational practice,

SCOPE AND SEQUENCE CHART
DOMAIN: GENERAL COMMUNITY FUNCTIONING

☐ Essential
▨ Negotiable

Essential and Negotiable Activities

	Kindergarten (Age 5)	Elementary School (Ages 6-11)	Middle School (Ages 12-15)	High School (Ages 16-19)	Transition (Ages 20-21)
Travel	Walking (wheeling) to/from destination Riding school/city bus Riding in a car Using caution with strangers/problem solving when lost Riding a bike	Walking (wheeling) to/from destination Riding school/city bus Riding in a car Using caution with strangers/problem solving when lost	Walking (wheeling) to/from destination Riding city bus/wheelchair van Riding in a car Using caution with strangers/problem solving when lost Riding a bike	Walking (wheeling) to/from destination Riding city bus/wheelchair van Riding in a car Using caution with strangers/problem solving when lost Riding a bike Taking a taxi	Walking (wheeling) to/from destination Riding city bus/wheelchair van Riding in a car Using caution with strangers/problem solving when lost Riding a bike Taking a taxi
General Shopping	Buying toys and games	Buying toys and games Buying shoes/clothes Buying gifts	Buying games Buying shoes/clothes Buying gifts Buying personal care items	Buying games Buying shoes/clothes Buying gifts Buying personal care items	Buying games Buying shoes/clothes Buying gifts Buying personal care items
Grocery Shopping	Buying a snack	Buying a snack/few items	Buying a snack/few items Buying some of the household groceries and supplies	Buying a snack/few items Buying some of the household groceries and supplies	Buying a snack/few items Buying some of the household groceries and supplies
Restaurant Use	Eating out in a restaurant (fast food, sit down, cafeteria)	Eating out in a restaurant (fast food, sit down, cafeteria) Eating/drinking items from vending machine	Eating out in a restaurant (fast food, sit down, cafeteria) Eating/drinking items from vending machine	Eating out in a restaurant (fast food, sit down, cafeteria) Eating/drinking items from vending machine	Eating out in a restaurant (fast food, sit down, cafeteria) Eating/drinking items from vending machine
Using Services		Using the pay phone Using the hair styling shop Using the post office Using health services	Using the pay phone Using the hair styling shop Using the post office Using health services Using the bank	Using the pay phone Using the hair styling shop Using the post office Using health services Using the bank	Using the pay phone Using the hair styling shop Using the post office Using health services Using the bank

Figure 1: An Example of a Scope and Sequence Chart from a Community-Referenced Curriculum Guide

particularly for students with moderate and severe intellectual disabilities. Throughout this discussion, we have continually paired community-referenced curricula with this particular segment of the student population. In many ways, they *are* inextricably linked. The community-referenced curricula evolved in response to the needs of this particular group of students. However, this historical linkage does not mean that a community-referenced curriculum has implications only for those students. We return to this matter in the final section of this chapter.

The Emergence of Community-Referenced Curricula

Not long ago, classroom instruction for students with moderate and severe disabilities was characterized by repeated practice trials on isolated skills derived from traditional developmental sequences in motor skills, language skills, and in mathematics and reading. Typical classroom activities for these students involved sorting objects, following basic directions, imitating movements and sounds, learning self-care skills, and later on for more sophisticated students, working on beginning concepts in mathematics and reading. As students approached secondary school age, prevocational programming was added to the curriculum, often requiring more sorting and nonfunctional "seat work." These skills were seldom integrated for students. Just as schools might assume that typical fourth graders can synthesize and integrate separate mathematics, language arts, and social studies lessons into their daily lives, we operated on a similar assumption that students with severe learning needs could integrate their separate lessons in motor skills, speech, and self-help and apply these skills to their daily lives. Just as typical students sometimes have difficulties seeing the relevance of their education, so do students with severe disabilities. The end result of this curricular approach was that programs usually led to the graduation of handicapped youth whose skill repertoires resembled those of very young children, rather than the repertoires of young adults ready to participate in the real world. Dissatisfaction with such results led to a community-referenced approach to curriculum development, which can be best understood by examining the array of conditions surrounding its emergence.

Contributions from applied research. Given its relatively short history, curriculum development for students with severe disabilities has made impressive strides. Not more than two decades ago, a rather small but influential group of professionals worked toward the development of model school curricula. Drawing upon a knowledge base central to their own interests, this group laid the foundation for today's curricular reform.[4] One of the dominant interests of this group was applied behavioral analysis. Application of the learning theory advanced by Skinner, who believes that much of human behavior can be explained by the events that immediately precede and follow it,[5] was seen in highly prescribed early intervention and language development programs[6] and thoroughly task-analyzed self-care and prevocational programs.[7] The overall goal was to demonstrate that persons with severe disabilities were capable of learning more complex skills than had been previously thought. Considering the fact that as late as the early 1970s the vast majority of students with severe disabilities were not considered "educable" and were therefore excluded from public school attendance, this was a particularly meaningful goal for the time.[8]

Early practices and educational goals were also influenced by the application of developmental or normative models of learning. Many early curricular materials for students with moderate and severe disabilities were based on the premise that while the rate of development of a child with mental retardation is slower than for "normal" individuals, it nevertheless follows the same predictable path of skill acquisition. Thus, teachers were asked to rely on checklists and curricular objectives that were based upon the development of very young children. Since it took students with moderate and severe disabilities much longer to learn the developmental tasks, it was not unusual to find a ten- or twelve-year-old still working on something prescribed for a two- or three-year-old (e.g., stacking rings, sorting shapes and colors). Although the theoretical orientation of the developmental model was different from that which had its roots in applied behavioral analysis, the intent behind its application was essentially the same: to demonstrate that persons with severe disabilities could benefit from instruction.

Normalization. The concept of "normalization" originated in Scandinavia during the late 1960s. Based on reforms in Denmark's residential services for persons with mental retardation, Bank-Mikkelson defined the normalization principle as "letting the mentally retarded obtain an existence as close to the normal as possible."[9] Nirje, also Scandinavian, endorsed the principle and further characterized it as "making available to the mentally retarded patterns and conditions of everyday life which are as close as possible to the norms and patterns of the mainstream of society."[10]

Wolfensberger offered a North American reformulation of the normalization principle that has had a lasting impact on human services for people with severe disabilities.[11] In the 1970s, when students with moderate and severe disabilities were gaining increased access to special education services, the notion of normalization as a guiding principle offered two important directions to the emerging curriculum. First, a curriculum could be designed to prepare these students for conditions of everyday living that were as close as possible to those experienced by the rest of society. Second, it encouraged the development and use of teaching procedures and educational environments that were reflective of normative expectations.

Parents, litigation, and legislation. To a great extent, the current emphasis on community-referenced curricula can be traced back to efforts made by parents of children with disabilities, both individually and collectively. In one of the most widely noted special education cases, the *Pennsylvania Association for Retarded Children v. Commonwealth of Pennsylvania* (PARC consent decree of 1972), parents were successful in having the court strike down state laws that worked to exclude children with severe disabilities from public schools. The PARC case and its enforcement mechanisms established standards that did more than address exclusionary practices. It set forth important principles of integration, active parent participation, and curricula designed to meet each individual's needs.[12]

Litigation of the early 1970s was followed in 1975 by P.L. 94-142, which guaranteed a free and appropriate public education for all children with disabilities. In this legislation, Congress recognized the deficiencies in educational services for students with severe disabilities and specifically noted that children "with the most severe handicaps who are receiving inadequate education" should be given priority.

Using the mechanisms provided by P.L. 94-142, parents continue to have a strong voice in determining what constitutes quality educational services. Through the Individual Education Program (IEP) process, parents now have the right to meet with professionals and participate in the development of their children's programs. At times, when requests for more functional, individually relevant programs have been rejected by school districts, parents have exercised the due process protections of P.L. 94-142. As a result, hearing officers and judges increasingly are being asked to make decisions about the appropriateness of curricular content. *Battles v. Commonwealth of Pennsylvania* not only illustrates this point, but also demonstrates how legal decisions have actually served to broaden the concept of formal education.[13] The court stated: "Where basic self-help and social skills such as toilet training, dressing, feeding and communications are lacking, formal education begins at that point."[14] In *Campbell v. Talladega County Board of Education*, the court specified that the school district must provide curricula which address needs in four areas: daily living activities, vocational activities, recreational activities, and social and community adjustment.[15] These cases, and others like them, represent some of the more recognized efforts of parents to influence curriculum development. Less overt, but not less significant, are the efforts being made on a daily basis across the country when parents and teachers come together to design an IEP which is satisfactory to all parties.

Exemplary models and a small, influential, professional network. The literature reveals a marked degree of professional consensus about the importance of school integration and community-referenced curriculum for students with moderate and severe disabilities. The widespread adoption of these curricular orientations has been explained by Tawney and Sniezek: "[B]ecause this was [and is] a relatively small field, because there were federal funds to support travel for group meetings, because close working relationships existed or developed quickly, there was a climate which fostered sharing of ideas and, consequently, widespread adoption of those resources that seemed most likely to have potential for educational benefit."[16]

Among the first nationally recognized teacher preparation programs in the area of severe disabilities were the University of Washington's nursery program for children who were deaf and blind, developed in 1966, and the University of Wisconsin's program for school-aged youth, which by 1972 had developed into a comprehensive undergraduate teacher-training sequence.[17] The number of teacher preparation programs grew rapidly, spurred on by the financial support of the U.S. Office of Special Education and Rehabilitative Services (then the Bureau of Education for the Handicapped). Nevertheless, the number of university professors, policymakers, and school administrators whose careers were devoted solely to improving educational services for students with severe disabilities remained rather small, particularly when compared with those colleagues interested in other disability groups.[18] A strong professional network began to develop, and eventually a national organization was formed in 1975—the Association for Persons with Severe Handicaps (originally named the American Association for the

Education of the Severely and Profoundly Handicapped). By 1987 it had grown to nearly 7000 members.

Increased attention to learning style. The shift to future-oriented goals of education brought about a renewed interest in the learning style of students with moderate and severe disabilities. With growing interest in teaching community living skills, there was a need to examine the curricular implications of students' basic learning characteristics. In particular, attention was drawn to the relatively slow learning pace of students with severe disabilities, and their apparent difficulties in generalization. It became obvious that the slow learning pace of some students left them hopelessly entangled in readiness sequences. They were never considered ready to learn the actual skills (such as reading and mathematics applications) because they had not sufficiently mastered the so-called prerequisites (e.g., shape and color discrimination, one-to-one correspondence). The curricular implications were clear: using normal developmental sequences with learners who have a significantly slower learning pace often resulted in a curriculum consisting of nonfunctional, isolated, and age-inappropriate tasks that did not lead to meaningful educational outcomes. Equally obvious were the curricular implications of students' difficulties with generalization. Teachers were operating under a high degree of instructional inference. That is, most instruction was carried out in classroom settings with artificial materials (workbooks, cardboard clocks, cardboard money, and yes, even cardboard buses), under the assumption that the skills taught under these conditions would transfer to the real settings. This practice, which was characterized as the "train and hope" strategy, could no longer be considered educationally tenable given the pressing need to prepare students for community life.[19]

Accountability. Public involvement, expectation, and scrutiny of the quality of general public education is evidenced by many events of recent decades: the rapid growth of science curriculum after Sputnik; the ongoing outcry over issues of discipline in our schools; the increased attention to graduates who can not read; worry about our nation's sagging achievement scores; and the current "excellence in education" movement.[20] To date, only a few attempts have been made to evaluate the outcomes of education for students with moderate and severe disabilities. Stanfield did a follow-up study of 100 graduates (labeled "moderately retarded") from a large California school district. His findings revealed that 44 percent of them were not involved in any postschool work or habilitation program. Another 40 percent were in sheltered workshop programs, while only 3 percent were in nonsheltered work settings.[21] He called for "guaranteed comprehensive postschool programming" as a means for remedying these unsatisfactory outcomes. Later follow-up studies revealed similar outcomes, but began to call for curricular reform within the existing school program. The need for increased community vocational training, longitudinal curricular sequences in the community living areas, improved home-school collaboration, and transition services from school to adulthood, were among the many recommendations contained in these reports.[22] Although this wave of follow-up studies merely confirmed what educators already knew, it set in motion an accountability mechanism that undoubtedly strengthened an already emerging community-referenced curriculum.

It is now apparent that the community-referenced curriculum is not a passing fad, but a promising practice that should have a lasting effect on educational services. For over a decade we have had the chance to see how community-referenced curricula have been implemented in our schools. Much has already been accomplished. Consider, for example, the postschool outcomes reported in the latest follow-up investigation of the Madison Metropolitan School District.[23] Of the thirty-two students with severe disabilities who graduated during the 1984-86 school years, twenty-nine are working in community settings. This is a marked contrast from the follow-up data supplied on Madison graduates from the 1971-78 school years, when fifty-three individuals graduated and only one worked in a community setting.

Lessons Learned from Implementing a Community-Referenced Curriculum

The accomplishments of the past decade have produced many important lessons about the implementation of community-referenced curricula—lessons that should influence our reform efforts for some time to come. What are some of these lessons?

The occasional field trip is not sufficient. By the time they graduate from high school, most nondisabled students are competent performers of many community living skills—crossing streets, riding the bus, handling money, using a wide range of community services and facilities. Their proficiency in these skills is not learned through systematic instruction in school but rather through casual exposure and the incidental teachings of family and peers. If the school sets out to teach nondisabled students about the "community," instruction usually takes the form of an occasional field trip.

Educators of students with severe disabilities have learned to make a distinction between community instruction and field trips. A field trip is an opportunity to expose large groups of students to events or settings that would not ordinarily be experienced in everyday life. Community instruction, on the other hand, is specifically designed to allow students to experience events and settings which are most common to everyday life. And, unlike field trips, community instruction seeks to go beyond mere exposure by providing concentrated and ongoing instruction at a particular site with the smallest possible group of students. Repeated community instructional sessions are deemed necessary in order to achieve significant educational outcomes. Thus one of the earliest lessons learned about community-referenced instruction for students with severe disabilities was that mere exposure to community environments was simply not pedagogically powerful enough.

While a one-time exposure to community settings is clearly not sufficient for some students to acquire essential community living skills, we have yet to reach reasonable consensus on how much community instruction is necessary. Should a student leave the school for instruction in street crossing everyday, once a week, or once a month? Should community vocational instruction consume 25, 50, or 75 percent of the weekly schedule of a high school student with severe disabilities? How much time should an elementary school student spend in community settings? Only a few rough guidelines based on the "best guesses" of experienced educators have begun to appear in the literature. Since students with moderate and severe disabilities represent a diverse group of learners, decisions about how much time should be spent in the community will need to take account of this diversity. Furthermore, today's teachers are being asked to respond to two major curricular imperatives: (a) to provide systematic instruction in the community to prepare students better for adult life; and (b) to maximize school integration and support the growth of social relationships between students with disabilities and their nondisabled peers. These imperatives are potentially in competition with each other, for the more time a student spends in the community, the less time he or she spends in school learning and developing relationships with nonhandicapped peers. Decision guidelines have to be sensitive to this tension and ensure that both imperatives are given sufficient consideration.

Logistical barriers can be overcome. During the initial phases of implementing a community-referenced curriculum, educators face many difficult decisions about logistics. Who will be responsible for contacting local businesses and industries to locate job training sites? How will transportation be handled? Who pays for the costs incurred by repeated instructional trips to the grocery store, restaurant, and YMCA? How will the teacher who has eight students with multiple disabilities provide effective community instruction? What about liability coverage for students when they are in the community? Can teaching assistants serve as instructors in the community? To address some of these issues, school districts have been able to rely on precedents existing within regular education. For example, many school districts have adapted school policies originally designed for field trips and work-study programs for use in community instruction. For other logistical problems, no precedent exists. Consider, for example, the teacher who has been assigned eight students who all use wheelchairs and therefore require vehicles with wheelchair lifts or ramps. Confounding these transportation difficulties is the district's policy indicating that teaching assistants are not permitted to conduct instruction unless they are in the presence of the classroom teacher. To resolve such difficulties the school district must rethink at least two significant policies or practices—the homogeneous grouping of students and the role of teaching assistants.

A number of useful resources are becoming available to educators who face logistical barriers in implementing community-referenced programs. Baumgart and VanWalleghem have outlined administrative solutions to staffing difficulties[24] while Hamre-Nietupski and colleagues suggest solutions to common barriers such as transportation, scheduling, costs, and homogeneous grouping.[25] An inescapable lesson is communicated through the suggestions of these authors: *logistical barriers cannot be overcome by teachers alone.* Of course, the short-term solutions made by teachers on a daily basis cannot be totally dismissed. Many of us are familiar with the teacher who holds a bake sale to fund community instruction, or the teacher who regularly uses a personal vehicle to transport students despite the fact that district policies are not necessarily supportive of this practice. But long-term solutions—those made with a full awareness and commitment to the unique needs of students—will not be reached until parents, teachers, and administrators work together in the problem solving process.

Educational goals must have validity. Decisions about what schools ought to teach are just as important for students with moderate and severe disabilities as for students without disability. Indeed, community-referenced curricula grew out of an effort to help teachers determine what to teach. Initially, the goal selection process seemed rather unencumbered: (a) identify a student, (b) select environments and activities in which the student functions now or will need to function in the future, and (c) match the performance of the student against the demands of the environment and determine which specific skills warrant instruction or adaptation.[26] Ideally, this process was to be applied to each individual student under the assumption that relevant community living skills might differ considerably from student to student. But current practice has strayed somewhat from this original premise. Educators are much more likely to ascribe to the notion that all community living activities are worthwhile by their very nature, and thus one "can't go wrong" when selecting from a list of such "functional" activities. Not all community-living skills, however functional, can be mastered during the school years, nor are all skills equally crucial to each individual's life.[27] As Meyer points out: "It is no longer enough to be pleased that we have taught something; we must be able to defend our choice of what we teach by showing that, somehow, the learner's quality of life and the reactions of others to that person are improved as a result of our efforts."[28]

The goals we select for students with severe disabilities will need to be influenced by many significant factors. First, we must recognize that not all community living activities can be sufficiently addressed during a student's educational career. Thus, the educator must work closely with parents to determine which goals have the highest priority at a given time. Second, whenever possible, we should avoid compensating for inadequacies in other human service systems. For example, many teachers report the need to compensate for the lack of recreational supports available to students. Hence, students are taught to bowl, ski, and play billiards as a part of their school programs because of the absence of access to typical recreation programs or extracurricular events and clubs. Similar curricular compensations have been made for inadequate postschool services. Until recently there were few continuing education options in technical schools, universities, community colleges, and adult education programs for students with severe disabilities. The human service agencies that might have filled this void have been equally bereft in their offerings, limiting options to highly restrictive sheltered workshops and day-activity programs. This lack of appropriate adult services has fostered a "now or never" approach to education; if a student does not receive systematic instruction on an important community living skill during his or her school years, it seems unlikely that such instruction will be provided during adulthood. Evidence of this "now or never" approach can be found in numerous curriculum guides which suggest that, by the graduation age of twenty-one students must learn to shop for groceries, prepare meals for the entire family, do laundry, and work in ten different job sites, sometimes long before most nonhandicapped students would be expected to engage in these activities. Surely, some of the compensation is justifiable when we consider students' learning styles. If it takes a student a significantly longer period of time to learn a critical skill, we may be induced to begin instruction earlier than normally expected. However, when we are primarily driven by the inadequacies in other service systems it might be best to work toward changing those systems.

Finally, educators have just begun to recognize the importance of student input and choice making.[29] As Guess and Siegel-Causey point out:

Conspicuously missing is the same intense effort to permit severely handicapped persons a reasonable degree of choice in what they would like to learn, or even the method in which the skill might be taught. Again, as the controller, we always assume to know what is best for our severely handicapped students. We presume to know what will enable them to function better in the world, but then are dismayed when they 1) do not learn *our* chosen tasks or do so slowly, or 2) fail to demonstrate competence of presumably learned skills in other settings or situations.[30]

We have reached a time where decisions about "what to teach" can no longer be based on a single criterion such as "functionality." Decision making will undergo much more scrutiny than it has in the past. Among the questions educators must be prepared to answer are: Why did you select this skill? Is it of value to the student and to significant others? Is it being taught solely because of the inadequacies of other service systems? And, how much input did the student have in the goal selection process?

Members of the community can make important contributions to the educational process. When the school broadens to encompass its community, members of that community take notice. After all, they are the clerks, the co-workers, and the bus drivers with whom students will routinely interact. Each member of the community is in an important position to contribute to the education of students with disabilities in casual and ongoing ways. A local example illustrates this point. Steven is a young man who lived in an institution, but because of his school program he received vocational training in the community. He was learning to wash dishes at a Pizza Hut, and was given assistance and supervision by his teacher. He understood most of the routine and, although his pace was considerably slower than that of nonhandicapped co-workers, the quality of his work was quite good. At times, without noticeable warning, Steven would become frustrated with his work and yell out or push away the dirty trays and dishes. Because of his limited speech, he was being taught how to express his needs and frustrations with hand gestures; but this gestural system had not totally replaced his more dramatic means of expression. On one occasion, Steven pushed over an entire rack of pans and dishes, producing enough commotion to capture the attention of every restaurant patron. The restaurant manager, not the teacher, intervened. In a firm, but matter-of-fact tone, he said, "Steven, why didn't you tell me you needed a break? Now let's pick these up." The manager had learned enough about Steven in order to feel comfortable interacting with him in this difficult situation. He had also learned to realize that the act was not malicious, and that terminating the work experience would serve no constructive purpose. Thus, with a commitment to Steven's growth, he continued to support the work experience, and eventually hired him the following year when Steven left high school at age twenty-one.

The involvement of community members in the educational process rarely happens by chance. Teachers play an important role in providing information and facilitating relationships between students and community members—a role that is just beginning to be understood and appreciated.

Attention must not be diverted from school integration. Unfortunately, many students with moderate and severe disabilities continue to be denied access to regular schools. They spend their days in segregated schools, cut off from the energizing social climate in which their nonhandicapped peers function. Some educators believe that the tremendous educational void caused by school segregation can be remedied by implementing a community-referenced curriculum, that getting out into the community is a sufficient integration experience and it does not really matter if the nonhandicapped persons are the same age or older. But it does matter; community-referenced instruction alone will never fill the void created by school segregation. In addition to implementing community-referenced programs for students with moderate and severe disabilities we must continue to work toward integration of those students into the life of the school. As Brown and his colleagues have stated:

The best way for physicians, secretaries, group home managers, waiters, architects, nurses, teachers of nonhandicapped students, school board members, legislators, and others to develop the skills and attitudes necessary to function effectively with and for severely handicapped persons is to grow up and attend school with them.[31]

Developing an appreciation of diversity and forming meaningful relationships with students considered handicapped is an effort that requires great diligence on the part of educators. It is clear that we cannot afford to have attention diverted from this important endeavor.

At Risk of Becoming an Appendage

After studying twenty-five special education programs in various school districts throughout the country, Bogdan concluded that many such programs have become "appendages to the school system rather than alterations of its structure and values." To avoid becoming an appendage, special education programs must apparently be willing to fit into the existing structure, even when doing so brings about significant educational costs to the students involved. Bogdan provides the following example:

Nowhere was this more evident than in one high school program I studied. This program for learning-disabled and neurologically impaired teenagers was housed in a school that honored academic achievement—both getting into college and, for slower students, graduating. The program helped students accumulate Carnegie units and pass minimum competency tests required for graduation. School personnel thought that the curriculum and state system were irrelevant to the students' needs, but they worked to get the students through. They drilled them for competency tests and pressed them to fit well enough into the mold to squeeze by. They bent examination rules, required daily rote memorization, and neglected curricula that might better prepare students for the world after high school.[32]

If becoming a part of the school requires conforming to its goals and its curriculum, what are the implications for students for whom "squeezing by" is not even within the realm of possibility? Must their programs be viewed as merely add-ons? Are community-referenced programs, then, at great risk of becoming mere appendages to the regular school curriculum? Our own experiences in schools where such programs are being developed, indicate that the answer is clearly "yes."

When put to the test, many school districts will acknowledge the "appendage status" of the community-referenced programs within their systems. Indeed, very few of their teachers, parents, and principals are actually aware that this type of curriculum is being offered and, if they are aware, they admit to knowing very little about its goals and associated content areas. When achievement scores are discussed at faculty meetings and at in-service meetings, rarely is there mention of student gains made in the community living areas. Similarly, the fact that Joanne, a student with severe disabilities, graduated into a job at Kenney's Shoes often goes without acknowledgement, while the National Merit Scholars are lavished with praise. And, when the district presents the broad range of curriculum offerings to the school board for review, noticeably absent is the community-referenced curriculum, although it has been in place for over five years. These are indications that, even in districts where a community-referenced curriculum has been formally adopted, it might still be omitted from the framework of the overall curriculum. It has a separate status of its own.

Several conditions seem to be imperatives if a community-referenced program is to avoid becoming an appendage and if it is to be seen as an integral part of the overall school program. First, it is important that school districts recognize the value of community living as a goal area and acknowledge that a portion of the student body, however small, may need direct preparation in this area. Second, the full scope of subject areas needs to be expanded and redefined in order to include such community living areas as domestic, general community, vocational, and recreation/leisure. Finally, classroom arrangements and student groupings need to be created so that all students have reasonable access to the full scope of relevant curricula and can learn together to the maximum extent possible. None of these conditions should be construed as a means of "watering down" the existing curriculum; indeed, that would work against the overall objective of offering a complete curriculum, one that excludes none, yet challenges all.

Before proceeding with a brief discussion of each of these conditions, it might be useful to recall that the concept of community-referenced curriculum, as we have described it, emerged out of a need to serve more effectively a small segment of the student body, namely students who experience moderate and severe disabilities. Since these students only recently began entering regular public schools, it should not be surprising that their curricular needs have not yet been adequately reflected within the existing public school structure. However, it is not too soon to institute a policy of engaging in *curricular planning with reference to a comprehensive educational framework that accounts for the great diversity of students who attend today's schools.* By doing so, what has been treated as an isolated program may be able to change from an appendage to an important part of the overall school program. We believe that enough groundwork has been laid to begin considering the relationship between a community-referenced curriculum and other components of the existing school curriculum. Moreover, we can not ignore the fact that, ready or not, increasing numbers of school districts are currently in the process of developing community-referenced curricula. Why should these districts follow previously established patterns by carrying out the curriculum revision process as if it bore no relationship to the rest of the school structure?

In the spirit of exploration we offer suggestions on how to incorporate a community-referenced curriculum into the total school program. To formulate our ideas about the current structure of schools, we have drawn heavily upon our own experiences and the numerous recent reports on American education. Particularly useful was John Goodlad's *A Place Called School*, a report based on "A Study of Schooling," involving an extensive investigation of 1,016 classrooms and interviews with 1,350 teachers, 8,624 parents, and 17,163 students.[33]

Valuing community living as a goal area. To become an integral part of the entire school program, community-referenced curricula will need to be recognized and valued by those who have the greatest influence on the overall curriculum—teachers, parents, school district officials, and the general public. If we accept what is written in the mission statements of numerous school districts and state education agencies, active community participation *is* seen as a valued goal of education. For example, consider the goals written by the New York State Board of Regents for elementary, secondary, and continuing education. Embodied in the list of goals are such statements as "to perform work in a manner that is gratifying to the individual and to those served," to exhibit the "capacity for creativity, recreation, and self-renewal," and to "maintain one's mental, physical, and emotional health."[34] These educational goals represent broad statements of purpose and can easily be interpreted to reflect the needs of a diverse population of students. Thus, educators intent on finding community-referenced goals in school mission statements will not have to look very hard to find them.

Goodlad suggests that educational goal statements can serve as a starting point for dialogue among school board members, parents, students, and teachers "in the needed effort to achieve a common sense of direction for their schools and to build programs of teaching and learning related to these goals."[35] One of the questions raised during these dialogues might be whether current educational goals are sufficiently inclusive, specifically, whether they address the needs of all students, including those with severe disabilities. Hopefully, when considering this issue, school districts will embrace the notion that some students would benefit greatly from direct preparation in the community-living areas and, in recognition of this fact, revise goal statements where necessary.

Redefining the scope and sequence of curriculum content. Although organized in many different ways, the full scope of school curriculum is frequently defined to include: Language Arts/English, Mathematics, Science, Physical Education, the Arts (Music, Drama, Visual Arts), Social Studies, Foreign Language, Home Economics, Industrial Arts, and Vocational/Career Education. Neither the scope, nor the sequence (which reflects the planned progression of learning experiences over time), have been adapted to include the content needs of students who require some direct preparation in the community-living areas. If the needs of this group are to be reflected in the full scope and sequence of curriculum content, strategies will be needed to broaden and perhaps redefine the existing curricular framework. We examine here three different strategies for accomplishing this task.

In the first strategy, the district continues to use the existing structure of the regular content areas and includes community living content only as it arises for all students. Thus, the student with severe disabilities may be exposed to "money handling," "community workers," "dressing for the weather," and "meal preparation," but only as these topics occur in units typically covered at particular grade levels. Using this strategy, the student, rather than the curriculum, does most of the accommodating. Because the district does not have an articulated scope and sequence for the community living areas, decisions to emphasize particular community living skills would occur on a "hit or miss" basis rather than as a part of a longitudinal sequence. This strategy closely resembles the "willingness to fit" paradigm discussed by Bogdan. While it may succeed in achieving a high level of social integration, it may fall short of providing a systematic and longitudinal plan to teach community living skills directly.

A second strategy is to present the community living areas as unique domains that carry the same status as language arts, social studies, and so forth, but with a general understanding that the applicability of its sequences remain limited to a small segment of the student population. Under this strategy, teachers attempt to protect the integrity of the community-referenced curriculum, first by selecting meaningful instructional goals, and then by looking for ways in which the goals might overlap with the regular content areas. The community living content is infused into the existing structure whenever such a curricular overlap occurs. For example, a leisure goal for Sonja might be to "work with wood." It is determined that, with adaptations, she could learn to sand pieces of wood, varnish them, and put them together to make small furniture items. The idea of this goal came from a community-referenced curriculum guide which contained a longitudinal sequence of learning experiences designed to strengthen one's leisure repertoire. After the goal is selected, a search is made through the regular content areas or classes, to determine if an overlap exists. In Sonja's case, she could become a student in the "cabinet making" portion of the industrial arts course (an instructional assistant would be provided to help carry out the modifications of the content and to supply additional teaching support). Unlike the curricular strategy described above, the student with severe disabilities is not expected to participate when the content does not overlap and/or lacks sufficient meaning (e.g., during fifty-minute lectures on design). Here, the integrity of the community-living curriculum is maintained, but social integration may be diminished as the student moves in and out of the regular curriculum (or classroom).

Finally, a third strategy might be to present community-referenced content areas and instructional strategies as unique domains carrying the same weight as other content areas *and* yet broaden their applicability to a wider range of students. This strategy would both protect the integrity of community-referenced curriculum and set the stage for achieving a high level of integration, making it the strategy of choice. It would be the most challenging strategy to implement because it involves altering the structure of some regular education content areas. Community-living content would combine with existing content areas like physical education, vocational education, and home economics. Curriculum sequences would be articulated that not only challenge students with severe disabilities, but would maintain the challenges that already exist for nonhandicapped students. Admittedly, this would involve a rather complicated process of curriculum revision. Indeed, it begins by recognizing that there are some overlaps among community-referenced curricula and the other content areas. For example, young children are expected to learn how to dress for outdoors and manage personal belongings and to become aware of community services and the roles of community workers. Older students are expected to learn about nutrition and how to plan balanced meals, and to become aware of the variety of careers and community service options available to adults. These are activities that apply to both students with severe disabilities and their nondisabled peers. The challenge in curriculum revision does not come from identifying these overlapping activities, but from acknowledging that they must be addressed differently for different students. While it has been argued that some students require direct and ongoing preparation in community living activities (e.g., actually learning how to prepare a meal, open a bank account, work in the central supply area of a hospital), the majority of students (the nonhandicapped population) does not require this same intensive treatment. It is not so much a difference in kind, but in degree. Thus, the challenge becomes defining the content areas broadly enough, and with sufficient variation, so that a full range of students can be served.

Possible scenarios for the type of variations we foresee in high schools and elementary schools are depicted in the following examples.

High School. On Monday, Tuesday, and Wednesday afternoons, Mr. Clift supervises community-internship experiences for a small group of Juniors from Maxwell High School. His group includes Frank, Becky, Montez, Carol, and Sam. Becky experiences a severe disability. The other students in the group have more typical learning styles. This semester the members of the group are interning at Terrace Labs, where they are learning science as well as career/vocational skills. Montez is in the top 5 percent of his class in his academic standing. Becky is described in her school records as profoundly mentally retarded and functions within the lowest 1 percent of the population based on most standardized measures. The educational needs of both students are met within a real community work environment.

As a strong science student, Montez leans towards a career in chemistry or mathematics. At Terrace, he learns and applies principles of chemistry as they pertain to the production of pharmaceutical products. As a research assistant to his mentor he assists with the research and production activities of the plant. Becky assists with the sterilization of test tubes and lab equipment under the supervision of a job coach. For Becky this assignment is the most challenging of her placements so far. She is increasing her social interaction skills as well as her endurance.

Elementary School. Elementary school classrooms often enlist many teaching and grouping practices that allow students with diverse needs to learn together. Small-group instruction, peer tutoring, and experiential learning are just a few of the strategies that Mr. Lee uses to ensure that Shawn and Jerry, two students with severe disabilities, are included in instructional sessions. Mr. Lee created a Hot Chocolate Business to use as a backdrop for his mathematics lessons. Each day during the mathematics class, Shawn and Jerry were assigned to the Hot Chocolate Business. Other groups of students—four at a time—were assigned on a rotating basis following a schedule devised by Mr. Lee and his instructional assistant. On Mondays, Tuesdays, and Thursdays, the instructional assistant would carry out in-classroom lessons drawing upon the money handling, communication, and social skills required to operate the Hot Chocolate Business. On Wednesdays, the students would walk two blocks to a grocery store where they purchased the supplies needed for the business, and on Fridays they opened the Hot Chocolate Business for sales during recess. A typical in-classroom lesson was outlined for the accomplishment of several objectives: (a) to teach the application of the mathematics concept that the nonhandicapped students were currently working on from the 4th grade curriculum (e.g., division with decimals); (b) to teach Jerry how to count money and use his calculator to determine the affordability of items; and (c) to teach Shawn how to manage the supplies by unpacking and stocking the hot chocolate packets and basic money handling skills. This type of experientially based lesson not only allowed the teacher to address learning objectives at varying levels of proficiency, but it also made learning much more interesting for the students involved.[36]

Creating inclusive and responsive classroom arrangements and student groupings. It is possible for a school to have a commitment to community living goals and to its curriculum content, but arrange instruction in such a way that community-referenced programs remain an appendage, rather than an integral part of the overall school structure. Students in need of a community-referenced instructional approach might still be separated from their peers, stigmatized as "nonacademically oriented" or "nondiploma" students, and locked into grouping arrangements that permit little contact with other students in the school. As conveyed in other chapters in this volume, there is no simple list of proven strategies to overcome obstacles to integration. Hopefully, inclusive school goals and curriculum sequences will help set the stage for expanding opportunities for students to learn in heterogeneous groups. There should not be a sharp distinction between groups of students, but rather a delivery system which allows students to access programs and content areas based on their individual needs. Thus, the fifteen students in a high school who happened to be labeled moderately and severely handicapped would not have one "program." They would have many different programs ranging from the student who spends 30 percent of his time in the vocational and community living domains (while the rest of the time is devoted to functional academics, the arts, and physical education) to the student who spends as much as 75 percent of her time in vocational and community living domains. Furthermore, when students with moderate and severe disabilities leave the school building for community instruction, they would not necessarily leave alone. As illustrated in the previous examples, they might be accompanied by nondisabled students who can benefit from career exploration that takes place in the real work settings, or consumer education that occurs in stores and local businesses.

Conclusion

Community-referenced curriculum has offered much promise in the education of students with severe disabilities. In the short period of time during which it has been implemented a great deal has been learned. Before we become too firmly entrenched in community-referenced curriculum development efforts and research agendas, it might be wise to pause and reflect upon how community-referenced curriculum and the education of students with severe disabilities interfaces with the broader spectrum of curricula in our schools. If becoming a part of the school requires conforming to its existing goals and its curriculum, many students will remain outsiders. Restructuring schooling to avoid program appendages will take conscious efforts—efforts that can be initiated either by those who work within the regular education structure or by those who have been on a separate path toward the design of community-referenced curricula.

Footnotes

1. For a perspective on how Lou Brown's work contributed to the formation of community living content areas, see Lou Brown, John Nietupski, Susan Hamre-Nietupski, "The Criterion of Ultimate Functioning," in *Hey, Don't Forget about Me! Education's Investment in the Severely, Profoundly, and Multiply Handicapped*, ed. M. Angele Thomas (Reston, VA: Council for Exceptional Children, 1976), pp. 2-15; Lou

Brown, Mary Beth Branston, Susan Hamre-Nietupski, Ian Pumpian, Nick Certo, and Lee Gruenewald, "A Strategy for Developing Chronological Age-Appropriate and Functional Curricular Content for Severely Handicapped Adolescents and Young Adults," *Journal of Special Education* 13 (1978): 81-90.

2. Barbara Wilcox and Tom Bellamy, *Design of High School Programs for Severely Handicapped Students* (Baltimore, MD: Paul H. Brookes, 1982).

3. Alison Ford, Patrick Dempsey, Jim Black, Linda Davern, Roberta Schnorr, and Luanna Meyer, *The Syracuse Community-Referenced Curriculum Guide for Students with Moderate and Severe Handicaps* (Syracuse, NY: Syracuse City School District, 1986).

4. James W. Tawney and Karen M. Sniezek, "Educational Programs for Severely Mentally Retarded Elementary-age Children: Progress, Problems, and Suggestions," in *Severe Mental Retardation: From Theory to Practice*, ed. Diane Bricker and John Filler (Reston, VA: Council for Exceptional Children, 1985), pp. 76-96.

5. B. F. Skinner, *Science and Human Behavior* (New York: Macmillan, 1953).

6. See, for example, William Bricker and Diane Bricker, "An Early Language Training Strategy," and Doug Guess, Wayne Sailor, Donald M. Baer, "To Teach Language to Retarded Children," in *Language Perspectives: Acquisition, Retardation, and Intervention*, ed. Richard Schiefelbusch and Lyle Lloyd (Baltimore, MD: University Park Press, 1974), pp. 431-68, 529-63; and William Bricker and Diane Bricker, "The Infant, Toddler, and Preschool Research and Intervention Project," in *Intervention Strategies for High Risk Infants and Young Children*, ed. T. Tjossem (Baltimore: University Park Press, 1976).

7. See, for example, Stanley W. Bijou and Donald M. Baer, *Child Development: Readings in Experimental Analysis* (New York: Appleton-Century-Crofts, 1967); Marc W. Gold, "Task Analysis of a Complex Assembly Task by the Retarded Blind," *Exceptional Children* 43 (1976): 78-85; idem, "Vocational Training," in *Mental Retardation and Developmental Disabilities: An Annual Review*, vol. 7, ed. J. Wortis (New York: Branner/Magel, 1975), pp. 254-64.

8. R. Paul Thompson, Barbara Wilcox, and Robert York, "The Federal Program for the Severely Handicapped: Historical Perspective, Analysis, and Overview," in *Quality Education for the Severely Handicapped*, ed. Barbara Wilcox and Robert York (Falls Church, VA: Counterpoint Handcrafted Books and Other Media, 1980), pp. 1-28.

9. N. E. Bank-Mikkelsen, "A Metropolitan Area in Denmark: Copenhagen," in *Changing Patterns in Residential Services for the Mentally Retarded*, ed. Robert Kugel and Wolf Wolfensberger (Washington, DC: President's Committee on Mental Retardation, 1969), p. 234.

10. Bengt Nirje, "The Normalization Principle and Its Human Management Implications," in *Changing Patterns in Residential Services for the Mentally Retarded*, ed. Kugel and Wolfensberger, p. 181.

11. Wolf Wolfensberger, *Normalization: The Principle of Normalization in Human Services* (Toronto: National Institute on Mental Retardation, 1972).

12. Frank J. Laski, "Judicial Address of Education for Students with Severe Mental Retardation: From Access to Schools to State-of-the-Art," in *Severe Mental Retardation*, ed. Bricker and Filler, pp. 36-48.

13. Ibid.

14. Ibid., p. 39.

15. Ibid.

16. Tawney and Sniezek, "Educational Programs for Severely Mentally Retarded Elementary-Age Children," p. 78.

17. Norris G. Haring, "Review and Analysis of Professional Preparation for the Severely Handicapped," in *Quality Education for the Severely Handicapped*, ed. Wilcox and York, pp. 180-201.

18. Ibid.

19. Trevor F. Stokes and Donald M. Baer, "An Implicit Technology of Generalization," *Journal of Applied Behavior Analysis* 10 (1977): 349-67.

20. National Commission on Excellence in Education, *A Nation at Risk: The Imperative for Educational Reform* (Washington, DC: U.S. Department of Education, 1983).

21. James S. Stanfield, "Graduation: What Happens to the Retarded Child When He Grows Up?" *Exceptional Children* 39 (1973): 548-52.

22. See, for example, Lou Brown, Betsy Shiraga, Alison Ford, Jan Nisbet, Pat VanDeventer, Mark Sweet, and Ruth Loomis, "Teaching Severely Handicapped Students to Perform Meaningful Work in Nonsheltered Vocational Environments," in *Special Education Research and Trends*, ed. Richard J. Morris and Burton Blatt (Elmsford, NY: Pergamon, 1986), pp. 131-89; Susan B. Hasazi, Lawrence R. Gordon, Cheryl A. Roe, "Factors Associated with the Employment Status of Handicapped Youth Exiting High School from 1979 to 1983," *Exceptional Children* 51 (1985): 455-69; and Dennis E. Mithaug, Chiyo N. Horiuchi, and Peter N. Fanning, "A Report on the Colorado Statewide Follow-up Survey of Special Education Students," *Exceptional Children* 51 (1985): 397-404.

23. Lou Brown, Patty Rogan, Betsy Shiraga, Kathy Zanella Albright, Kim Kessler, Fred Bryson, Pat VanDeventer, and Ruth Loomis, *A Vocational Follow-up Evaluation of the 1984 to 1986 Madison Metropolitan School District Graduates with Severe Intellectual Disabilities* (Seattle, WA: Association for Persons with Severe Handicaps, 1987).

24. Diane Baumgart and John VanWalleghem, "Staffing Strategies for Implementing Community-Based Instruction," *Journal of the Association for Persons with Severe Handicaps* 11 (1986): 92-102.

25. Susan Hamre-Nietupski, John Nietupski, Paul Bates, and Steve Maurer, "Implementing a Community-Based Education Model of Moderately/Severely Handicapped Students: Common Problems and Suggested Solutions," *Journal of the Association for the Severely Handicapped* 7 (1982): 38-43.

26. Lou Brown, Mary Beth Branston, Susan Hamre-Nietupski, Ian Pumpian, Nick Certo, and Lee Gruenewald, "A Strategy for Developing Chronological Age-Appropriate and Functional Curricular Content for Severely Handicapped Adolescents and Young Adults," *Journal of Special Education* 13 (1978): 81-90.

27. For discussions of educational validity, see Luanna H. Voeltz and Ian M. Evans, "Educational Validity: Procedures to Evaluate Outcomes in Programs for Severely Handicapped Learners," *Journal of the Association for the Severely Handicapped* 8 (1983): 3-15; and Ian M. Evans and Luanna H. Meyer, "Basic Life Skills," in *School Psychology: The State of the Art*, ed. James E. Ysseldyke (Minneapolis: National School Psychology In-service Training Network, 1984), pp. 37-56.

28. Luanna H. Meyer, "Foreword," in Robert J. Gaylord-Ross and Jennifer F. Holvoet, *Strategies for Educating Students with Severe Handicaps* (Boston: Little, Brown, 1985), pp. 5-6.

29. See Mayer Shevin and Nancy K. Klein, "The Importance of Choice-making Skills for Students with Severe Disabilities," *Journal of the Association for the Severely Handicapped* 9 (1984): 159-66; and Doug Guess and Ellin Siegel-Causey, "Behavioral Control and Education of Severely Handicapped Students: Who's Doing What to Whom? and Why?" in *Severe Mental Retardation*, ed. Bricker and Filler, pp. 230-44.

30. Guess and Siegel-Causey, "Behavioral Control and Education of Severely Handicapped Students," 234-35.

31. Lou Brown, Alison Ford, Jan Nisbet, Mark Sweet, Anne Donnellan, and Lee Gruenewald, "Opportunities Available When Severely Handicapped Students Attend Chronological Age Appropriate Regular Schools," *Journal of the Association for Persons with Severe Handicaps* 8 (1983): 20.

32. Robert Bogdan, " 'Does Mainstreaming Work?' Is a Silly Question," *Phi Delta Kappan* 64 (February 1983): 427-28.

33. John I. Goodlad, *A Place Called School: Prospects for the Future* (New York: McGraw-Hill, 1984).

34. *New York State Plan (1987-89): Educating Children with Handicapping Conditions in New York State* (Albany, NY: New York Department of Education, 1986).

35. Goodlad, *A Place Called School*, p. 51.

36. The example of the "Hot Chocolate Business" unit was adapted from actual classroom instruction conducted by David Smukler while he was completing an internship at Ed Smith Elementary School in Syracuse, New York. This instructional program is also described in Alison Ford and Linda Davern, "Moving Forward with School Integration: Strategies for Involving Students with Severe Handicaps in the Life of the School," in *Integration Strategies for Persons with Handicaps*, ed. Robert Gaylord-Ross (Baltimore: Paul H. Brookes, in press).

CHAPTER VII

Teaching Alternatives to Aggression

ARNOLD P. GOLDSTEIN

Violence in America's schools has for several years posed a largely unresolved national problem of the first magnitude—to teacher and student victims, to school property, to the community, and to the educational process in general. Approximately 270,000 physical assaults occur annually in primary and secondary schools in the United States, and approximately $500 million in damage from vandalism, arson, and theft are visited upon school property each year. The number of assaults on teachers has grown steadily, and reached a level that led Block to describe the increasingly common "battered teacher syndrome."[1] But 78 percent of personal victimization in schools (rape, assault, larceny) are students[2] and, while the level of such victimization seems to have stabilized or even decreased slightly in very recent years, their absolute level remains very high and still largely resistant to significant reduction.[3] Much the same may be said about aggression directed toward school property—a dramatic and consistent increase during the 1960s and 1970s, a stabilization at (or slight decrease to) very high levels in the early 1980s. We refer here to such acts as trespass, breaking and entering, theft of school property, property destruction, fires, and bomb threats. Perhaps it suffices to indicate that in the last thirty-five years the number of students in average daily attendance in American public schools has increased by approximately 100 percent, and the cost of school arson during this period has increased by approximately 1,000 percent.[4] As we have noted elsewhere,

The human and economic costs of aggression toward people and property in America's schools is very substantial. After decades of what, at least in retrospect and probably in reality, seem like negligible incidence rates, both classes of aggression increased precipitously during the late 1960s and early

1970s. Their plateauing at very high levels since that time can give us little cause for comfort. In fact, there are several reasons to suspect that even these apparent current levels may be serious underestimates.[5]

Teacher and school administration response to aggressive, disruptive, difficult youngsters in America's secondary and elementary schools has characteristically involved heavy reliance on one or another methods designed to reduce or inhibit such negative behaviors, with relatively little companion effort explicitly directed toward increasing the frequency of alternative constructive behaviors. We have, in fact, become reasonably competent as a profession in at least temporarily decreasing or eliminating fighting, arguing, teasing, yelling, bullying, and similar acting-out, off-task behaviors. But we have attended rather little to procedures designed to teach negotiation skills; constructive responses to failure; management of peer-group pressure; means of dealing effectively with teasing, rejection, accusations, anger, and so forth. The technology of interventions for decelerating negative behaviors will not detain us long in the present chapter. It is a technology well summarized and examined in a number of recent sources.[6] Two of the most heavily relied upon decelerative approaches, and paradoxically two of the least effective in terms of long-term results, do deserve a special word of comment. They are corporal punishment and verbal reprimands.

On grounds of either humaneness or efficacy, we would assert that corporal punishment has no place in the contemporary classroom. Stated simply, if extremely, we believe a child should never be hit by an adult, whether the hitting is labeled paddling, spanking, beating, or an assault. Though such overt aggression by school personnel is legal in forty-three states, the seven states which have outlawed corporal punishment in their public schools have done so quite recently, and several other states are considering such legislation. Hopefully, more and more state legislatures and local school boards will come to realize that, as several investigators have demonstrated, hitting a child (a) suppresses behavior mostly only until the hitter leaves, (b) teaches youngsters the unfortunate lesson "might makes right," and not infrequently leads to (c) overt counteraggression.

Reprimands are a second concretization of what Weber et al. term the intimidation classroom management strategy, and a popular one at that.[7] White found that in every grade after the second, the rate of teacher reprimands exceeded the rate of teacher praise and, in absolute terms, the rate of teacher reprimands was a constant reprimand every two minutes across all elementary and junior high school grades.[8] Thomas et al. have replicated these findings.[9]

Both reprimands and corporal punishment certainly have their champions and neither are lacking in at least some empirical support of their efficacy.[10] It is also clear, however, that their effectiveness often is quite temporary, and a complex function of a large number of considerations, including the likelihood, consistency, immediacy, duration, and severity of their occurrence, as well as a number of characteristics of the punishing agent.

A central point with regard to the several means in use for reducing problematic classroom behaviors—whether corporal punishment, reprimands, or such more benign punishers as extinction, time out and response cost—is that none teaches alternative constructive responses. They suppress, but offer no substitutes. As we have commented elsewhere,

A reprimand or a paddling will not teach new behaviors. If an aggressive youngster literally is deficient in the ability to ask rather than take, request rather than command, negotiate rather than strike out, all the scolding, scowling, spanking, and the like possible will not teach the youngster the desirable alternative behaviors. Thus, punishment, if used at all, must be combined with teacher efforts which instruct the youngster in those behaviors he knows not at all.[11]

The remainder of the present chapter is devoted to this prosocial instructional goal. Constructive alternatives to aggression are being effectively taught to disruptive youth, and thus we will seek to describe in detail the procedures, materials, and evaluation evidence which essentially constitute this contemporary prosocial skills training approach.

Prosocial Skills Training

The roots of prosocial skills training lie within both education and psychology. The notion of literally seeking to teach prosocial behaviors has often, if sporadically, been a significant goal of the American educational establishment. The character education movement of the 1920s and more contemporary moral education and values clarification programs are three prominent examples, and there are others.[12] Add to this institutionalized educational interest in prosocial behavior enhancement, the hundreds of interpersonal and prosocial skills courses taught in over 2,000 community colleges, and the hundreds of self-help books oriented toward similar skill-enhancement goals which are available to the American public, and it becomes clear that the formal and informal educational establishment in America provided fertile soil and explicit stimulation within which the prosocial skills training movement could grow.

Much the same can be said for American psychology, as it too laid the groundwork in its prevailing philosophy and concrete interests for the development of this new movement. The learning process has above all else been the central theoretical and investigative concern of American psychology since the late nineteenth century. This focal interest also assumed major therapeutic form in the 1950s, as psychotherapy practitioners and researchers alike came to view psychotherapeutic treatment more and more in learning terms. The very healthy and still expanding field of behavior modification grew from this joint learning-clinical focus, and may be appropriately viewed as the immediately preceding psychological context in which prosocial skills training came to be developed. In companion with the growth of behavior modification, psychological thinking increasingly shifted from a strict emphasis on remediation to one that was equally concerned with prevention, and the basis for this shift included movement away from a medical model concept toward what may most aptly be called a psychoeducational perspective. Both of these thrusts gave strong impetus to the viability of the prosocial skill-training movement.

Perhaps psychology's most direct contribution to prosocial skills training came from social learning theory, and in particular from the work conducted and stimulated by Albert Bandura. Based upon the same broad array of modeling, behavioral rehearsal, and social reinforcement investigations which helped stimulate and direct the development of our own approach to skill training, Bandura comments:

The method that has yielded the most impressive results with diverse problems contains three major components. First, alternative modes of response are repeatedly modeled, preferably by several people who demonstrate how the new style of behavior can be used in dealing with a variety of . . . situations. Second, learners are provided with necessary guidance and ample opportunities to practice the modeled behavior under favorable conditions until they perform it skillfully and spontaneously. The latter procedures are ideally suited for developing new social skills, but they are unlikely to be adopted unless they produce rewarding consequences. Arrangement of success experiences, particularly for initial efforts at behaving differently, constitute the third component in this powerful composite method. . . . Given adequate demonstration, guided practice, and success experiences, this method is almost certain to produce favorable results.[13]

Other events of the 1970s provided still further stimulation for the growth of the prosocial skills training movement. As noted earlier, very high levels of violence toward persons and property emerged and grew in America's 84,000 schools during this period. The inadequacy of prompting, shaping, and related operant procedures for adding new behaviors to individuals' behavioral repertoires was increasingly apparent. The widespread reliance upon deinstitutionalization which lay at the heart of the community mental health movement resulted in the discharge from America's public mental hospitals of approximately 400,000 persons, the majority of whom where substantially deficient in important daily functioning skills.

A further impetus to our own interest in prosocial skills training is its apparent prescriptive utility for lower socioeconomic status trainees in particular. As we have commented in this regard elsewhere,

Lower-class child rearing and life style, with their emphasis upon action, motor behavior, consequences rather than intentions, and their reliance upon external example and authority and a restricted verbal code, ill prepare such persons for successful involvement in traditional [insight-oriented interventions] but, we speculated, might prepare them very well for an [approach] which was responsive to such life-style characteristics. This would be an approach which was brief, concrete, behavioral, actional, authoritatively administered, and which required imitation of specific overt examples, taught role-taking skills, and provided early, continuing, and frequent reinforcement for enactment of seldom used but adaptive skill behaviors. These are the defining characteristics of Structured Learning.[14]

These factors (i.e., relevant supportive research, high and growing levels of school violence, the incompleteness of operant approaches, large populations of grossly skill-deficient individuals), all in the context of historically supportive roots in both education and psychology, came together in the thinking of the present writer and others as demanding a new intervention, something prescriptively responsive to these several needs. Prosocial skill training was the answer, and a movement was launched.

Our involvement in this movement, a prosocial skill training approach we have termed Structured Learning, began in the early 1970s. At that time, and for several years thereafter, our studies were conducted in public mental hospitals with long-term, highly skill-deficient, chronic patients. As our research program progressed, and demonstrated with regularity successful skill enhancement effects,[15] we shifted our focus from teaching a broad array of interpersonal and daily living skills to adult, psychiatric inpatients to a more explicit concern with skill prosocial training for aggressive individuals. Our trainee groups included spouses engaged in family disputes violent enough to warrant police intervention, child abusing parents, and, most especially, overtly aggressive adolescents,[16] and elementary school children.[17]

SKILL DEFICIENCY AND AGGRESSIVE BEHAVIOR

A substantial body of literature has in fact directly demonstrated that aggressive youngsters display widespread interpersonal, planning, aggression management, and other prosocial skill deficiencies. Freedman et al. examined the comparative skill competence levels of a group of chronically aggressive juvenile delinquents and a matched group (age, IQ, social background) of nonoffenders in response to a series of standardized role play situations.[18] The offender sample responded in a consistently less skillful manner. Spence constituted comparable offender and nonoffender samples, and videotaped their individual interviews with a previously unknown adult.[19] The offender group evidenced significantly less (a) eye contact, (b) appropriate head movements, and (c) speech, as well as significantly more fiddling and gross body movement. Conger et al. add further to this picture of skill deficiency. They conclude from their evidence that juvenile delinquents, as compared to nondelinquent cohorts,

had more difficulty in getting along with peers, both in individual one-to-one contacts and in group situations, and were less willing or able to treat others courteously and tactfully, and less able to be fair in dealing with them. In return, they were less well liked and accepted by their peers.[20]

Not only are adjudicated delinquents discriminable from their nondelinquent peers on a continuum of skill competence, but much the same is true for youngsters who are "merely" chronically aggressive. Patterson et al. observe:

The socialization process appears to be severely impeded for many aggressive youngsters. Their behavioral adjustments are often immature and they do not seem to have learned the key social skills necessary for initiating and maintaining positive social relationships with others. Peer groups often reject, avoid, and/or punish aggressive children, thereby excluding them from positive learning experiences with others.[21]

As Patterson et al. appear to be proposing, the social competence discrepancy between aggressive youngsters and their nonaggressive peers has early childhood roots according to evidence provided by Mussen et al.[22] Boys who later become delinquent in their longitudinal study, were appraised by their teachers as less well-adjusted socially than their classmates as early as third grade. They appeared less friendly, responsible, or fair in dealing with others, and more impulsive and antagonistic to authority. Poor peer relations (less friendly toward classmates, less well-liked by peers) were further developmental predictors of later delinquency. Thus, it may be safely concluded that prosocial skill deficiencies of diverse (especially interpersonal) types markedly characterize both the early development and adolescent behavior of delinquent and aggressive youngsters to a degree that significantly differentiates them from their nondelinquent, nonaggressive peers.

In these several ways, therefore, it is clear that the aggressive youngster characteristically displays substantial deficits in a broad array of prosocial psychological skills. The remediation of such deficits looms as an especially valuable goal.

Structured Learning Procedures
ASSESSMENT

Structured Learning, as is true for all approaches to prosocial skills training, begins with assessment of trainees' levels of proficiency-deficiency in the array of skills which constitute the curriculum in this approach. We have found it useful to estimate levels of skill deficiency by employing, alone or in combination, four methods of assessment: interviews, direct observations, behavioral testing, and skill checklists.

Interviews. Since a youngster's behavior affects peers, family, relatives, employers, and school personnel, these other people, if available, are prime sources for information about the youngster's skill proficiency or deficiency. Thus, in addition to the obvious value of skill-relevant interviewing of the youngsters themselves, useful information may be obtained, with the youngster's permission, from interviews conducted with these real-life figures.

Direct observation. There are very often, intentionally or otherwise, important discrepancies between what people say they do, or would do, in a given situation and how they actually behave. Valuable information about skill proficiency or deficiency may be obtained by actually observing the youngsters functioning in school, at home, or elsewhere in their interpersonal world. What do they actually *do* when their peers tease them, a parent disciplines them, an employer points out an error, a teacher asks them to volunteer for an activity? Clearly, such behavioral information is an especially valuable piece of the assessment picture.

Behavioral testing. One weakness of direct observation is that circumstances that allow youngsters to show whether or not they possess a given skill, and are willing and able to use it, may not occur during observation. While the tester or observer is present, for example, peers, parents, employers, and others may "be on their best behavior" or otherwise act unrepresentatively. When direct observation of skill use is not by itself sufficient for adequate skills assessment, an alternative is behavioral testing. This assessment approach involves creating, by role play, simulation, play acting, or in imagination, the types of situations that in real life would require competent skill use for solution, and then observing what youngsters do. While the artificial nature of behavioral testing compared to direct observation in the school, home, or community is a drawback, it can be applied to all potential trainees in a standardized manner. If the situations are well chosen and realistically portrayed, this method can elicit important information about skill proficiency and deficiency.

Skill checklists. We have consistently found skill deficiency information obtained directly from youngsters to be a particularly worthwhile part of the assessment picture. It tells us not only in which skills they estimate they are strong or weak, but via the act of sharing this information with us, also lets us know a bit about their motivation to change. There are reliable instruments of value for this purpose.[23]

SKILL DEVELOPMENT

Following assessment to establish skill proficiency-deficiency, the Structured Learning approach may then be effectively used. It consists of the didactic procedures recommended by Bandura, based upon empirical, social learning research.[24] These procedures are modeling, role playing, performance feedback, and transfer training.

Modeling. Structured Learning requires first that trainees be exposed to expert examples of the behaviors we wish them to learn. The six to twelve trainees constituting the Structured Learning group are selected based upon their shared skill deficiencies. Each potentially problematic behavior is referred to as a skill. Each skill is broken down into four to six different behavioral steps. The steps constitute the operational definition of the given skill. Using either live acting by the group's trainers or audiovisual modeling displays, actors portray the steps of that skill being used expertly in a variety of settings relevant to the trainee's daily life. Trainees are told to watch and listen closely to the way the actors in each vignette follow the skill's behavioral steps.

Role playing. A brief spontaneous discussion almost invariably follows the presentation of a modeling display. Trainees comment on the steps, the actors, and very often, on how the situation or skill problem portrayed occurs in their own lives. Since our primary goal in role playing is to encourage realistic behavior rehearsal, a trainee's statements about his or her individual difficulties using the skill being taught can often develop into material for the first role play. To enhance the realism of the portrayal, the main actor is asked to choose a second trainee (co-actor) to play the role of the significant other person in his or her life who is relevant to the skill problem. It is of crucial importance that the main actor seek to enact the steps he or she has just seen and heard modeled.

The main actor is asked to describe briefly the real skill problem situation and the real person(s) involved in it, with whom he or she could try these behavioral steps in real life. The co-actor is called by the name of the main actor's significant other during the role play. The trainer then instructs the role players to begin. It is the trainers' main responsibility, at this point, to be sure that the main actor keeps role playing and that he or she attempts to follow the behavioral steps while doing so.

The role playing is continued until all trainees in the group have had an opportunity to participate, even if all the same steps must be carried over to a second or third session. While the framework (behavioral steps) of each role play in the series remains the same, the actual content can and should change from role play to role play. It is the skill-deficiency problem as it actually occurs, or could occur, in each trainee's real-life environment that should be the content of the given role play. When completed, each trainee should be better armed to act appropriately in the given reality situation.

Performance feedback. Upon completion of each role play, a brief feedback period ensues. The goals of this activity are to let the main actor know how well he or she followed the skill's steps or in what ways he or she departed from them, to explore the psychological impact of his enactment on the co-actor, and to provide the main actor with encouragement to try out his or her role play behaviors in real life. In these critiques, the behavioral focus of Structured Learning is maintained. Comments must point to the presence or absence of specific, concrete behaviors, and not take the form of general evaluative comments or broad generalities.

TRANSFER OF TRAINING

Several aspects of the Structured Learning sessions described above have, as their primary purpose, increasing the likelihood that learning in the training setting will transfer to the trainee's actual real-life environment, whether it is his or her classroom, school yard, home, or neighborhood.

Provision of general principles. Transfer of training has been demonstrated to be facilitated by providing trainees with general mediating principles governing successful or competent performance on the training and criterion tasks. This procedure has typically been operationalized in laboratory contexts by providing subjects with the organizing concepts, principles, strategies, or rationales that explain or account for the stimulus-response relationships operative in both the training and application settings. The provision of general principles to Structured Learning trainees is operationalized in our training by the presentation in verbal, pictorial, and written form of appropriate information governing skill instigation, selection, and implementation principles.

Overlearning. Overlearning is a procedure whereby learning is extended over more trials than are necessary merely to produce initial positive changes in the trainee's behavior. The overlearning, or repetition of successful skill enactment in the typical Structured Learning session is quite substantial, with the given skill taught and its behavioral steps modeled several times, role played one or more times by the trainee, observed live by the trainee as every other group member role plays it, read by the trainee from a blackboard and on the Skill Card, written by the trainee in his or her Trainee's Notebook, practiced in vivo one or more times by the trainee as part of the formal homework assignment, practiced in vivo one or more times by the trainee in response to skill-oriented, intrinsically interesting stimuli introduced into his or her real life.

Identical elements. In perhaps the earliest experimental concern with transfer enhancement, Thorndike and Woodworth concluded that when there was a facilitative effect of one habit on another, it was to the extent that, and because, they shared identical elements.[25] Ellis and Osgood have also emphasized the importance for transfer of similarity between the training and application tasks.[26] The greater the similarity between physical and interpersonal stimuli in the Structured Learning setting and stimuli in the home, school, or other setting in which the skill is to be applied, the greater the likely transfer.

The "real-lifeness" of Structured Learning is operationalized in a number of ways. These operational expressions of identical elements include (1) the representative, relevant, and realistic content and portrayal of the models, protagonists, and situations in the live modeling or modeling tapes, all designed to be highly similar to what trainees are likely to face in their daily lives; (2) the physical props used in, and the arrangement of, the role-playing setting to be similar to real-life settings; (3) the choice, coaching, and enactment of the co-actors as protagonists to be similar to real-life figures; (4) the manner in which the role plays themselves are conducted to be as responsive as possible to the real-life interpersonal stimuli to which the trainee will actually respond with the given skill; (5) the in vivo homework; (6) the training of living units (e.g., all the members of a given class or group home as a unit.)

Stimulus variability. Positive transfer is demonstrably greater when a variety of relevant training stimuli are employed.[27] Stimulus variability is implemented in our Structured Learning studies by rotating group leaders across groups, rotating trainees across groups, having trainees re-role play a given skill with several different co-actors, having trainees re-role play a given skill across relevant settings, and using multiple homework assignments for each given skill.

Real-life reinforcement. Given successful implementation of both appropriate Structured Learning procedures and the transfer enhancement procedures examined above, positive transfer may still fail to occur. As has been repeatedly shown, stable and enduring performance in application settings of newly learned skills is very much at the mercy of real-life reinforcement contingencies.[28]

We have found it useful to implement several supplemental programs outside the Structured Learning setting which can help to provide the rewards or reinforcements trainees need so that their new behaviors are maintained. These programs include provision for both external social reward (provided by people in the trainee's real-life environment) and self-reward (provided by the trainee himself or herself). In several schools, juvenile detention centers, and other agencies, we have actively sought to identify and develop environmental or external support by holding orientation meetings for staff and for relatives and friends of trainees (i.e., the real-life reward and punishment givers). The purpose of these meetings was to acquaint significant others in the trainees' life with Structured Learning theory, procedures, and skills. Most important in these sessions is the presentation of procedures whereby staff, relatives, and friends can encourage and reward trainees as they practice their new skills. We consider these orientation sessions for such persons to be a major value for transfer of training. Frequently, environmental support is insufficient to maintain newly learned skills. It is also the case that many real-life environments in which trainees work and live will actively resist the trainees' efforts at behavior change. For this reason, we have found it useful to include in our transfer efforts a program of self-reinforcement. Trainees can be instructed in the nature of self-reinforcement and encouraged to "say something and do something nice for yourself" if they practice their new skill well. All of these demonstrated transfer-enhancing techniques, as well as a substantial number of other potentially fruitful techniques, are examined at length in a small number of recent writings devoted to this all-important concern with generalization and endurance of treatment effects.[29]

AGGRESSION-ALTERNATIVE PSYCHOLOGICAL SKILLS

By means of the four procedures just described, we have in a number of investigations taught several aggression-alternative skills to aggressive, disruptive, difficult youngsters in secondary and elementary school settings,[30] as well as in facilities for incarcerated delinquents. The full skill curriculum developed by us for adolescents includes the skills shown in Table 1.

For instructional purposes each of the skills that constitute the curriculum is broken down into a small number of behavioral steps. The steps *are* the skill. They are what the trainers model and what each trainee role plays. Behavioral steps associated with three of the skills in the table are given here as illustrations:

Expressing affection
1. Decide if you have warm, caring feelings about the other person.
2. Decide whether the other person would like to know about your feelings.
3. Decide how you might best express your feelings.

TABLE 1
Aggression-alternative Skills for Adolescents

Group	Skills	Group	Skills
I. Beginning Social Skills	1. Listening 2. Starting a Conversation 3. Having a Conversation 4. Asking a Question 5. Saying Thank You 6. Introducing Yourself 7. Introducing Other People 8. Giving a Compliment	IV. Skill Alternatives to Aggression	22. Asking Permission 23. Sharing Something 24. Helping Others 25. Negotiation 26. Using Self-control 27. Standing Up for Your Rights 28. Responding to Teasing 29. Avoiding Trouble with Others 30. Keeping Out of Fights
II. Advanced Social Skills	9. Asking for Help 10. Joining In 11. Giving Instructions 12. Following Instructions 13. Apologizing 14. Convincing Others	V. Skills for Dealing with Stress	31. Making a Complaint 32. Answering a Complaint 33. Sportsmanship after the Game 34. Dealing with Embarrassment 35. Dealing with Being Left Out 36. Standing Up for a Friend 37. Responding to Persuasion 38. Responding to Failure 39. Dealing with Contradictory Messages 40. Dealing with an Accusation 41. Getting Ready for a Difficult Conversation 42. Dealing with Group Pressure
III. Skills for Dealing with Feelings	15. Knowing Your Feelings 16. Expressing Your Feelings 17. Understanding the Feelings of Others 18. Dealing with Someone Else's Anger 19. Expressing Affection 20. Dealing with Fear 21. Rewarding Yourself	VI. Planning Skills	43. Deciding on Something to Do 44. Deciding What Caused Problem 45. Setting a Goal 46. Deciding on Your Abilities 47. Gathering Information 48. Arranging Problems by Importance 49. Making a Decision 50. Concentrating on a Task

4. Choose the right time and place to express your feelings.
5. Express affection in a warm and caring manner.

Dealing with an accusation
1. Think about what the other person has accused you of (if it is accurate, inaccurate, if it was said in a mean way or in a constructive way).
2. Think about why the person might have accused you (have you infringed on his or her rights or property?).
3. Think about ways to answer the person's accusations (deny, explain your behavior, correct other person's perceptions, assert, apologize, offer to make up for what happened).
4. Choose the best way and do it.

Dealing with group pressures
1. Think about what the other people want you to do and why (listen to other people, decide what the real meaning is, try to understand what is being said).
2. Decide what you want to do (yield, resist, delay, negotiate).
3. Decide how to tell the other people what you want to do (give reasons, talk to one person only, delay, assert).
4. Tell the group what you have decided.

RESEARCH EVALUATION

Starting in 1970, our research group has conducted a systematic research program oriented toward evaluating and improving the effectiveness of Structured Learning. Approximately sixty investigations have involved a wide variety of trainee populations: adult schizophrenics, geriatric patients, child-abusing parents, and such change-agent trainees as mental hospital staff, police, and persons employed in industrial contexts. We have also done studies with young children[31] and in recent years with aggressive and other behaviorally disordered adolescents.[32]

With regard to adolescent trainees, Structured Learning has been successful in enhancing such prosocial skills as empathy, negotiation, assertiveness, following instructions, self-control, and perspective taking. Beyond these straightforward demonstrations that Structured Learning promotes skill acquisition for youngsters, these studies have also highlighted other aspects of the teaching of prosocial behaviors. In an effort to capitalize upon adolescent responsiveness to peer influence, Fleming demonstrated that gains in negotiating skill are as great when the Structured Learning group leader is a respected peer as when the leader is an adult.[33] Litwack, more concerned with the skill-enhancing effects of an adolescent anticipating that he will later serve as a peer leader, showed that such helper role expectation increases the degree of skill acquired.[34] Apparently, when the adolescent expects to teach others a skill, his own level of skill acquisition benefits, a finding clearly relevant to Reissman's helper therapy principle. Trief demonstrated that successful use of Structured Learning to increase perspective-taking skill (i.e., seeing matters from other people's viewpoint) also leads to consequent increases in cooperative behavior.[35] The significant transfer effects both in this study and in other investigations have been important signposts in planning further research on transfer enhancement in Structured Learning.[36]

As in earlier efforts with adult trainees, the value of teaching certain skill combinations has begun to be examined. Aggression-prone adolescents often get into difficulty when they respond with overt aggression to authority figures with whom they disagree. Responding to this type of event, Golden successfully used Structured Learning to teach such youngsters resistance-reducing behavior, defined as a combination of reflection of feeling (the authority figure's) and assertiveness (forthright but nonaggressive statement of one's own position).[37] Jennings was able to use Structured Learning successfully to train adolescents in several of the verbal skills necessary for satisfactory participation in more traditional, insight-oriented psychotherapy.[38] And Guzzetta was successful in providing means to help close the gap between adolescents and their parents by using Structured Learning to teach empathic skills to parents.[39] Investigations conducted by Spatz-Norton and by Zimmerman combined Structured Learning with complementary interventions and demonstrated thereby substantial effects upon adolescent trainee prosocial behaviors beyond that following either intervention employed singly.[40]

The overall conclusions drawn from these several empirical evaluations of our work with adolescent as well as other trainees are twofold.

1. *Skill acquisition.* Across diverse trainee populations (clearly including aggressive adolescents in urban secondary schools and juvenile detention centers, as well as younger children) and target skills, skill acquisition is a reliable training outcome, occurring in well over 90 percent of Structured Learning trainees. While pleased with this outcome, we are acutely aware of the manner in which gains demonstrable in the training context are rather easily accomplished, given the potency, support, encouragement, and low threat value of trainers in this context, but that the more consequential outcome question by far pertains to trainee skill performance in real-world contexts (i.e., skill transfer).

2. *Skill transfer.* Across diverse trainee populations, target skills, and applied (real-world) settings, skill transfer occurs with approximately 45-50 percent of Structured Learning trainees. Studies have indicated that across several dozen types of training and psychotherapy involving many different types of clients, the average transfer rate on follow-up is between 15 percent and 20 percent of clients seen.[41] The 50 percent rate consequent to Structured Learning is a significant improvement upon this collective base rate, though it must immediately be underscored that this cumulative average transfer finding also means that the gains shown by the half of our trainees were limited to in-session acquisition. Of special consequence, however, is the consistently clear manner in which skill transfer in our studies was a function of the explicit implementation of laboratory derived transfer-enhancing techniques, such as those described earlier.

Concurrent with or following our development of the Structured Learning approach to prosocial skills training, similar programs have emerged to enhance skill competency by focusing in large part on prosocial training for aggressive youngsters.[42] The instructional techniques that constitute each of these skills training efforts derive from social learning theory and typically consist of instructions, modeling, role playing, and performance feedback, with ancillary use in some instances of contingent reinforcement, prompting, shaping, or related behavioral techniques.

FUTURE DIRECTIONS

A systems perspective. Our view of prosocial skills training—or any psychoeducational interventions—is that its components optimally will perpetually evolve and never reach a sense of completion or closure. The modest success of skills training with regard to transfer and maintenance effects is sufficient basis for being sharply dissatisfied with its customary operational definition. What profitably might be added to the basic foursome of constituent techniques, and what optimally ought to be deleted? We believe there are two planes along which potentially viable treatment components may be experimentally added and deleted. Horizontal additions and deletions refer to new training components utilized with the trainee himself or herself. We are currently seeking to discern whether the potency of our basic prosocial skills training package (modeling, role playing, performance feedback, transfer training) will be significantly increased if, in addition to direct teaching of prosocial behavior, we simultaneously teach prosocial values (by means of Kohlberg's moral education techniques) and anger inhibitors (by means of relaxation and self-statement disputation training),[43] that is, not only what to do instead of aggression (prosocial values and behaviors), but also how to manage or reduce the underlying anger. These are but mere examples of other existing or to be developed techniques which can be meaningfully tested as possible additions to existing operational definitions of prosocial skills training.

But skills training does not occur in an environmental vacuum. There are always several other players on the stage of interpersonal competency—parents, peers, employers, siblings, friends, teachers, strangers, antagonists. Rather than simply seek to train the main actor—the prosocial skills training trainee—we may also intervene vertically and seek to impact directly on those figures in the trainee's real world whose own behavior may significantly influence the trainee's skill competency. With reference to aggressive adolescents, our recent monograph on school violence presents an example of a systems, ecological, or vertical intervention research strategy.[44] School violence, we held, would yield most fully when, in addition to the several suggested interventions targeted directly to the aggressive youngster, equally energetic attention was directed to the teachers involved; the school administration; the youngster's parents; the school board and other relevant persons in the school community; and even at the broader state and federal levels. We have not yet tested this particular highly comprehensive implementation of a constructive treatment design, but we see it as an extended example of a research strategy that may be particularly fruitful when utilized in a prosocial skills training context.

Prescriptive utilization. The efficacy of prosocial skills training may also be enhanced by adherence, in both its investigation and implementation, to a prescriptive, tailored, or differential ingredients strategy. Here the effort is made to be responsive to trainee channels of accessibility, learning styles, group-relevant behaviors, and personality characteristics when defining the specific training procedures to be used. Prescriptiveness also may be reflected in the spacing, duration, and pacing of the group's sessions; the trainers to be employed; the skills to be taught (their difficulty, sequencing, and relevance to trainee motivation) and other training parameters. In short, prescriptive utilization of prosocial skills training seeks to discern and employ optimal characteristics of the training enterprise *for particular trainees.* This research and practice strategy parallels directly analogous viewpoints productively advanced earlier with regard to education[45] and psychotherapy.[46] There are in particular a number of aspects of prosocial skills training we wish to highlight as especially heuristic targets of this prescriptive viewpoint, i.e., dimensions of the skill training enterprise where individualization may particularly enhance trainee skill competency. All of these suggestions, however, are speculative products of skills training experiences, and are in need of direct empirical scrutiny.

There is, first, the nature of trainees' skill deficiencies. It is not enough to employ multilevel, multimodal deficit assessment techniques (behavioral observation, role play tests, skill inventories, structured interviews) in order to identify reliably the particular skills in which the youngster is deficient.[47] It is also necessary to be prescriptively responsive in our remedial efforts to the fact that there are three different ways in which an individual may be deficient in any given skill. As Ladd and Mize have stated,

First, children may lack knowledge or concepts of appropriate social behaviors . . . or they may possess concepts atypical of their peer group. . . . At least three forms of social knowledge may be represented in a skill concept, each of which is viewed as necessary for effective social functioning: (a) knowledge of appropriate goals for social interaction, (b) knowledge of appropriate strategies for reaching a social goal, and (c) knowledge of the context(s) in which specific strategies may be appropriately applied. . . . Second, children may lack, perhaps as a result of insufficient practice of the skills, actual behavioral abilities. . . . Finally, some children may be deficient in giving themselves feedback about their interpersonal encounters. Specifically, these children may lack the ability (a) to monitor and evaluate their own behavior and its effects on others . . . and (b) to make inferences or attributions about their interpersonal successes and failures that are conducive to continued effort, adaptation, and self-confidence in social interactions.[48]

Selection of target skills might optimally reflect not only such typical parameters as the skill(s) in which the trainee is deficient, the degree of deficiency, and the interpersonal and environmental contexts in which the deficiency manifests itself, but also the particular nature (knowledge, behavior, feedback) of the deficit. To do so has clear and direct implications for the prescriptive specification of just what the trainee is to be taught.

Our decade-long experience with Structured Learning has provided additional leads for studying the prescriptive individualization of the skills training process. In all our investigations we have energetically sought to adapt the four skills training components to the particular receptivity channels and optimal learning styles of the particular trainees involved. Depending in large measure on such trainee qualities, our modeling displays have been either audio, video, or live; role playing has varied in length, simplicity, and repetitiveness; performance feedback has been directive, especially gentle or lengthy; and transfer training has been operationalized as a function of the trainee's available community resources, homework opportunities, and abstraction capacity.

With aggressive adolescents, we have prescriptively evolved toward groups no larger than five or six; briefer initial structuring of group procedures; live modeling by the trainers; use of two or three *different* vignettes when modeling; heightened levels of trainer activity, directiveness, and control; increased use of token or material reinforcers; employment of visual depictions of target skills steps; added reliance on preannounced rules for group management; adolescent-relevant target skills; and adolescent-experienced skill trainers.

There is one additional and perhaps especially important way in which prosocial skills training is optimally employed in a prescriptive manner. The "next generation" of prosocial skills training interventions will, we believe, be offered as part of a larger intervention package into which it is meaningfully integrated. An example of such a multifacetted intervention is our own Aggression Replacement Training in which the Structured Learning approach to skills training (a behavioral intervention) is offered on an extended basis simultaneously with trainee participation in Anger Control Training (an affective intervention) and Moral Education (a cognitive intervention) in a prescriptive effort to remediate the multiple deficits of chronically aggressive, incarcerated adolescents.

Trainee motivation. We believe that prosocial skills training research and practice have not given sufficient attention to the relevance of trainee motivation for skill competency and its development. It is as if, in Hullian terms of several years ago, our focus has been almost exclusively on habit strength at the expense of drive, in a context in which, as Hull amply demonstrated, behavior was a multiplicative function of both.[49] It is important that future investigative efforts in this domain seek to redress this imbalance, and thus examine means for the substantial enhancement of skill competency motivation—a matter very often of special relevance for aggressive adolescents and younger children. In addition to appropriate contingent reinforcement, the value of which is well established in a skills training context, trainee motivation may be enhanced in conjunction with three different events which unfold sequentially during the skills training process: the establishment of the trainer-trainee relationship, the selection of appropriate target skills, and the establishment of certain motivation-relevant group parameters.

Trainer-trainee relationship. It is a truism in such interpersonal influence contexts as psychotherapy, counseling, and education that client or student motivation to do "the work" of the process is in part driven by the steam of a positive relationship with the change agent involved. Ladd and Mize comment in this regard:

As in any pedagogical undertaking, it is likely that the success of a social skill training program also depends on the quality of the relationship established between the child and the instructor. Even the most well-designed and all-inclusive training program may be rendered ineffective if it is conducted in an overtly didactic, mechanical, and uninviting manner. Rarely, however, have previous social skill training investigators alluded to instructor characteristics of the instructor-child relationship as important aspects of the skill training process.[50]

Thus, it might seem, we ought appropriately to conclude, consistent with the prevailing truism for other change endeavors, that a warm, close, personal empathic trainer-trainee relationship may well substantially potentiate aggressive adolescent trainee skill acquisition. But all truisms are not necessarily true, and, in fact, by their very comprehensiveness they deny or minimize the opportunity for a differentiated, prescriptive perspective on such matters. A host of clinicians have speculated that therapeutic progress of diverse sorts with aggressive adolescents would, in fact, be advanced by a very different kind of (especially initial) helper-helpee relationship—one of *low* empathy, high impersonality, and careful avoidance of emotional exploration.[51] Edelman and Goldstein examined this proposition empirically, and indeed found quite substantial support for the prescriptive utility in such pairings of low empathy (plus high genuineness) helper behavior.[52] Thus, we support the generalization that trainee motivation and consequent skill acquisition are likely influenced substantially by the quality of the trainer-trainee relationship. But precisely what kind(s) of relationships are optimal in this context remains very much an open question, with considerable speculation and some beginning evidence combining to point to a type of relationship quite different from that characteristically aspired to in most other change endeavors.

Skill selection. Which skills shall be taught, and who will select them? This is as much a motivational as a tactical question, for to the degree that the youngster is enabled to anticipate learning skill competencies *he* feels he needs, *he* discerns as presently deficient but of likely utility in his real-world relationships, his motivation is correspondingly enhanced. We have operationalized this perspective in our Structured Learning skills training by means of a process we call "negotiating the curriculum." First, we avoid the option of serving as unilateral skill selector for the trainee. In doing so we concur with Schinke, who observes:

Seldom recognized in interpersonal skills training with adolescents is how values influence client referral and problem definition. Decisions about desirable skills are weighted by personal preferences, moral judgments, and ethical constraints.[53]

We similarly avoid the cafeteria-like option of denying the potential value of our skill-relevant expertise and knowledge and laying out the entire skill curriculum and simply asking the trainer to select those he wishes. Either unilateral approach, we feel, is inadequate; the first delimits trainee motivation, the second denies trainer expertise. Instead, we utilize a curriculum selection procedure which allows both parties to participate actively. We begin by having the trainer (if he or she knows the trainee well) and the trainee each independently complete their respective versions of the Structured Learning Skills Inventory.[54] Then much the same as when an academic advisor and a student meet to juxtapose and reconcile their respective tentative course programs for the next semester for the student, the skills trainer and trainee compare, contrast, examine, and select from their Skills Inventories in such a manner that trainer beliefs about what the trainee needs, and trainee beliefs about his or her own deficiencies and desired competencies are mutually reflected. We feel this procedure is motivation-enhancing. Whether it in fact serves this important function is indeed a question worth careful examination.

Group procedures. Our concern above in optimizing trainee participation in the skill selection process is an example of seeking to enhance the trainee's task-associated intrinsic motivation. But extrinsic task characteristics may also profitably be mobilized toward the goal of maximizing inducements for active, on-task trainee participation. While we as yet have little empirical evidence in support of the group procedure recommendations we are about to make, they indeed appear to us to be reliable extrinsic means for enhancing trainee motivation. Where are the group sessions held? In most schools and institutions we try to seek a special place, associated in the trainee's thinking with particular privileges or opportunities (e.g., teacher's lounge, student center, recreation area), and yet not a place so removed in its characteristics from the typical skill application settings in which trainees function as to reduce the likelihood of skill transfer. When will the group meet? If it is not judged to be too great an academic sacrifice, we attempt to schedule skills training sessions when what the youngsters will have to miss in order to attend the sessions is an activity they do not especially enjoy (including certain academic subjects), rather than free play, lunch, gym, or the like. Who will lead the group? For our initial, program-initiating groups in particular, we seek to utilize as trainers those teachers, cottage parents, members of the institutional staff, or others we deem to be most stimulating, most tuned to the needs and behaviors of aggressive adolescents (but not the most overtly empathic, for reasons described earlier), and in general most able to capture and hold the attention of participating youngsters. Since the impact of the initial meeting(s) of the initial group bears upon not only the motivation and performance of trainees in *that* group, but also rapidly through the school's or institution's grapevine, upon the interest, motivation, and eventually, performance of youngsters who constitute subsequently formed groups, the group leadership skills of the first trainers employed can have far-reaching motivational consequences. Which skill shall be taught first? This is a crucial decision, one of special relevance to trainee motivation. In addition to reflecting the give and take of the negotiated skill curriculum, the first skill taught is optimally one very likely to yield immediate, real-world reward for the trainee. It must "work"; it must pay off. While some trainers prefer to begin with the simpler conversation skills, as a sort of warm up or break in, our preference is to try to respond to both simplicity and reward potential. The "felt need" of the trainee for the near-future value of a given skill, therefore, weighs especially heavily in our initial skill selection decisions.

The last two decades have seen the initiation and growth of a new movement in contemporary education and psychology—prosocial skills training. The present chapter has examined the roots of this movement, and the development of one of its concrete expressions, our Structured Learning approach. By means of Structured Learning, and related techniques, chronically aggressive adolescents and younger children are reliably being taught prosocial alternative behaviors and, to a growing degree, are able to transfer and maintain such newly learned skills in real-world settings. Prosocial skills training is a healthy movement, soundly based in empirical research, and pragmatically offering much to the educator striving to deal constructively with chronically aggressive students.

Footnotes

1. Alfred Bloch, "The Battered Teacher," *Today's Education* 66 (1977): 58-62.

2. M. Joan McDermott, *Criminal Victimization in Urban Schools* (Albany, NY: Criminal Justice Research Center, 1979).

3. Arnold P. Goldstein, Steven J. Apter, and Berj Harootunian, *School Violence* (Englewood Cliffs, NJ: Prentice-Hall, 1984).

4. R. J. Rubel, *Unruly School: Disorders, Disruptions, and Crime* (Lexington, MA: D. C. Heath, 1977).

5. Goldstein, Apter, and Harootunian, *School Violence*, p. 5.

6. C. M. Charles, *Building Classroom Discipline* (New York: Longman, 1984); Edmund T. Emmer, Carolyn M. Evertson, J. P. Sanford, B. S. Clements, and M. E. Worsham, *Classroom Management for Secondary Teachers* (Englewood Cliffs, NJ: Prentice-Hall, 1984); Carolyn M. Evertson, Edmund T. Emmer, B. S. Clements, J. P. Sanford, and M. E. Worsham *Classroom Management for Elementary Teachers* (Englewood Cliffs, NJ: Prentice-Hall, 1984); Wilford A. Weber, John Crawford, Linda A. Roff, and Catherine Robinson, *Classroom Management* (Princeton, NJ: Educational Testing Service, 1983).

7. Weber et al., *Classroom Management*.

8. Mary A. White, "Natural Rates of Teacher Approval and Disapproval in the Classroom," *Journal of Applied Behavior Analysis* 8 (1975): 367-72.

9. John D. Thomas, Ian E. Presland, M. Dilys Grant, and Ted L. Glynn, "Natural Rates of Teacher Approval and Disapproval in Grade 7 Classrooms," *Journal of Applied Behavior Analysis* 11 (1978): 91-94.

10. Saul Axelrod and Jack Apsche, *The Effects of Punishment on Human Behavior* (New York: Academic Press, 1983); Ron Van Houten, Paul A. Nau, Sandra MacKenzie-Keating, Dorothy Sameoto, and Betty Colavecchia, "An Analysis of Some Variables Influencing the Effectiveness of Reprimands," *Journal of Applied Behavior Analysis* 15 (1982): 65-83.

11. Arnold P. Goldstein and Harold Keller, *Aggressive Behavior: Assessment and Intervention* (New York: Pergamon Press, 1987).

12. See, for example, Clive Beck, *Moral Education in the Schools: Some Practical Suggestions* (Toronto: Ontario Institute for Studies in Education, 1971); Peter McPhail, J. R. Ungoed-Thomas, and Hilary Chapman, *Learning to Care: Rationale and Method of the Lifeline Program* (Niles, IL: Argus Communications, 1975); Fred Newmann and Donald Oliver, *Clarifying Public Issues: An Approach to Teaching Social Studies* (Boston: Little, Brown, 1970); John Wilson, *Practical Methods of Moral Education* (London: Heinemann Educational Books, 1972); William Glasser, *Schools without Failure* (New York: Harper and Row, 1969); Gerald Weinstein and Mario Fantini, *Toward Humanistic Education: A Curriculum of Affect* (New York: Praeger, 1970).

13. Albert Bandura, *Aggression: A Social Learning Analysis* (Englewood Cliffs, NJ: Prentice-Hall, 1981), p. 253.

14. Arnold P. Goldstein, *Psychological Skill Training* (New York: Pergamon Press, 1981), p. 16.

15. Ibid.

16. Arnold P. Goldstein, Robert P. Sprafkin, and N. Jane Gershaw, *Skill Training for Community Living: Applying Structured Learning Therapy* (New York: Pergamon Press, 1976).

17. Ellen McGinnis and Arnold P. Goldstein, *Skillstreaming the Elementary School Child* (Champaign, IL: Research Press, 1984).

18. Barbara J. Freedman, Lisa Rosenthal, Clyde P. Donahoe, Jr., David G. Schlundt, and Richard M. McFall, "A Social-Behavioral Analysis of Skill Deficits in Delinquent and Nondelinquent Adolescent Boys," *Journal of Consulting and Clinical Psychology* 46 (1978): 1448-62.

19. Susan H. Spence, "Differences in Social Performance between Institutionalized Juvenile Male Offenders and a Comparable Group of Boys without Offense Records," *British Journal of Clinical Psychology* 20 (1981): 163-71.

20. John J. Conger, Wilbur C. Miller, and Charles R. Walsmith, "Antecedents of Delinquency, Personality, Social Class, and Intelligence," in *Readings in Child Development and Personality*, ed. Paul H. Mussen, John J. Conger, and Jerome Kagan (New York: Harper and Row, 1965), p. 442.

21. Gerald R. Patterson, John B. Reid, R. R. Jones, and R. E. Conger, *A Social Learning Approach to Family Intervention* (Eugene, OR: Castalia Publishing Co., 1975), p. 4.

22. Paul H. Mussen, John J. Conger, Jerome Kagan, and James Geiwitz, *Psychological Development: A Life-Span Approach* (New York: Harper and Row, 1979).

23. See, for example, Arnold P. Goldstein, Robert P. Sprafkin, N. Jane Gershaw, and P. Klein, *Skillstreaming the Adolescent* (Urbana, IL: Research Press, 1980); Thomas M. Stephens, *Social Skills in the Classroom* (Columbus, OH: Cedar Press, 1978); Hill Walker, Scott McConnell, D. Holmes, Bonnie Todis, J. Walker, and N. Golden, *The Walker Social Skills Curriculum* (Austin, TX: Pro-Ed, 1983); Herbert C. Gunzburg, *Progress Assessment Chart of Social Competence* (London: SEFA Publications, 1980); M. Kohn, B. Parnes, and B. L. Rosman, *Kohn Social Competence Scale* (New York: Martin Kohn Publisher, 1979); Johnny Matson, Karen Esveldt-Dawson, and Alan E. Kazdin, "Validation of Methods for Assessing Social Skills in Children," *Journal of Clinical Child Psychology* 12 (1983): 174-80.

24. Bandura, *Aggression: A Social Learning Analysis.*

25. Edward L. Thorndike and Robert S. Woodworth, "The Influence of Improvement in One Mental Function upon the Efficiency of Other Functions," *Psychological Review* 8 (1901): 247-61.

26. Henry Ellis, *The Transfer of Learning* (New York: Macmillan, 1965); Charles E. Osgood, *Method and Theory in Experimental Psychology* (New York: Oxford University Press, 1953).

27. See, for example, Mary F. Callantine and J. M. Warren, "Learning Sets in Human Concept Formation," *Psychological Reports* 1 (1955): 363-67; Carl P. Duncan, "Transfer after Training with Single versus Multiple Tasks," *Journal of Experimental Psychology* 55 (1958): 63-72; Eugene Shore and Lee Sechrest, "Concept Attainment as a Function of Number of Positive Instances Presented," *Journal of Educational Psychology* 52 (1961): 303-7.

28. See, for example, W. Stewart Agras, "Behavior Therapy in the Management of Chronic Schizophrenia," *American Journal of Psychiatry* 124 (1967): 240-43; Ronald P.

Gruber, "Behavior Therapy: Problems in Generalization," *Behavior Therapy* 2 (1971): 361-68; Roland G. Tharp and Ralph Wetzel, *Behavior Modification in the Natural Environment* (New York: Academic Press, 1969).

29. S. Epps, B. J. Thompson, and M. P. Lane, "Procedures for Incorporating Generalization Programming into Interventions for Behaviorally Disordered Students" (Ames, IA: Unpublished manuscript, 1985); J. P. Galassi and M. D. Galassi, "Promoting Transfer and Maintenance of Counseling Outcomes," in *Handbook of Counselling Psychology*, ed. Steven D. Brown and Robert W. Lent (New York: Wiley, 1984); Arnold P. Goldstein and Frederick Kanfer, *Maximizing Treatment Effects* (New York: Academic Press, 1979); Goldstein and Keller, *Aggressive Behavior*; Paul Karoly and John J. Steffan, *Improving the Long-term Effects of Psychotherapy* (New York: Guilford Press, 1980).

30. Goldstein et al., *Skillstreaming the Adolescent*; McGinnis and Goldstein, *Skillstreaming the Elementary School Child*.

31. Jeffrey W. Hummel, "Teaching Preadolescents Alternatives to Aggression Using Structured Learning Training under Different Stimulus Conditions" (Doct. diss., Syracuse University, 1980); Carl R. Swanstrom, "An Examination of Structured Learning Therapy and the Helper Therapy Principle in Teaching a Self-Control Strategy in School Children with Conduct Problems" (Doct. diss., Syracuse University, 1978).

32. See, for example, Arnold P. Goldstein et al., *Skillstreaming the Adolescent*; Arnold P. Goldstein, B. Glick, S. Reiner, D. Zimmerman, T. Coultry, and D. Gold, "Aggression Replacement Training: A Comprehensive Intervention for Juvenile Delinquents." *Journal of Correctional Education* 37 (1985): 120-26.

33. Donald Fleming, "Teaching Negotiation Skills to Preadolescents" (Doct. diss., Syracuse University, 1976).

34. Stephen E. Litwack, "The Helper Therapy Principle as a Therapeutic Tool: Structured Learning Therapy with Adolescents" (Doct. diss., Syracuse University, 1976).

35. P. Trief, "The Reduction of Egocentrism in Acting-out Adolescents by Structured Learning Therapy" (Doct. diss., Syracuse University, 1976).

36. See, for example, R. Golden, "Teaching Resistance-Reducing Behavior to High School Students" (Doct. diss., Syracuse University, 1975); Litwack, "The Helper Therapy Principle as a Therapeutic Tool"; R. Raleigh, "Individual vs. Group-Structured Learning Therapy for Assertiveness Training with Senior and Junior High School Students" (Doct. diss., Syracuse University, 1977).

37. Golden, "Teaching Resistance-Reducing Behavior to High School Students."

38. Rick L. Jennings, "The Use of Structured Learning Techniques to Teach Attraction-Enhancing Interviewee Skills to Residentially Hospitalized, Lower Socioeconomic, Emotionally Disturbed Children and Adolescents: A Psychotherapy Analogue Investigation" (Doct. diss., Syracuse University, 1975).

39. Roberta A. Guzzetta, "Acquisition and Transfer of Empathy by the Parents of Early Adolescents through Structured Learning Training" (Doct. diss., Syracuse University, 1974).

40. C. Spatz-Norton, "The Effect of Self-Statements and Structured Learning Training of Empathy upon Aggressive Behavior and Prosocial Conflict Resolution in Aggressive Elementary School Aged Males" (Master's thesis, Syracuse University, 1984); D. Zimmerman, "Enhancing Perspective-Taking and Moral Reasoning via Structured Learning Therapy and Moral Education with Aggressive Adolescents" (Master's thesis, Syracuse University, 1984).

41. Arnold P. Goldstein and Frederick Kanfer, *Maximizing Treatment Effects* (New York: Academic Press, 1979); Karoly and Steffan, *Improving the Long-term Effects of Psychotherapy.*

42. See, for example, Winthrop R. Adkins, "Life Skills: Structured Counseling for the Disadvantaged," *Personnel and Guidance Journal* 49 (1970): 108-16; idem, "Life Coping Skills: A Fifth Curriculum," *Teachers College Record* 75 (1974): 507-26; Michael Argyle, Peter Trower, and Bridget Bryant, "Explorations in the Treatment of Personality Disorders and Neuroses by Social Skill Training," *British Journal of Medical Psychology* 47 (1974): 63-72; P. Elardo and M. Cooper, *AWARE: Activities for Social Development* (Reading, MA: Addison-Wesley, 1977); Bernard G. Guerney, Jr., *Relationship Enhancement* (San Francisco: Jossey-Bass, 1977); M. A. Hare, "Teaching Conflict Resolution Situation" (Paper presented at the meeting of the Eastern Community Association, Philadelphia, 1976); Robert C. Hawley and Isabel Hawley, *Developing Human Potential: A Handbook of Activities for Personal and Social Growth* (Amherst, MA: Education Research Associates, 1975); J. S. Hazel, J. B. Schumaker, J. A. Sherman, and J. Sheldon-Wildgen, *ASSET: A Social Skills Program for Adolescents* (Champaign, IL: Research Press, 1981); H. Heiman, "Teaching Interpersonal Communications," *North Dakota Speech and Theater Association Bulletin* 2 (1973): 7-29; Thomas M. Stephens, *Social Skills in the Classroom* (Columbus, OH: Cedars Press, 1978).

43. Goldstein et al., "Aggression Replacement Training"; Spatz-Norton, "The Effect of Self-Statements and Structured Learning Training of Empathy upon Aggressive Behavior and Prosocial Conflict Resolution in Aggressive Elementary School Aged Males"; Zimmerman, "Enhancing Perspective Taking and Moral Reasoning via Structured Learning Therapy and Moral Education with Aggressive Adolescents."

44. Goldstein, Apter, and Harootunian, *School Violence.*

45. Lee J. Cronbach, "How Can Instruction Be Adapted to Individual Differences?" in *Learning and Individual Differences*, ed. R. M. Gagné (Columbus, OH: Charles C. Merrill, 1967); Berj Harootunian, "Teacher Training," in *Prescriptions for Child Mental Health and Education*, ed. Arnold P. Goldstein (New York: Pergamon Press, 1978); David E. Hunt, "Matching Models for Teacher Training," in *Perspectives for Reform in Teacher Education* (Englewood Cliffs, NJ: Prentice-Hall, 1972); George G. Stern, *People in Context* (New York: Wiley, 1970).

46. Goldstein, ed. *Prescriptions for Child Mental Health and Education*; Arnold P. Goldstein and Norman Stein, *Prescriptive Psychotherapies* (New York: Pergamon Press, 1976); Peter A. Magaro, "A Prescriptive Treatment Model Based upon Social Class and Premorbid Adjustment," *Psychotherapy: Theory, Research, and Practice* 6 (1969): 57-60.

47. Alan S. Bellack, "Behavioral Assessment of Social Skills," in *Research and Practice in Social Skills Training*, ed. Alan S. Bellack and Michel Hersen (New York: Plenum, 1979); Larry Michelson and Randy Wood, "Behavioral Assessment and Training of Children's Social Skills," *Progress in Behavior Modification* 9 (1980): 241-291.

48. Gary Ladd and Jacquelyn Mize, "A Cognitive-Social Learning Model of Social Skill Training," *Psychological Review* 90 (1983): 129-30.

49. Clark Hull, *Principles of Behavior* (New York: Appleton-Century-Crofts, 1943).

50. Ladd and Mize, "A Cognitive-Social Learning Model of Social Skill Training," p. 153.

51. Sidney I. Dean, "Treatment of the Reluctant Client," *American Psychologist* 13 (1958): 627-30; Arnold P. Goldstein, Kenneth Heller, and Lee B. Sechrest,

Psychotherapy and the Psychology of Behavior Change (New York: Wiley 1966); Fritz Redl and David Wineman, *The Aggressive Child* (New York: Free Press, 1957); Robert L. Schwitzgebel, "Short-term Operant Conditioning of Adolescent Offenders on Socially Relevant Variables," *Journal of Abnormal Psychology* 72 (1967): 134-42; Charles W. Slack, "Experimenter-Subject Psychotherapy: A New Method of Introducing Intensive Office Treatment for Unreachable Cases," *Mental Hygiene* 44 (1960): 238-56.

52. Eric Edelman and Arnold P. Goldstein, "Prescriptive Relationship Levels for Juvenile Delinquents in a Psychotherapy Analog," *Aggressive Behavior* 10 (1984): 269-78.

53. Steven P. Schinke, "Interpersonal Skills Training with Adolescents," in *Progress in Behavior Modification*, vol. 11, ed. Michel Hersen and Alan S. Bellack (New York: Academic Press, 1981), p. 81.

54. Goldstein et al., *Skillstreaming the Adolescent*.

CHAPTER VIII

Classroom Organization for Diversity among Students

SUSAN B. STAINBACK AND WILLIAM C. STAINBACK

One of the most widely studied and most controversial issues in classroom organization is the question of whether homogeneous or heterogeneous ability grouping is most beneficial for students. This issue cuts across the current literature in both special and regular education, affecting students considered normal as well as those labeled "disabled."

It has been estimated that homogeneous between-class ability grouping is used in over 75 percent of the schools in the United States.[1] Two of the primary assumptions on which homogeneous ability grouping is based are (a) that students achieve more when grouped with peers of similar academic ability, and (b) that students of lower ability will develop a more positive self-concept because they do not have to compete with brighter students for recognition.[2] These two assumptions have been the target of investigations for more than half a century.

The Evidence from Research

Student achievement. There is widespread allegiance to the practice of homogeneous grouping. Yet, as noted by Slavin, "almost without exception [research reviews] from the 1920s to the present have come to the same general conclusion: that between-class ability grouping has few if any benefits for student achievement."[3] Although the studies in these reviews involved primarily homogeneous class arrangements in regular rather than in special education, the findings have considerable implication for the viability of homogeneous grouping of lower-ability students in special education classes and programs.

In a meta-analysis of the literature on homogeneous grouping in special education classes, Carlberg and Kavale found that students in mild disability categories had higher achievement when not placed in special homogeneous classrooms, and that the negative effect of placement in special classes was particularly pronounced for slow learners.[4] In a review of special class homogeneous placements on the basis of ability, Madden and Slavin, like Carlberg and Kavale, found support for placing slow learners and mildly handicapped students in regular classes.[5]

We are concerned here with between-class ability grouping as an issue of classroom organization. While the vast majority of research studies and reviews of research do not support achievement benefits of between-class homogeneous grouping, there are exceptions. A few studies and reviews of research in both special and regular education support the claim of increased student achievement in homogeneously grouped classes.[6] As pointed out by Madden and Slavin in their review of such investigations, the difference in the findings may be due to the way the researchers organized and conducted their studies and reviews, especially in those studies dealing with special education.[7] For example, it appears that when researchers compared well-organized heterogeneous regular education classrooms (where individualized, cooperative, and adaptive learning programs were used) with homogeneously organized special education classes, their findings were nearly always in favor of the heterogeneous regular class arrangements. However, when heterogeneous regular class arrangements were compared to homogeneous special class arrangements with little or no attention to what actually happened in the classrooms, the results were generally mixed and contradictory.

Self-concept. The assumption that a higher self-concept is held by students with low ability when placed in classes with peers of similar ability has been used as a justification for homogeneous ability-grouped classes. However, in a recent review of the research, Dawson concluded: "The preponderance of the research fails to support this prediction."[8]

Kulik found positive effects on self-esteem when considering three studies of slow learners who were placed in remedial programs.[9] However, this finding was in direct conflict with a more comprehensive meta-analysis of fifty studies in which slow learners were placed in segregated homogeneously grouped special and remedial classrooms. In this more comprehensive study, Carlberg and Kavale found that slow learners in homogeneously grouped special classes performed significantly more poorly on social and personality measures than did slow learners in heterogeneous regular classes.[10]

Oakes found that students homogeneously grouped into low tracks in secondary schools had poor attitudes about themselves, while heterogeneously grouped class members had mixed attitudes toward themselves.[11] In another study, Mann found that students in low-ability classes gave only negative answers about themselves when asked why they were in a low-ability class.[12] The perception of an adolescent student moved from a heterogeneous elementary class group to a homogeneously grouped "low track" when entering junior high was captured by Schafer and Olexa:

I felt good when I was with my [elementary] class, but when they went and separated us that changed us. That changed our ideas, the way we thought about each other, and turned us to enemies toward each other because they said I was dumb and they were smart.[13]

In general, the idea that improved self-concept results from placing students who have learning difficulties with other low-ability peers has not been substantiated by research.

Recent national reports addressing the issue of ability grouping in classrooms also have not supported the common practice of homogeneous placement of students. The National Coalition of Advocates for Students concluded that the benefits of homogeneous grouping are questionable.[14] Goodlad's report on his "Study of Schooling" concluded that not only is homogeneity (interclass grouping) not advantageous for bright students but may also result in significant achievement loss of the slowest students: "The continuation of this folly [homogencous class grouping] tempts me to urge its mandatory abolition so that ill-informed people will be forced to refrain from its use."[15]

It should be noted that the research and national reports to date have focused primarily on students classified as "low ability," "slow learning," or "mildly handicapped." Few, if any studies have focused on the issue of heterogeneous versus homogeneous grouping for students classified as "severely retarded" or "multiply handicapped." Heterogeneous regular class placement for such students has only recently begun and is not yet widespread. There is, however, increasing evidence that even students with very severe handicaps can benefit from placement in regular classrooms.[16]

Finally, there is a small but growing number of professionals who argue that whether we group students homogeneously or heterogeneously is fundamentally not a research issue.[17] It is a much larger issue related to the kind of society we want to support. If we want to foster an integrated society, then students need to be integrated throughout their school years in order to provide opportunities to learn how to accept each other and live together in positive and productive ways. We need integrated schools where students of different abilities, disabilities, and racial and socioeconomic backgrounds can learn and play side by side. The issue for these professionals is not whether heterogeneous or homogeneous grouping is best, but rather how heterogeneous classrooms can be made to work to the advantage of all students in their academic, social, and emotional development.

Classroom Organization to Accommodate Diversity

We now turn to a consideration of organizational procedures that can be used to accommodate the diversity among students in heterogeneously organized classes. A number of "best practices" have begun to emerge as ways of addressing the needs of a diverse student group. The procedures we discuss here are focused on meeting the full range of differences present in a class. They are not only procedures for students considered "disabled." Instead, it is recognized that every student, regardless of label or assignment to a categorical group, is unique and worthy of individual consideration with regard to his or her educational needs.

1. *Recognizing students according to their interest, needs, and abilities.* Within public schools today most recognition is "norm-referenced," based on competition and comparisons with a peer group.[18] Recognition is given to those students who excel in performance in relation to their classmates. Positive attention and recognition is generally given for such accomplishments as writing the best poem, getting the highest score, winning a game, or ranking in the highest percentile on a standardized test.

In a heterogeneous class structure the use of such student recognition is questionable. Because of the diversity in characteristics, skills, and uniqueness among class members, each student can draw upon a different set of resources for the competition. These underlying differences can make competition with peers for recognition futile for some students, regardless of the effort expended, while other students require minimal effort to receive recognition. Unfortunately, recognition and success based on competition with peers can result in decreased motivation and even a negative attitude toward learning and achievement for many students. In a heterogeneous class the emphasis should be on motivating students to compete against their own highest level of achievement rather than against the achievements or performance of others who have a different set of potential resources from which to draw.[19]

We do not intend to imply that all forms of competition between peers are inappropriate. Much of the enjoyment in some school activities is based on competition. However, in heterogeneous classrooms competition that allows every student an opportunity to be considered a worthwhile player should be encouraged, and the evaluation of success should be based on the individual resources of each participant.

2. *Fostering student interdependence.* In heterogeneous classrooms, individual students and small groups of students are often called upon to function without continuous direct teacher guidance. Fostering interdependence can help in the development of natural networks of support that enable students to function without direct teacher guidance.[20]

Natural networks of support can be facilitated by encouraging students to share with each other and to teach each other through various cooperative learning activities, buddy systems, tutoring programs, and through natural and informal friendships. When natural networks of support develop, students learn to meet the needs of one another naturally without teacher intervention. For example, a student who has a mobility problem may receive peer assistance in getting out of the building when the fire alarm rings, and in turn may provide comfort to a classmate confused or upset by the alarm. Everyone requires some type of support in certain situations and likewise everyone can provide some type of support to others. To help heterogeneously organized classrooms function smoothly and to foster good citizenship we need to encourage students to recognize the needs of others and to support each other when necessary.

3. *Integrating support services.* Without the assistance of support staff, teachers often cannot deal with the diversity of needs exhibited in a heterogeneous group of students. Traditionally, specialized support staff (e.g., school psychologists, physical therapists, occupational therapists, speech correctionists, and experts in reading, learning, and behavior) have concentrated their time on direct service to students. Students needing assistance are taken to an isolated section of the classroom to engage in intensive one-to-one or small-group activities. The resource room to which students with learning or behavior difficulties are frequently taken for specialized help is a common example.

Due to a growing recognition of its inefficiency and ineffectiveness, there has recently been a shift away from this isolated service model and toward a more integrated service model.[21] In this integrated model, the specialist works with students in the natural and integrated setting (the regular classroom) in which students are typically involved and where there are people with whom they are naturally associated. This arrangement increases the chances that what is being taught can become an integral part of the students' daily curriculum and activities, which can in turn help the generalization and maintenance of the skills being learned.

In the integrated school program, the specialist provides a model for and teaches the individual student as well as modeling for and teaching the student's teacher and peers, thus increasing the number of individuals who can provide cues and assistance to the student. The experiences needed by the student can be fostered not only by specialized personnel at direct service times but also by others with whom the student is in contact throughout the day. An important ancillary benefit is that teachers and peers learn skills they can use with other students and friends who need the kind of assistance being provided.

In an integrated model the focus of services also requires consideration. In addition to focusing on individual students who require their services, the specialists can also assist the teacher in adapting classroom procedures and activities so as to be responsive to the varied individual interests, needs, and capabilities of all class members. Whether singled out for specialized services or not, all students benefit when more instructional time of teachers and specialists is available.

A word of caution about the integrated support services model is necessary. When specialists work directly with a student having learning and behavior difficulties in regular classrooms, they need to be careful not to embarrass or draw undue attention to particular students and their difficulties. Some students are very sensitive to having a specialist work with them in front of their classmates, especially if the specialist is identified as a "special" educator with expertise in helping students who are "disturbed," "disordered," or "retarded." This problem can generally be avoided if the specialist (a) is identified as an expert in an instructional area (e.g., individualization of instruction, reading, mathematics, community-referenced instruction) and (b) is available to help any students needing assistance rather than only students with a specific label.

4. *Locating instructional and related activities in normal settings for all students.* To maintain heterogeneous classroom arrangements, no classroom or school location should be reserved for special groups of students. For instance, certain areas should not be utilized so as to become associated with student subgroups (e.g., the left back corner of the room for students who cannot read, the left wing of the building for students with handicaps, the outer play field for behaviorally disordered students, or the room behind the stage for activities for gifted students).

If certain classroom spaces or school locations are reserved for specific activities, the locations should be associated with the instructional focus or function for which they are used.[22] In most cases it is more normalized, more functional, and less stigmatizing to students to refer to locations according to their instructional focus or function rather than to associate those locations with categories of students such as the "retarded."

Another location concern is that students who require the expertise of specialized support personnel should receive such assistance in the natural classroom environment whenever possible.[23] Pulling students out of their classrooms and away from their peers can cause undue attention to them and can disrupt their education. Reynolds and Wang have used the term "disjointed incrementalism" to refer to the discontinuities or interruptions that occur when students are pulled from regular classrooms to travel to and from various locations for specialized services.[24] Furthermore, when specialized services occur in the classroom, teachers, aides, peers, and others can become involved in ensuring that the instructional programming or related services are carried out as an integral part of a student's education throughout the school day rather than only when the student is taken to "special" and often nonnormalized locations.

5. *Using large and small groups for most activities.* In order to meet the individual needs of students in heterogeneous classrooms, individual one-to-one teaching and individual learning activities may *not* always be the most efficient or most effective approaches. There are advantages to teaching students in groups.[25] Individual (i.e., single student) activities reduce the overall amount of teacher-student interaction possible, deny students opportunities for peer modeling and skill sharing, and decrease opportunities for socialization, cooperation, and communication. While individual teaching or work may be necessary for any student at certain times and for certain

activities, properly organized group activities can be highly effective in fostering achievement of unique learning goals of students.

While many types of heterogeneous within-class grouping practices can be effective,[26] the selection of any specific grouping arrangement is influenced by the goal(s) to be achieved, the type of activity involved, and the characteristics of the students. Within-class heterogeneous grouping allows for shared responsibility among students and makes it possible for peers to learn from and help each other. By offsetting the stereotyping and stigmatization that often result when students are associated with a particular ability, disability, or achievement group, heterogeneous group structuring can promote better understanding of individual differences and similarities among all students.

In structuring within-class heterogeneous group activities, both the group activity and the goal must be selected so as to allow all students to function as contributing members of the group while fostering their individualized learning objectives.[27] Every student should be given the opportunity to be challenged and to be successful within the group structure if learning and positive peer interactions and attitudes are to be facilitated. Heterogeneous group activities must be of sufficient complexity to have components that each group member can use as a source of learning and contributions.[28]

Caution is advised in deciding who can successfully participate in such group activities. Unfortunately, we sometimes determine that an activity is too complex or difficult for some students when it really is not.[29] Often the problem arises from our inability to adapt the activity, for example, by adding easier and smaller components so that all students can participate successfully and by providing the assistance necessary for them to participate to the fullest extent possible. Students are sometimes excluded unnecessarily or are excused from numerous group activities because it is believed they could not perform "adequately." With careful planning, most if not all students can participate to some extent in group activities that might at first glance appear to be too complex or difficult for them. The exact opposite is true in some cases, for some students are not challenged enough in traditional group projects. It is just as important for group activities to be challenging for students who learn rapidly as it is to accommodate students who learn at a slow pace. Such challenges can be arranged by adding more difficult steps or activities to the group project.

The type of group structure to be used is also important to

consider. Some researchers recommend that group activities should be cooperative in nature to promote positive peer interaction, understanding, and camaraderie along with individualized success.[30] Cooperative group structuring involves assigning the group a common goal that requires participating students to coordinate their skills and efforts to achieve a goal such as the construction of a map of the United States. Cooperative learning can bring students of various achievement and intellectual levels together while allowing each student to work at his or her own individual level and pace. Positive interaction and enhanced achievement are obtained since, if the group goal is to be reached, all students must coordinate their efforts to that end. On the other hand, when students are instructed to work alone with the purpose of outperforming their peers (competition) or meeting a set criterion (individualistic learning), the initial tendency toward the rejection of some students, particularly those who have difficulties in learning, is perpetuated and increased.

While heterogeneous grouping should be used whenever possible, homogeneous grouping based on instructional content, ability, achievement, interest, or other criteria may be appropriate and useful in some cases.[31] Certain curricular activities, particularly in an area such as mathematics, are based on an understanding of a rigorous, systematic, internal organization of facts and concepts that requires a background of experiences and skills to relate to the information presented. In such cases, within-class homogeneous grouping of students according to achievement level may be beneficial. Also, individual teaching or learning activities may at times be needed and appropriate. However, such approaches are often vastly overutilized. In most instances, students can be successful and derive major benefits when heterogeneous within-class grouping is used.

6. *Organizing classrooms physically to accommodate various teaching and learning approaches.* To accommodate students with diverse needs, heterogeneously organized classrooms must be arranged so that a variety of instructional activities can easily be used.[32] If a classroom can only accommodate one type of instructional format (e.g., the lecture), it is usually not very conducive to meeting diverse learning needs and styles. Classrooms can be more accommodating when they are arranged to permit individualized and small-group activities, noisy and quiet activities, and various types of lectures, film presentations, and discussion. Successful heterogeneous classrooms therefore often have furniture that can easily be arranged in different ways, carpeted and uncarpeted floor space, and areas that can be opened up, closed in,

or screened off depending on the needs of the students when working on different tasks.

7. *Arranging for access to a variety of materials and equipment.* Materials such as worksheets, books, charts, and displays of varying instructional levels, print size, vocabulary difficulty, complexity, and age appropriateness may be needed to meet the instructional needs of a heterogeneous student group.[33] For example, large print materials may be useful for students who are visually impaired or who are beginning readers. Some students, including those who are distractable, may need worksheets in mathematics with only one or a few problems per sheet or worksheets with heavy black lines drawn around the problems on which they are to concentrate. Instructional equipment such as braille or standard typewriters, tape recorders, and various types of computers may be useful in the heterogeneously organized classroom. An audio converter computer may be used to translate verbal directions to written form for hearing-impaired students, may provide immediate feedback and reinforcement for students who require immediate gratification to remain motivated, may be used to clarify the function and importance of the written word to the beginning reader, or may provide needed support to the dependent learner.

8. *Arranging class schedules according to student needs and the involvement of specialized instructional staff.* Variation among students in a heterogeneously organized classroom will influence scheduling. Some students may be able to complete assignments easily and quickly. The teacher will need to schedule other challenging activities to provide them opportunity to fulfill their potential to the greatest extent possible. Other students may require longer periods of study because they work at a slower pace or because they are unable to concentrate on a task for an extended period. However, it is important also to assist students to modify their learning characteristics if possible. For example, for students who work slowly or have difficulty concentrating, the teacher may want to reduce gradually the length of some work sessions while at the same time instructing the students in various techniques to improve speed and concentration.

The availability and involvement of specialized instructional staff also influence the development of the classroom schedule. For example, specialized staff are considered most effective when they are associated with and facilitate normally scheduled class activities.[34] A reading specialist would likely best be scheduled during reading activities, a physical therapist during physical education, and a speech therapist or a speechreading specialist during activities involving oral communication skills. In this way, specialized staff can work within normal classroom activities that are related to their areas of expertise to help any students who need special assistance and to assist the classroom teacher in making the entire structure of the classroom more flexible and accommodating in regard to their specialty area.

While research on homogeneous versus heterogeneous grouping tends to indicate that best classroom organization practices would involve assigning students to heterogeneously grouped classrooms, the rationale for such a recommendation goes far beyond the findings of individual research studies. As noted by Slavin, heterogeneous class grouping is desirable "even if for no other reason than that separating students by ability goes against the grain of our democratic, egalitarian ideals."[35]

However, simply placing students in heterogeneous class arrangements is not enough. Within these classes all students, disabled or nondisabled, should be provided educational programs geared to their unique interests, needs, and capabilities, and challenged to be the best they can be. In order to accomplish this purpose, the most effective instructional practices for dealing with student diversity in a classroom must be identified and implemented.

FOOTNOTES

1. N. Raze, *Overview of Research on Ability Grouping* (San Mateo, CA: County Office of Education, 1985).

2. Jeannie Oakes, *Keeping Track: How Schools Structure Inequality* (New Haven, CT: Yale University Press, 1986).

3. Robert E. Slavin, "Ability Grouping and Student Achievement in Elementary Schools: A Best-Evidence Synthesis," *Review of Educational Research* 57 (Fall 1987): 293-336.

4. Conrad G. Carlberg and Kenneth Kavale, "The Efficacy of Special Versus Regular Class Placement for Exceptional Children," *Journal of Special Education* 14 (Fall 1980): 295-309.

5. Nancy A. Madden and Robert E. Slavin, "Mainstreaming Students with Mild Academic Handicaps: Academic and Social Outcomes," *Review of Educational Research* 53 (Winter 1983): 519-69.

6. Chen-Lin Kulik and James A. Kulik, "Effects of Ability Grouping on Secondary School Students: A Meta-Analysis of Evaluation Findings," *American Educational Research Journal* 19 (Fall 1982): 415-28; Douglas Marston, "The Effectiveness of Special Education: A Time Series Analysis of Reading Performance in Regular and Special Education Settings," *Journal of Special Education* 21 (Winter 1987): 13-26.

7. Madden and Slavin, "Mainstreaming Students with Mild Academic Handicaps."

8. Margaret M. Dawson, "Beyond Ability Grouping," *School Psychology Review* 16 (August 1987): 348-69.

9. Chen-Lin Kulik, "Effects of Interclass Ability Grouping on Achievement and Self-esteem" (Symposium paper presented at the annual meeting of the American Psychological Association, Los Angeles, 1985).

10. Carlberg and Kavale, "The Efficacy of Special versus Regular Class Placement for Exceptional Children."

11. Oakes, *Keeping Track.*

12. M. Mann, "What Does Ability Grouping Do to the Self Concept?"

13. Walter E. Schafer and Carol Olexa, *Tracking and Opportunity* (Scranton, PA: Chandler, 1971).

14. National Coalition of Advocates for Students, *Barriers to Excellence: Our Children at Risk* (Boston: National Coalition of Advocates for Students, 1985).

15. John I. Goodlad, *A Place Called School* (New York: McGraw-Hill, 1984).

16. Marsha Forest, ed., *More Education Integration* (Downsview, Ontario: G. Allan Roeher Institute, 1987).

17. Douglas Biklen, "The Myth of Clinical Judgment," *Journal of Social Issues,* 44 (March 1988): 127-40; Steven Taylor, "Caught in the Continuum: A Critical Analysis of the Principle of the Least Restrictive Environment," *Journal of the Association for Persons with Severe Handicaps* 13 (Spring 1988): 41-53; Susan B. Stainback, William C. Stainback, and Marsha Forest, eds., *Educating All Students in the Mainstream of Regular Education* (Baltimore: Paul Brookes, forthcoming).

18. James Tucker, "Curriculum-Based Assessment: An Introduction," *Exceptional Children* 52 (November 1985): 199-204; James Ysseldyke and Sandra Christenson, *The Instructional Environment Scale* (Austin, TX: PRO-ED, 1986).

19. Ibid.

20. Forest, *More Education Integration.*

21. James Sternat, John Nietupski, Rosalie Messina, Steve Lyon, and Lou Brown, "Occupational and Physical Therapy Services for Severely Handicapped Students: Toward a Naturalized Public School Service Delivery Model," in *Educational Programming for the Severely and Profoundly Handicapped,* ed. Ed Sontag, Judy Smith, and Nick Certo (Reston, VA: Division of Mental Retardation, Council for Exceptional Children, 1977).

22. Stainback, Stainback, and Forest, *Educating All Students in the Mainstream of Regular Education.*

23. Lou Brown, Mary B. Granston, Sue Hamre-Nietupski, F. Johnson, Barbara Wilcox, and L. Gruenewald, "A Rationale for Comprehensive Longitudinal Interaction between Severely Handicapped Students and Nonhandicapped Students and Other Citizens," *AAESPH Review* 4 (Spring 1979): 3-14.

24. Maynard C. Reynolds, Margaret C. Wang, and Herbert J. Walberg, "The Necessary Restructuring of Special and Regular Education," *Exceptional Children* 53 (February 1987): 391-98.

25. Mary E. D'Zamko and Lynne Raiser, "A Strategy for Individualizing Directed Group Instruction," *Teaching Exceptional Children* 18 (Spring 1986): 190-96.

26. Dawson, "Beyond Ability Grouping."

27. David W. Johnson and Roger T. Johnson, "Mainstreaming and Cooperative Learning Strategies," *Exceptional Children* 52 (April 1986): 553-61; Roger T. Johnson and David W. Johnson, "Building Friendships between Handicapped and

Nonhandicapped Students: Effects of Cooperative and Individualistic Instruction," *American Educational Research Journal* 18 (1981): 416-24; Robert E. Slavin, Marshall Leavey, and Nancy A. Madden, "Combining Cooperative Learning and Individualized Instruction," *Elementary School Journal* 84 (1984): 4102.

28. D'Zamko and Raiser, "A Strategy for Individualizing Directed Group Instruction."

29. Mary Falvey, "Curriculum Design and Adaptations," in *Educating All Students in the Mainstream of Regular Education*, ed. Stainback, Stainback, and Forest.

30. Johnson and Johnson, "Mainstreaming and Cooperative Learning Strategies"; Johnson and Johnson, "Building Friendships between Handicapped and Nonhandicapped Students"; Slavin, Leavey, and Madden, "Combining Cooperative Learning and Individualized Instruction."

31. Slavin, "Ability Grouping and Student Achievement in Elementary Schools."

32. Margaret C. Wang and Herbert J. Walberg, *Adapting Instruction to Individual Differences* (Berkeley: McCutchan Publishing Corp., 1985).

33. Carolyn M. Evertson, Edmund T. Emmer, Barbara S. Clements, Julie P. Sanford, Murray E. Worsham, *Classroom Management for Elementary Teachers* (Englewood Cliffs, NJ: Prentice-Hall, 1985).

34. Brown et al., "A Rationale for Comprehensive Longitudinal Interactions between Severely Handicapped Students and Nonhandicapped Students and Other Citizens."

35. Slavin, "Ability Grouping and Student Achievement in Elementary Schools."

CHAPTER IX

Vocational Education for Students with Handicaps

ROBERT GAYLORD-ROSS

Vocational education refers to the preparation of persons for a particular type of occupation, whereas in general education the total person is educated in the numerous curricular domains of arts, sciences, physical culture, and so forth. A basic premise of vocational education is that a rather circumscribed training curriculum will lead to the preparation and placement of a student in an occupation for which that training is appropriate. For this reason, vocational education entails a temporal proximity between training and job procurement. A secondary student might receive vocational education during grades 11 and 12 and obtain a permanent position as a bookkeeper upon graduating from high school. Vocational education may involve instructional activities well in advance of job procurement, even in the primary grades, but most of its activities occur immediately before placement.

During the past century, a large number of vocational training schools have appeared in the United States in a wide variety of educational settings, including universities, community colleges, high schools, vocational-technical schools, and adult education facilities.[1] In these settings students learn technical skills in order to be proficient in a specific occupation. Federal, state, and local governments have made substantial commitments to vocational education.[2] Federal assistance began with the Morrill Act (1862), which established land grant colleges to offer formal instruction in the agricultural and mechanical arts. In 1917, the Smith-Hughes Act assigned resources for preparing youth for work rather than for college. It also mandated that federal, local, and state agencies form a partnership in vocational education. Largely in response to the *vocational* needs of returning veterans after World War I, the federal role in vocational preparation grew, buttressed by the Smith-Sears Act of 1918 and the Vocational Rehabilitation Act of 1920. From 1917 to 1963, federal activity in vocational education continued to expand. The aerospace race between the United States and the Soviet Union provoked a need for skilled technicians and engineers, and the National Defense Education Act of 1958 provided a major infusion of funding for technical education. Five years later, the Vocational Education Act of 1963 (and its amended version in 1968) made an important shift from training for specific occupations (e.g., agriculture, home economics) to focusing on the diverse needs of youth to be served by vocational education.[3] It funded new efforts in curriculum development, research, demonstration, and teacher training. Most important, the act set aside 10 percent of federal funds for handicapped students and 15 percent of its funds for disadvantaged populations. Furthermore, the act emphasized the flexibility in the changing occupational marketplace and encouraged vocational preparation programs to shift their offerings accordingly. More recent vocational legislation, the Carl Perkins Act of 1984 (PL 98-524), as in previous acts, passed federal funds to state and local districts for equipment, staff, and buildings. PL 98-524 earmarks 10 percent of its funds for handicapped students and 22 percent for disadvantaged learners. In fact, a total 57 percent of its funds is allocated for special groups.

Of particular importance is the confluence of the language of Public Laws 94-142 and 98-199 (pertaining to special education), Public Law 98-524 (pertaining to vocational education), and Public Laws 93-112 and 96-602 (pertaining to rehabilitation) all of which encourage education in the least restrictive environment. This may mean work experiences in business settings and occupational training courses in regular public schools where handicapped students are trained alongside nonhandicapped students and co-workers. Although federal laws relating to vocational education have encouraged serving students in the least restrictive environment, they have not mandated that education should take place in integrated settings. Therefore, there is much variation across local school districts with respect to providing vocational education in integrated settings.

Vocational Education for Students with Mild Handicaps

Vocational education for students with mild handicaps typically consists of three components: occupational training, career counseling, and assessment.[4] The student is usually assessed during the beginning of the secondary years. Many standardized assessment instruments are available with which to identify a person's occupational abilities and preferences. Although these standardized instruments have some value, current vocational assessment emphasizes the pooling of formative data from on-the-job work experiences in order to construct valid portraits of the individual's vocational skills and interests.[5] The assessment information collected should be fed into the career counseling process. Formal and informal methods of counseling may be used to increase the student's awareness and motivation to obtain fulfilling employment. School counselors, teachers, vocational educators, and parents may play a role in career counseling. Mildly handicapped students often have the skills to learn a trade or a profession, but without systematic support they lack the awareness, opportunity, or motivation to enter a career path toward meaningful employment. Particularly in the case of the disadvantaged and mildly handicapped students, there may be few role models for successful employment in their social world. Also, they may simply have come to believe that they have few opportunities. Furthermore, the availability of well-paid illegal activities, such as trafficking in narcotics, may be much more appealing to the youth than entry-level, low-paying, manual labor jobs. One secondary vocational training program that assists mildly handicapped youth in securing adult employment has used an effective strategy to counter youthful disillusionment.[6] The Community Vocational Training Program uses the concept of "career ladder" when forging vocational training relationships with businesses. A large corporation, like California AAA, serves as a community training site for mildly handicapped students during their last semester of school. The company agrees to hire capable students selectively from the program. When hired, the students are reassured that they may have a lifetime career in the company, with opportunity for promotions, pay raises, and benefits. Thus, the initial job is not viewed as a "dead-end" slot, but rather as a possible first rung on an ascending career ladder.

Work experience is an important component of a vocational education program for the mildly handicapped student. In addition to teaching specific occupational skills, the primary goal of work experience is to teach the student general work behaviors like grooming, following directions, punctuality, stamina, and social skills—behaviors that usually prove to be most important in predicting job success. Interestingly, persons with mild handicaps often have more difficulty in displaying general work behaviors than individuals with more severe disabilities. We have used the term "serious vocational handicaps" to refer to the disabled individual who is at risk for job retention and who typically needs a substantial amount of supervision to acquire new skills at the work site.[7] Individuals with serious vocational handicaps may have disabilities ranging from mild to profound impairments. A successful experience program is probably the most effective way for them to practice and master the critical general work behaviors. Work experience sometimes results in permanent placements. In the statewide "workability" program in California placements for work experience resulted in a permanent job for about 30 percent of the students.[8] Thus, a secondary vocational training program may sometimes be a useful vehicle for the successful transition to employment.

While vocational education programs have grown steadily over the years, recently there have been criticisms about the efficacy of vocational education.[9] The number of graduates employed, particularly in the field in which they received training, is often small. Further, the occupational offerings in vocational programs are often inflexible and unresponsive to the changing market demands for particular trained personnel. A high school may offer courses in airplane and auto mechanics when there are no jobs in these fields in the surrounding communities. At the same time, health service occupations may be booming but the school offers no courses in this field. Employers indicate that their main skill priority for new employees is the presence of general work behaviors but that they cannot obtain a sufficient pool of workers with those behaviors, even in the midst of high unemployment. Furthermore, many companies have developed large training programs for new employees, thus relying less on previous training in vocational programs.

The role of vocational education in the overall curriculum has yet to be resolved. In particular, the "core curriculum" or "basic education" movement has called for a greater emphasis on teaching the three Rs and other basic skills. From this view, vocational education and other offerings like driver education or home economics are viewed as "frills" that may be expended in order to increase basic educational (i.e., academic) offerings. In addition, many educational critics like Goodlad feel that too many students are unnecessarily placed in vocational tracks and are thus denied the opportunities for higher education and for higher-status, higher-paying occupations.[10] In some cases, educators feel there is an ethnic, gender, racial, and class bias in such tracking.

If vocational education is to survive and grow, it must answer such stinging critiques. Most importantly, there needs to be a demonstration that essential academic content can be taught in vocational contexts. Research and demonstration efforts need to document how academic skills are infused within the vocational curriculum in both occupational training and work experience courses. For example, my colleagues and I have observed that many mildly handicapped students appear to be more motivated to learn and perform in real work settings than in the classroom. This seems to be particularly true for adolescents who may have had a series of academic failures and have become bored within the confines of the classroom. Finally, the career ladder notion ought to be implemented and validated to show that vocational education does not prematurely track students into low-level, dead-end occupations. Effective transition programs should develop partnerships with interested corporations. Longitudinal career plans may be designed and implemented. Ideally, mildly handicapped individuals will progress up meaningful career ladders as they simultaneously engage in postsecondary education in order to advance their careers and academic abilities.

Vocational Education for Students with Severe Handicaps

Persons with severe handicaps include the disabilities of mental retardation (moderate, severe, profound) and autism. Because of their significant cognitive impairments, typically these persons have been excluded from traditional vocational education courses. The general belief has been that they lacked the basic reading, writing, thinking, or motor skills to participate in the activities of those courses. Thus, the development of a vocational curriculum for students with severe handicaps was typically left to the special education teacher. Although PL 94-142 requires that all handicapped students have at least one vocational objective in their individual educational programs, there has been much variation in complying with this regulation, as well as confusion as to what a vocational objective is. Most teachers of students with severe handicaps have interpreted vocational activity to mean some task like sorting papers or working with nuts and bolts. The student would often have to repeat the assembly task in a production-like manner. If there was future planning it usually meant preparing the students for tasks that would be found in the local sheltered workshop.

Brown and his colleagues initiated a virtual revolution in curriculum development for students with severe handicaps (see chapter 3). Brown raised the question of the ultimate environment(s) in which the person will live as an adult. In the vocational context, professionals have been trying to develop alternatives to workshops in nonsheltered work settings. Then, the teacher of primary or secondary severely handicapped students would develop vocational activities for her students to prepare them for nonsheltered work as adults. This approach led to the strategy of making an environmental inventory of the different work settings in the local community. The skills needed in these potential employment sites were then identified and taught. It appears that the new community-based integrated vocational programming for students with severe disabilities may transform the face of vocational education for all students and the traditional opportunities for work in the community that have generally been available to people with severe disabilities.

THE RATIONALE FOR NONSHELTERED EMPLOYMENT

Not too long ago, sheltered workshops were seen as both a necessary and desirable work option for individuals with severe handicaps. They offered many adults the opportunity to engage in real work tasks and to earn money. When compared with the alternatives, the sheltered workshops were certainly superior to staying at home all day or attending a nonwork activity center. Today, the vocational field largely considers sheltered workshops to be unacceptable alternatives for persons with severe handicaps. The main reason is that the workshop attended only by handicapped persons is not an integrated setting. The segregated nature of the facility has become less acceptable as more students are graduated from integrated school programs. Parents of these students have come to expect programs for them to be integrated. Sending their son or daughter to a sheltered workshop would be viewed as a step backward after years of integration. Sheltered workshops also have not met the promise of providing a continuum of services. It had been expected that a steady flow of adults would progress from workshops to nonsheltered employment. Research has shown that people tend to remain in workshops for long periods of time, and many people, particularly those with severe disabilities, never leave at all.[11] The better workers also tend to remain in these sheltered settings because they are needed to meet the often exacting production demands at the workshop. Still another problem is that many sheltered workshops in the United States are having difficulty procuring a sufficient number of contracts. Thus, the participants spend many of their program hours in idle time or in nonwork activities. Finally, sheltered work does not offer a true employment position. Participants are paid well below minimum wage level and are not employees of a real company. Some feel that many, if not all, persons with severe handicaps are capable of regular, competitive employment, and that they have been unable to develop to their fullest in sheltered workshops with respect to economic employment and social integration.

Vocational Programming for Students with Severe Handicaps
TRAINING STRATEGIES

Vocational activities for students with severe handicaps used to mean working in the classroom on assembly-line tasks. But as the goals shifted from sheltered to nonsheltered work, such tasks were no longer considered preparatory. Instead, the focus shifted to how to prepare students for the real world of work. Some teachers tried to simulate a real work setting in a classroom by creating a miniature workshop or garden. While valuable tasks can be learned in such simulated settings, it has been shown that severely handicapped students have poor ability in generalizing from one setting to another. More importantly, a real work setting is dramatically different from a school simulation because of the adult supervisors and co-workers present, the more stringent demands and work patterns, and the odors, materials, and physical ecology of the site.[12] Therefore, training for vocational preparation, and for other domains like residential and community living, has moved increasingly from the school to the community. In the primary grades, students with severe handicaps may spend 20 percent of their training time in the community. By the time they are in secondary school this training time may increase to 80 percent.[13]

The establishment of a community vocational training program is no easy feat. Approval from school administrators must be gained to teach students off-campus. The type of supervision provided at the work site must be detailed. Teachers must approach employers to request that students be permitted to train at their sites. Many teachers feel inadequately prepared to establish a community training program of this nature.

There are a number of different models for training students at a work site. If it is the student's first experience, there will probably be a need for close supervision by an instructor. A community classroom may be established where two to four students are carefully instructed by a teacher or a paraprofessional.[14] Initially, the students work in close proximity to the teacher. As the three- to six-month training period progresses, the students work more independently as they are spread around the work site and the instructor supervises them intermittently.

Some students may progress to a work experience where they are alone at a work site without an instructor constantly present. The instructor may visit once a week for an hour to observe how well the student is advancing. In this and the community classroom model, a major aim of the program is to transfer supervision from the instructor to the co-workers at the site. One of the key things to be gained in work experience is to learn how to socialize and take supervision from co-workers. The work experience should teach other invaluable work skills like response rate, working on task for longer durations, breaktime behaviors, and punctuality. Even if the specific job tasks are different from a restaurant to an office, the general work behaviors required in the two settings should be similar. Consequently, one work training experience can make quite a difference in learning general work behaviors. A series of different work experiences should insure that these behaviors are learned with different settings, people, and materials and should increase the probability of their generalization to future permanent employment positions in adulthood.

When a teacher identifies the skills needed to work in a number of employment settings in the community, she can then conduct training in a number of ways. To identify particular employment sites and related skills the most straightforward approach is to obtain a work site in which the employer has committed to hire a particular student. Exact information can then be collected as to what jobs, skills, and rules to teach. Subsequently, on the training end, it might be possible to bring the student to the work site before he is employed, and train him for one week, one month, or one year in the requisite skills. This approach is the simplest and also the one most likely to bring successful results. The problem of generalizing from one setting to another does not arise, since the person is trained in the criterion setting.

Unfortunately, it is usually not possible to procure a particular job well before graduation. Even if one could, vocational education should be broader in preparation so that a person is capable of working at more than one site. Thus, the most likely approach for job preparation is to identify the main types of work sites that offer the possibility of employment for a particular student. In a particular community there may be many job possibilities in restaurants, hospitals, and offices. Jobs at these sites may include food preparation, maintenance work, and simple clerical tasks like photo duplication. The teacher could then establish an on-site vocational training program[15] so that during the secondary years each student receives at least six months of training in each of the possible work settings. For example, suppose Abby showed an interest in and ability for food preparation and maintenance work, but not office work. The teacher could arrange for one work experience in two different sites, allowing Abby to engage in food preparation and maintenance work. It would be quite fortuitous if the employer at one of the sites decided to hire Abby upon completion of the work experience. It is more likely, though, that these two secondary work experiences would teach many of the job skills for adult employment.

Horner has developed a model which attempts to promote the generalization of skills from one setting to another.[16] The "general case" model would identify the skills for food preparation work, for example, and then have the student train in at least two restaurants. The materials and tasks would vary considerably across the two or three restaurants. By varying tasks, materials, and settings, Horner predicts that the student will generalize these skills to future employment settings. The general case model is a scientifically elegant approach to promoting generalization. Many teachers will not have the resources to move a group of students through a series of training experiences in such a rigorous way. In this case the teacher should try to give each student an experience in the main employment sites in their community.

VOCATIONAL ASSESSMENT

The history of vocational education and rehabilitation has placed a strong emphasis on assessment. In fact, in many schools the main vocational service a student may receive is a vocational assessment, which attempts to find out a person's underlying work abilities, his employment preferences, and the specific work skills he has acquired. Assessments for nonhandicapped and mildly handicapped persons have often included paper and pencil tests or manipulations of equipment which may take hours or days. In either case a summative assessment is made of the individual's skills and abilities. Usually, a recommendation is made about the specific or general type of work a person may be suited for. These traditional approaches to vocational assessment appear to have little utility for persons with severe handicaps.[17] Most importantly, the severely handicapped individual is usually unable to complete the paper-and-pencil tests, to follow the test instructions, or to manipulate the materials successfully. Also, there is a serious question about whether a one-time test situation is a valid predictor of job readiness or job success.

A preferable approach to vocational assessment uses a formative evaluation of the student in a series of work experiences.[18] For example, after a student completes three work experiences in a restaurant, office, and factory, a review is made of the type of work setting in which the student performs best. Performance is determined according to which type of job the student and his family prefer, and in what sort of skills he displays the most proficiency. This information can be gathered from the observations of instructors and co-workers. Some instruments, like the Vocational Assessment Curriculum Guide, can be used by the supervisor at the work site to inventory a wide range of job skills.[19] Finally, preference and proficiency information is pooled by an assessment team which includes teachers, parents, and adult service personnel to decide what would be the best kind of employment position for the graduating youth.[20] Irvin has discussed the advantages of such formative, curriculum-referenced approaches to assessment.[21] The student is observed repeatedly as he performs familiar training tasks in familiar settings. Thus, the assessment is reliable and has good face and content validity. In curriculum-referenced assessment the training regime and the assessment process merge into an ongoing evaluation which tells the teacher how to modify her instructional techniques. In turn, through monitoring the training process, the assessment reports what instructional techniques work with particular vocational tasks and settings. This information should be invaluable to educators and employers in planning future vocational tasks and settings. Traditional summative, vocational assessments have been criticized for producing impressive reports that sit on shelves and have little impact on vocational programming. Curriculum-referenced assessment gathers information while the student is engaged in real work activities. This information can be fed directly back into future vocational education efforts by indicating underlying abilities, occupational preferences, extant skills, and effective instructional techniques.

TRANSITION

Much attention has been given to the transition of disabled youth from school to adulthood. The focus on transition has arisen because of the dropping off of services from school to adulthood and the high rates of unemployment among disabled adults. Federal legislation in 1984 (PL 98-199) amends the Education for All Handicapped Act of 1975, supplies funding for new transition programs, and suggests planning for the movement to adult services. Specifically, an Individualized Transition Plan (ITP) should be developed for the graduating student. The plan is an extension of the normal IEP except that it brings together professionals from school and adult services to plan for the transitional process. A main goal of the ITP is to secure nonsheltered employment for the graduating student. Another goal is to institute recreational and independent living programs for the times when the individual is not at work.

Planning for the transition to work is a challenging process. The vocational assessment information from the series of work experiences should be pooled to assist in making a placement decision. The process will be much easier if the employer at the last work experience is interested in hiring the student for permanent employment and if everyone agrees that this would be an excellent placement. A complete definition of transition operates at two levels. One level is the actual instructional delivery process where a teacher, for example, may provide on-the-job training for a school teacher so that the individual accurately performs all of the job tasks. These client-level transition services may include: teaching, counseling, behavior modification, and employer education. The second level of transition entails that interagency linkages will be formed between school and adult service agencies.[22] For example, the vocational component of a school program may place and train its students with disabilities in permanent employment during their final years of school. When the students leave, the school district may transfer pertinent records to a targeted adult service agency such as the local Association for Retarded Citizens. This agency would then provide ongoing vocational services for the individuals who had already been placed in permanent employment. It would also attempt to place and train any other individuals who were not already placed in nonsheltered employment. Thus, successful interagency linkage ensures that youth in transition do not "fall between the cracks" of service agencies. It guarantees lifelong longitudinal programming that begins in the local schools and continues through adulthood.

The relationship between community living and work has only recently been explored.[23] In our Employment Retention Program we have observed a wavering commitment by families in relation to their support for their children working.[24] Initially, most families (natural parents, foster parents, or group home support staff) are very receptive to the idea of community employment. Understandably, when they learn more about the placement process, concerns are expressed pertaining to Social Security benefits, working unusual or long hours, and the change from the child-student status (with associated dependencies) to the more independent adult-worker status. These observations point to the clear need for family members to become actively involved in the decisions that affect the school-to-work transition. Also, there is a great need for family involvement during secondary vocational training so that parents can observe their child working in a real employment setting and they can begin to set expectations for his or her nonsheltered employment in future years. Perhaps most importantly, the adult service system needs to respond to the concerns expressed by parents.

ADULT EMPLOYMENT OPTIONS

There are a number of types of employment options for adults with severe handicaps. Despite the inherent limitations of sheltered workshops, they will continue to remain as options for some time to come. If current trends continue, however, we should expect to see a gradual shift of persons and funds from sheltered to nonsheltered employment and a dramatic decrease in the number of high school graduates who enter the sheltered workshop system. The main approach to nonsheltered employment is competitive employment. In competitive employment an individual handicapped person works in a real work setting with all nonhandicapped co-workers. The person is paid at least minimum wage and is a regular employee. In the past, many adult handicapped persons have been placed by rehabilitation agencies in competitive employment situations. The persons usually have had mild handicaps like learning disabilities or cerebral palsy with normal cognitive functioning, so that there was little required in the way of extra on-the-job training. Typically the person was expected to learn the position informally under the direction of a supervisor or co-worker. Sometimes there was a need for adaptations in equipment or job responsibilities in order to secure the position.

In Will's model of the three bridges to transition, a person may find and learn a job with no specialized services.[25] In fact, Hasazi, Gordon, and Roe found that mildly handicapped youth most frequently found jobs through personal networking with friends and families, not through employment agencies.[26] A second bridge to transition involves "time-limited" services. Here, an employment agency may open a case upon receiving a referral. The agency might vocationally assess, counsel, place, and train the individual. After the person has successfully held the job for a three- to six-month period, the agency, usually the department of vocational rehabilitation, will "close" the case and thereafter no further services are provided. While such work rehabilitation programs have achieved a certain amount of success, they have not addressed the issue of employment for persons with serious vocational handicaps like severe mental retardation, emotional disturbance, or multiple handicaps. These individuals usually need lifelong vocational services.

A new concept of "supported work" has emerged in order to offer the assistance necessary to attain nonsheltered work for individuals with severe handicaps. In the competitive work setting, it usually entails having an instructor accompany the handicapped person to the job on the first day of work. The instructor has already learned how to perform the job and now teaches the student all the specific job tasks and general work behaviors required for successful employment. The first few days or weeks may require the instructor to be with the handicapped employee continuously to provide one-to-one assistance and instruction. As time passes and the employee gradually learns the job, the instructor fades out of the work site so that the person spends more time independently. During the fading process, the instructor makes sure that proper supervision is turned over to one or more of the co-workers. After weeks or months the instructor may have completely left the work setting. At that time the instructor will monitor the progress of the worker through ongoing follow-up visits or phone calls.

A second type of supported work model has a group of handicapped persons perform work in a nonsheltered context. For example, a work crew might travel around the community to perform landscaping or housecleaning tasks. An enclave would have a small group of handicapped employees work as a unit within a factory. A major drawback of crews and enclaves is the degree of separateness or isolation created by these models within these community settings. Members of the community see *groups* of people with disabilities rather than individuals. The groups may vary in size from four to ten and there is usually constant supervision from an instructor (with little fading). Another feature that holds to the separateness of these models is that the persons in crews or enclaves usually are not employees of the company and typically earn a subminimum wage. Yet crews and enclaves offer a more integrated alternative to sheltered work.

Another option for nonsheltered work has stirred a great deal of controversy. Volunteer work has placed persons with quite severe handicaps in actual work settings. The person may produce at such a slow pace, perhaps 1 percent of the normal workers' rate, that the employer may not wish to hire him or her as a wage earner. In such cases, Brown has defined the primary goal of nonsheltered work as a socialization experience where the person can have age-appropriate interactions with nonhandicapped peers.[27] For Brown, payment for work is an important but secondary goal for some individuals. Others have voiced strong objections to work without pay.[28] There is a long history of the peonage of handicapped persons and if volunteer work were permitted, employers would take advantage of this and opt for not paying their handicapped workers. While the potential for abuse is present, in the absence of a right to work, volunteer work offers a realistic, and perhaps temporary, work option for persons with the most severe disabilities. If nonsheltered employment entails minimum wage or substantial pay, then many handicapped persons will be excluded from such possibilities. If carefully monitored, an employment service system should be able to distinguish between regular pay, subminimum wage, and volunteer work. Pumpian, West, and Shepard have developed an extended adult education program for adults with severe handicaps.[29] Based in the local community college, the participants receive a comprehensive program of vocational, recreational, and community living instruction. The individual is rotated through different work experiences for as long as a five-year vocational assessment period. When appropriate paid work positions are procured, the individual is duly placed (at minimum or subminimum wage). Sometimes extended volunteer positions are obtained.

There has been an exciting growth of nonsheltered work options for disabled adults. For many of the leaders and advocates in the supported employment movement, nonsheltered work is the only alternative for disabled adults. For others in the adult service field, supported employment is just one option along a continuum of services which may include day activity centers, sheltered workshops, and supported employment. Ferguson, Ferguson, and Jones have expressed concern that individuals with the most severe disabilities may be excluded from nonsheltered work because of the perpetuation of the continuum notion.[30] In addition, even within the supported employment options of individual and group programming, some have concerns that certain individuals are being placed in unduly restrictive enclave and crew contexts, rather than using individualized placements. For example, Zivolich has developed a comprehensive supported employment program in Orange County, California.[31] After placing over 200 mentally retarded individuals in nonsheltered settings over a three-year period, Zivolich and his colleagues have decided to drop group placement models, which they feel are too socially restrictive, and to continue only with individual placements.

Challenges to Employment

ECONOMIC FACTORS

During the past five years there has been a large national movement to secure more and better employment for persons with disabilities. Vocational education plays a large part in the movement in order to prepare persons during the school years for employment or to provide on-the-job training and supervision when they become adults. Most of the discussion concerning supported employment has been focused at the individual level. There has been a singular fervor to establish programs to find jobs for persons with handicaps. It is often useful to take a broader look at related factors which affect employment.

The state of the economy is a major economic factor affecting the employment of handicapped persons. I found that the main reason cited in Western Europe for not pursuing nonsheltered options was the high rate of unemployment.[32] Certainly when unemployment rises it places more workers in competition with each other and with handicapped workers. O'Brien and Stern have pointed out that in the United States a 4 percent unemployment rate is effectively a zero rate.[33] At that point there should be no serious competition for jobs. As the unemployment rate rises, there is increasing tension and scarcity of jobs. In the queue of job seekers, persons requiring the least amount of training are the most desirable to employers. Workers with handicaps usually require more training so their rank on the hiring queue is often low. The type of on-the-job training provided by a supported work program may offset this concern since the employer is freed from much training responsibility.

Although unemployment is cited by educators, employers, and others as the reason for sheltered employment, this may not present the complete picture. For example, I found that Switzerland had an amazingly low unemployment rate of 1 percent, yet adult employment services were completely sheltered.[34] High unemployment can be used as a rationalization for a no-change policy in adult work options. For nonsheltered work to expand, there needs to be a strong political movement with clearly defined goals. High unemployment may certainly hinder placement activities. In Italy, it was reported to be the greatest deterrent to job placement. Yet, the Italians continued to make impressive strides in placing mentally handicapped adults in nonsheltered employment. In fact, Halpern has reported how aggressive placement agencies can have much success in the midst of high rates of unemployment.[35] At the same time that unemployment can be relatively high at a macroeconomic level (for the nation, state, or city) it still may be possible for an employment program to have a highly successful placement rate. One reason for this is that in the middle of high unemployment, employers still have difficulty finding workers with good general work behaviors. For example, the Pathways program for mentally handicapped adults was originally established in the midst of very high unemployment in Cardiff, Wales.[36] It has now expanded to twenty cities throughout England and Wales. When a supported employment program has established its credibility for placing good workers with adequate training and supervision, an employer will often be calling the program back for more of their workers.

A second economic issue relates to the type of work which handicapped persons may obtain. By and large, persons with developmental disabilities have obtained unskilled or semiskilled entry-level positions in fields like food service and janitorial work. Sensory and physically impaired persons who are cognitively able have been able to attain a wide range of jobs from low to very high skilled positions (although there still is a 70 percent unemployment rate within these disability groups).

The majority of newly created jobs in the United States are at the entry level and are low-paying (below $7,000 per year). On one hand, this might be a promising development for developmentally disabled adults, who in the past have entered this type of employment. Also, given recent progressive changes in social security laws for disabled persons, individuals should not lose their medical benefits on social security if they make less than $12,000 per year. On the other hand, obtaining only these positions, which are often devalued by the general public, might serve to perpetuate a negative image of people with disabilities and keep them at the low end of society. The notion of career ladders may play a useful role in countering this restrictive employment pattern and the potential disillusionment among youth who foresee their futures in this limited manner. An employment agency may develop partnerships with corporations that may start a person at an entry-level paying position, but gradually advance the person up the corporate structure.[37] Siegel and his colleagues have in fact found that successful individuals within their employment program may effectively serve as role models for the career ladder process.[38]

This role of economics is a part of vocational education. Educators must not only become familiar with training and job development techniques; they should also have a grasp of the bigger employment picture. O'Brien and Stern have presented a thorough review of economic incentives and disincentives for employing disabled persons.[39] We need to have a better understanding of the complex interplay of program and economic factors.

JOB RETENTION

As difficult as it may be to place a handicapped individual in competitive employment, it may be even more challenging to retain him or her in that position. When layoffs occur the handicapped person may be the first one fired, although this is not necessarily the case, as Halpern has shown.[40] Job maintenance problems for handicapped (and nonhandicapped) workers usually stem from two reasons. The person may display disruptive behaviors like fighting or swearing, or may be resistant to instructions or regulations at the site. A supported work program may institute a social and behavioral program on site to remediate the problem. Sometimes only one occurrence of an assaultive behavior will lead to termination so that behavior intervention may be too little, too late. Yet, we have had success in training co-workers to carry out behavior management programs.[41] The other major reason for job loss is working too slowly or too inefficiently. The worker can usually be trained to perform with an acceptable rate of errors. Many handicapped persons, though, are either physically frail or are not skilled in working rapidly. A slow work rate translates into inefficient production and the likelihood of termination. The supported employment instructor might use special reinforcement and prompting techniques to elevate the response rate. If change is not soon forthcoming, the employer may have no other choice but to terminate the person. On the other hand, it may be possible to redefine the job through job-sharing procedures so that the handicapped person does more job tasks which he is capable of completing accurately and rapidly, and omits tasks in which he is less proficient.[42] Such job sharing may be done informally among co-workers and sometimes requires the support and direction of the employer. Recent experiences suggest that many difficulties in job retention can be overcome when the right amount and intensity of support is provided by the supported employment instructor.

Primary Vocational Education

Probably because of the proximity between secondary school and adult employment, the main thrust of vocational education activity comes at the secondary level. Yet, increasingly longitudinal models for career education which begin at the primary level are being developed.[43] For example, Brolin has described primary-grade, career-awareness activities where the student learns about possible careers through reading or hearing successful disabled workers speak at their school. Career-awareness activities are followed in the middle school by career-exploration activities, where a student may shadow a person on the job for a day or might perform simple jobs around school. Career awareness and career exploration are excellent program ideas for expanding the work possibilities and heightening motivation for employment. Besides providing information, they offer role models for disabled children and set their future career sites.

The most straightforward approach to primary vocational education is to identify the general work behaviors in future work environments. Then, the teacher should make sure that behaviors such as rate, stamina, following directions, accuracy, on-task performance, generalization across materials and settings, waiting in line, sorting, and socializing are included in the daily activities. Besides incorporating general work behaviors in the curriculum, specific vocational activities may be established where the student performs clerical tasks in the office, or shelving tasks in the library, with the teacher being careful to select tasks in which nonhandicapped children are also involved.[44] The activities may last five to thirty minutes a day. Their key characteristics include: working in multiple settings and not just the classroom; working alongside a variety of nonhandicapped persons, including adults; and doing real (not make-believe) work. While these types of vocational education activities should prove useful for primary students, just *what* vocational education is for the primary student with moderate and severe handicaps is still in need of more complete resolution.

The Italian Illustration

While the United States is presently quite caught up in the supported work movement for nonsheltered employment, Italy has been involved with competitive employment for mentally handicapped persons for over ten years.

In the late 1960s and 1970s Italy, like many countries in the West, was experiencing a political and cultural turmoil. The war in Vietnam was a prominent concern and focal point of public debate, but all areas of life and culture were examined. One political issue that emerged addressed the quality of life of mentally ill and mentally handicapped persons. Most of these persons were treated in dreadful institutional hospitals or in special segregated schools in the community. As the plight of mentally ill and mentally handicapped persons was included within the political agenda of the left, a strong antisegregation movement developed. It was felt that such persons must be treated in their local community and in integrated schools. Thereafter, the large institutions were closed and social services were reorganized at the local level. In 1971, Italy adopted landmark legislation which promised that all handicapped students would be educated in a regular public school. In fact, this legislation went much further than our own PL 94-142. It did not just encourage education in the least restrictive environment. Rather, it stipulated that all handicapped students, except in extreme cases of physical or behavioral difficulties, would be educated in a regular school *and* in a regular classroom. At present, 80-95 percent (depending on the school district) of handicapped students are educated in integrated school settings.

From this massive scholastic integration experience, there simultaneously emerged a work integration movement. The movement was limited to a number of cities in the north—Parma, Genoa, Bologna, Milan, and Trento. An attempt was made to find nonsheltered employment for as many handicapped persons as possible. Organized through the local health departments, a vital coalition of unions, professionals, and left-wing political parties pushed for competitive employment. The northern Italian experience has been highly successful. In Parma, over 250 mentally handicapped persons currently work in nonsheltered settings.

What specific lessons can be learned from the northern Italian experience? First, when a group of powerful political and professional forces coalesce they can produce revolutionary changes in delivery systems. Second, a system of stipends to cover salaries for up to one year and a quota system to induce employers to employ handicapped persons can have salutary effects. In some cases, the United States has stipend programs that cover salaries up to three months. We also have a tax credit system to entice employers to hire handicapped persons. These incentives are not as large as those in Italy. Although the quota system sounds encouraging, it is largely bypassed for people with mental handicaps in other countries in Europe and in other parts of Italy. Third, in spite of the advances Italy has made in nonsheltered employment, there have been setbacks. As Vincenzo Bagnasco, a leader of the integration movement in Parma has said, "competitive employment is *fragile*." That is, work integration is different from school integration. Once a policy has been formulated and students placed in a regular public school, the system is likely to remain integrated. Employment always poses ongoing vicissitudes of unemployment, worker effectiveness, and employer attitudes. In Parma, as in most of Europe, the rates of unemployment have increased dramatically during the late 1970s and early 1980s. Also, more conservative political coalitions have failed to champion the integration theme. Consequently, the proportion of mentally handicapped persons in competitive employment in Parma has decreased dramatically from 60 percent of those served in 1975 to 25 percent in 1985.[45] As stated previously, high unemployment can be used as a rationalization to avoid developing nonsheltered work options. Yet, when such a program is put in place, the rate of unemployment can modulate its range of effectiveness considerably. Fifth, in terms of vocational preparation, there are few instances of systematic instruction being used as part of a training program in Italy. The learning of work tasks occurred on the job through informal observation and trial and error. It was my feeling that if systematic instruction procedures were used to their fullest, even more persons, with more severe disabilities, could be employed in business settings.

Overall, Italy has a system that maximizes integration at school and work. Preparation for employment evolves out of a school experience where handicapped students can develop their social skills through interactions with nonhandicapped students in the regular class. In some cities like Genoa, a systematic series of work experiences occurs during the late adolescent years. Finally, the individual may be placed in permanent, competitive employment with a variety of support vehicles from the mental health agency, the union, and economic subsidies. The Italian system is not a perfect one, and has certainly been influenced by high unemployment, but it exemplifies the possibility of creating viable comprehensive systems.

Concluding Remarks

Whenever a movement unfolds it tends to espouse a singular focus to the exclusion of other considerations. In the present case, with all of the programs dealing with vocational education, transition, and supported work, we run the danger of losing sight of the total individual. Halpern has warned of such a piecemeal approach and suggests that substantive efforts also be given to community living variables like residential skills, leisure activity, social networks, and so forth.[46] After a student leaves school it is important to plan for the student's other activities besides work. Many of the jobs handicapped persons obtain are part time, hence the importance of filling up the rest of the day with *useful* activities rather than just sitting at home and watching television. By the same token, while community living programs can almost always be successful in offering recreational and other community living activities, these efforts will be incomplete without opportunities for meaningful work. The problem of obtaining nonsheltered employment, is a great challenge. Presently, there is no right to a job as there is a right to attend a free school or a right to access public buildings. Full employment is not likely to exist in a capitalist economy and we have seen how the economic marketplace can affect placement efforts. Furthermore, we are just beginning to understand the support systems needed to maintain persons with serious vocational handicaps in community jobs. In spite of these challenges, the fruits of successful employment are immense. When a person is gainfully employed, his or her status in society changes tremendously. The person now does not have welfare dependence added to his particular disability label. The person is a respected, employed citizen who happens to have a particular disability. The true social integration of persons with handicaps will occur when persons mingle as relative coequals.[47] Social interactions based on mutual exchange rather than caretaking will emerge when persons become active participants in the work place. Vocational education can play a significant role not only in securing nonsheltered employment but also in facilitating the complete socialization of the handicapped individual.

Footnotes

1. William E. Kiernan and Michael E. Pyne, "Hard to Train: A History of Vocational Training for Special Needs Youth," in *Prevocational and Vocational Education for Special Needs Youth*, ed. Kevin P. Lynch, William E. Kiernan, and J. R. Stark

(Baltimore: Paul H. Brookes, 1982); Allen Phelps and James Fraser, "Legislative and Policy Aspects of Vocational Special Education," in *Vocational Education for Persons with Special Needs*, ed. Robert Gaylord-Ross (Palo Alto, CA: Mayfield Publishing Co., 1988).

2. Cory Gaylord-Ross, Joyce Forte, and Robert Gaylord-Ross, "The Community Classroom: Technological Vocational Training for Students with Serious Handicaps," *Career Development for Exceptional Individuals* 9 (1986): 24-33.

3. Phelps and Fraser, "Legislative and Policy Aspects of Vocational Special Education."

4. Robert Gaylord-Ross, Shep Siegel, Hyun S. Park, and William Wilson, "Secondary Vocational Training," in *Vocational Education for Persons with Special Needs*, ed. Gaylord-Ross.

5. Robert Gaylord-Ross, Joyce Forte, Keith Storey, Cory Gaylord-Ross, and Devi Jameson, "Community-referenced Instruction in Technological Work Settings," *Exceptional Children* 54 (1987): 112-21.

6. Shep Siegel, Karen Greener, Joanne Prieuer, and Robert Gaylord-Ross, "The Community Vocational Training Program," *Career Development for Exceptional Individuals*, in press.

7. Gaylord-Ross, Forte, and Gaylord-Ross, "The Community Classroom."

8. Gail Zittel, "Work-Ability: A State Transition Program," *American Rehabilitation* 1 (1985): 50-55.

9. Robert J. Flynn, "Effectiveness of Conventional and Alternative Vocational Education with Handicapped and Disadvantaged Youth: A Research Review," in *Prevocational and Vocational Education for Special Needs Youth*, ed. Lynch, Kiernan, and Stark; John T. Grasso and James R. Shea, "Effects of Vocational Education Programs: Research Findings and Issues," in *Planning Papers for the Vocational Education Study*. Vocational Education Study Publication No. 1 (Washington DC: National Institute of Education, 1979).

10. John I. Goodlad, *A Place Called School: Prospects for the Future* (New York: McGraw-Hill, 1984).

11. G. Thomas Bellamy, Larry E. Rhodes, Phil E. Bourbeau, and David M. Mank, "Mental Retardation Services in Sheltered Workshops and Day Activity Programs: Consumer Outcomes and Policy Alternatives" (Paper presented at the National Working Conference on Vocational Services and Employment Opportunities, Madison, WI, April, 1982).

12. Janis Chasdey-Rusch and Frank Rusch, "The Ecology of the Workplace," in *Vocational Education for Persons with Special Needs*, ed. Gaylord-Ross.

13. Wayne Sailor, Ann Halvorsen, Jackie Anderson, Lori Goetz, Kathy Gee, Kathy Doering, and Pam Hunt, "Community Intensive Instruction," in *Education of Learners with Severe Handicaps: Exemplary Service Strategies* (Baltimore: Paul H. Brookes, 1985).

14. Robert Gaylord-Ross, "The Role of Assessment in Transitional, Supported Employment," *Career Development for Exceptional Individuals* 9 (1986): 129-34.

15. Alice Wershing, Cory Gaylord-Ross, and Robert Gaylord-Ross, "Implementing a Community Vocational Training Model: A Process for Systems Change," *Education and Training of the Mentally Retarded* 21 (1986): 130-37.

16. Robert H. Horner, James Sprague, and Barbara Wilcox, "General Case Programming for Community Activities," in *Design of High School Programs for Severely Handicapped Students*, ed. Barbara Wilcox and G. Thomas Bellamy (Baltimore, MD: Paul H. Brookes, 1982), pp. 61-98.

17. Robert Gaylord-Ross, "Vocational Integration for Persons with Mental Handicaps: A Cross-cultural Perspective," *Research in Developmental Disabilities* 8 (1987): 531-48.

18. Gaylord-Ross et al., "Community-referenced Instruction in Technological Work Settings."

19. Frank R. Rusch, Richard P. Schutz, Dennis Mithaug, Harry E. Steward, and Dave Mar, *Vocational Assessment and Curriculum Guide* (Seattle, WA: Exceptional Education, 1982).

20. Gaylord-Ross et al., "Community-referenced Instruction in Technological Work Settings."

21. Larry Irvin, "Vocational Assessment," in *Vocational Education for Persons with Special Neeeds*, ed. Gaylord-Ross.

22. Madeleine Will, *OSERS Programming for the Transition of Youth with Disabilities: Bridges from School to Working Life* (Washington, DC: U.S. Department of Education, 1984).

23. Dan Close and Thomas Keating, "Community Living and Work," in *Vocational Education for Persons with Special Needs*, ed. Gaylord-Ross.

24. Robert Gaylord-Ross, Cory Gaylord-Ross, Chris Hagie, Penny Musante, and Devi Jameson, "Considerations and Outcomes in Transitional, Supported Employment," *Career Development for Exceptional Individuals* 11 (1988): 42-50.

25. Will, *OSERS Programming for the Transition of Youth with Disabilities*.

26. Susan B. Hasazi, Lawrence Gordon, and Cheryl Roe. "Factors Associated with the Employment Status of Handicapped Youth Exiting from High School from 1979-1983," *Exceptional Children* 51 (1985): 455-69.

27. Lou Brown, Betsy Shiraga, Jennifer York, Kim Kessler, Beth Strohm, Patricia Rogan, Mark Sweet, Kathy Zanella, Pat VanDeventer, and Ruth Loomis, "Integrated Work Opportunities for Adults with Severe Handicaps: The Extended Training Option," *Journal of the Association for the Severely Handicapped* 9 (1984): 262-69.

28. G. Thomas Bellamy, Larry W. Rhodes, Barbara Wilcox, John Albin, David M. Mank, Shawn M. Boles, Robert H. Horner, Mary Collins, and James Turner "Quality and Equality in Employment Services for Adults with Severe Disabilities," *Journal of the Association for the Severely Handicapped* 9 (1984): 270-77.

29. Ian Pumpian, Elizabeth West, and Holly Shepard, "The Training and Employment of Persons with Severe Handicaps," in *Vocational Education for Persons with Special Needs*, ed. Gaylord-Ross.

30. Philip M. Ferguson, Dianne L. Ferguson, and David Jones, "Generations of Hope: Parental Perspectives on the Transition of Their Children from School to Adult Life," in *Transition Planning and Adult Services: Perspectives on Policy and Practice*, ed. Philip M. Ferguson (Eugene, OR: Center on Human Development, 1987), pp. 81-119.

31. Steven Zivolich "Full Employment Initiative for Persons with Severe Disabilities in Orange County" (Unpublished manuscript, Developmental Disabilities Center, Orange, CA, 1987).

32. Gaylord-Ross, "Vocational Integration for Persons with Mental Handicaps."

33. Jerry O'Brien and David Stern, "Economic Issues in Employing Persons with Disabilities," in *Vocational Education for Persons with Handicaps*, ed. Robert Gaylord-Ross (Mountain View, CA: Mayfield Publishing Co., 1988).

34. Gaylord-Ross, "Vocational Integration for Persons with Mental Handicaps."

35. Andrew S. Halpern, "General Unemployment and Vocational Opportunities for EMR Individuals," *American Journal of Mental Deficiency* 78 (1973): 123-27.

36. Gaylord-Ross, "Vocational Integration for Persons with Mental Handicaps."

37. Siegel et al., "The Community Vocational Training Program."
38. Ibid.
39. O'Brien and Stern, "Economic Issues in Employing Persons with Disabilities."
40. Halpern, "General Unemployment and Vocational Opportunities for EMR Individuals."
41. Gaylord-Ross et al., "Secondary Vocational Training."
42. Ibid.
43. Conn Brolin, *Vocational Preparation for Persons with Handicaps* (Columbus, OH: Bell and Howell, 1982); G. M. Clark, *Career Education for the Handicapped Child in the Elementary School* (Denver: Love Publishing Co., 1979).
44. Thomas Haring, Blair Roger, Mellanie Lee, Cathy Breen, and Robert Gaylord-Ross, "Social Language Training for Moderately Handicapped Students," *Journal of Applied Behavioral Analysis* 19 (1986): 159-71.
45. Gaylord-Ross, "Vocational Integration for Persons with Mental Handicaps."
46. Andrew S. Halpern, "Foundations of Transition," *Exceptional Children* 57 (1985): 479-86.
47. Phil Strain, "Modification of Sociometric Status and Social Interaction with Mainstreamed Mild Developmentally Disabled Children," *Analysis and Intervention in Developmental Disabilities* 1 (1981): 157-70.

CHAPTER X

Evaluating Special Education Programs: Process and Outcome

IAN M. EVANS AND ELVERA M. WELD

General Issues In Evaluation

Program evaluation began in the mid-1960s, due to the development of social intervention programs under the administrations of Presidents Kennedy and Johnson. Innovative social programs were expensive and thus it was inevitable that better estimates of their real contribution should be demanded by policymakers. Soon this call for accountability extended to other areas where the outcomes had traditionally been either taken for granted (such as education in general) or poorly articulated (such as psychotherapy). Thus, early evaluation efforts were focused on the investigation of large-scale, national programs, using the sophisticated quantitative methods of basic social sciences. A particularly strong influence on evaluation methodology was a monograph by Campbell and Stanley[1] that outlined the strengths and weaknesses of various experimental and quasi-experimental research designs in terms of their ability to establish the social intervention as the unequivocal cause of the benefits.

In recent years, however, it has been realized that the evaluation of a program requires more than testing the hypothesis that the program itself was responsible for change. This move beyond formal experimentation to the description and documentation of the benefits achieved was fostered by clarifying the difference between *summative*

Preparation of this chapter was partially supported by a Cooperative Agreement from the U.S. Department of Education, Office of Special Education and Rehabilitation Services. This material does not necessarily reflect the position or policy of the U.S. Department of Education, and no official endorsement should be inferred. Portions of this chapter originally formed Technical Report No. 14, *The Evaluation of Special Education: A School District's Perspective*, Project SPAN, SUNY-Binghamton, New York, 13901.

evaluation (analyzing the results of a program in order to influence decisions about its continuation), and *formative* evaluation (the use of empirical data to fine-tune the workings of a program so that it has a better chance of achieving its stated purpose). While summative evaluation, resembling applied experimentation, may be important for long-term policymaking, formative evaluation seems to be more useful to administrators.[2] Evaluation concerns both the program (its process—how it is designed and how it works) and individual outcomes. Both can be measured by objective means, but the judgment of worth is subjective. The value that one places on a given educational outcome is a function of the similarity of the outcome with what was expected.[3] In regular education the expected achievements of students are clear-cut, for there is quite general agreement on the aspects of an academic program that students are expected to master. Students with handicaps, however, by definition are not expected to achieve at grade level, and thus there are no widely accepted academic standards whereby their performance can be judged. In fact, professional expectations regarding handicapped individuals' potential vary widely. For instance, physicians are much more pessimistic than educators regarding the future job possibilities and living arrangements of mentally retarded students.[4] Thus, it is possible that teachers, school administrators, parents, and even students themselves may be satisfied with educational attainment that is less than optimal simply because prior expectations were low.

It is interesting to note that the concept of the Individualized Educational Plan (IEP) reflects professional recognition that there are no a priori standards for students in special education—the IEP process creates personal curriculum goals for each student. One way of evaluating a student's progress, therefore, could be in terms of the number of IEP goals actually achieved in a given year. While there is some merit to this suggestion, much hinges on the appropriateness of the original goals identified. It is possible that teachers would feel subtle pressure to set easily attainable annual goals for their students. Outcome evaluation is a threatening activity in many ways, since the evaluation of students ultimately permits the evaluation of teachers, of programs, of curricula, and of administrators. If professionals can overcome this reluctance to subject their own activities to scrutiny, the benefits for students are considerable.

In this chapter we assume that the typical educator is really most interested in steadily enhancing the quality of a school's special education programs. Rather than looking for global judgments, today's professionals should be seeking data to guide decision making at various levels, such as curriculum revision, allocation of resources, or innovation in school routines. This approach is in accord with the strong empirical tradition that has emerged in the field of special education. Because there are so many individual variations in students with handicaps, and so many different effective instructional strategies, it is not feasible to demonstrate, through research, the absolute superiority of one particular teaching method. While using approaches that have already received empirical support would be desirable, special education teachers wishing to adopt an empirical stance must still rely on student performance measures to guide their teaching. Our purpose here is to elaborate on these assumptions in order to provide teachers, administrators, and policymakers with a conceptual foundation for evaluating special education programs.

A School District's Perspective

In order to provide a realistic context throughout this chapter we refer to a study of school administrators that we conducted as a component of a research program to develop an outcome measure for evaluating special education. The purpose of the survey was to gain some understanding of how educational administrators view the evaluation of special education. It was felt that this knowledge would be useful for developing an assessment strategy that would be acceptable to its potential users. We interviewed a select group of administrators within one district—a district with a total pupil enrollment of about 6,600, of which some 500 students are in special education. Among the group members, chosen because they represented various divisions of administrative responsibility for handicapped students, were building principals, a department chair, the directors of evaluation, special services, and other support divisions, and members of the school board. A formal interview protocol provided structure, but deviations from it were encouraged as additional issues of interest emerged. The interviewer could thus pursue each administrator's unique perceptions and insights. The tape-recorded interviews were transcribed and read by independent judges to ascertain their common features.

The respondents were all highly supportive of special education services (although this perhaps reflected a selection bias), and firmly committed to quality services for students with disabilities. At the same time, however, concern for program evaluation was noticeably absent. The measurement of student progress or any practical outcome was obviously not a task that engaged much, if any, of their time and attention. On a number of occasions the interviewer's use of the term "evaluation" was interpreted as an evaluation of the individual students (i.e., to determine eligibility for services).

The respondents were asked if they were aware of any external requests for evaluation, such as from the State Education Department, from consumer groups, or the Federal Government. Despite our feeling that accountability is in the air, no one in this group acknowledged ever experiencing pressure for outcome evaluation. They did emphasize that there was general evaluation of the district's *compliance* with legal statutes for special education, and also that parents had been an effective force for change. As one principal remarked:

We were audited by the State and someone came down and went through the entire program, evaluating compliance and so forth. But you know what else is an influence is the knowledgeable parents who are coming together, forming support groups, and not wanting their kids to be shortchanged. And there's nothing wrong with that, because that's what makes us examine our program and make sure we provide what we should be providing, regardless of what it costs. It's because of these people that things have changed.

In general, there was a sense of going through bureaucratic motions about much of the information that was gathered on students, but no felt demand for data that would really impact decisions other than meeting state criteria. One comment from an individual involved in the formal testing program captures this situation:

I don't know what the State does with that information [Metropolitan Achievement Test Scores]. I don't know what we do with it. I don't think we do anything with it, other than send it to the State and then they send us money, which is not a bad trade.

Obviously tests, with their standardized scores and known norms, represent one of the most common forms of outcome measurement used in regular education and special education. However, there are special problems associated with the evaluation of handicapped children by such measures.

Individual Evaluation
UNIQUE FEATURES OF EVALUATING SPECIAL EDUCATION STUDENTS

At the most basic level there should be little difference between evaluating students with handicaps and those without. As one respondent in our study replied to a question concerning the goals of special education: "The goals are to enable students to maximize potential, earn a living, enjoy free time, lead a productive life, treat other people humanely, and develop intellectual skills. Of course, those are the same for any youngster." Because of the long tradition of emphasis on basic intellectual skills and general academics in regular education, the school's role in preparing children for life's exigencies is indirect. The strong presumption that the purpose of schooling is to provide academic training is reflected in a recent study.[5] Mothers of nonhandicapped children ranked school subjects first, and communication skills second, as the skills that "best prepare your child for later life." Mothers of severely handicapped students rated communication skills as most important. They also mentioned such skills as personal hygiene, motor skills, and self-help skills (dressing, preparing food) that were never mentioned by mothers of nonhandicapped students. Both groups of parents, incidentally, reported satisfaction with the curricula provided for their children and believed that the public schools *were* preparing their children for the future.

It seems clear that the parents of nonhandicapped children expect that daily living skills will be automatically acquired by their offspring and that classroom instruction is properly focused on academic and intellectual skills. The attainment of these skills can be readily measured by achievement tests, which reflect formal cognitive operations, such as reading or mathematics, but not such desirable cognitive attributes as critical thought or creativity. The ease and convenience of standardized educational and psychological tests have resulted in their widespread acceptance as an index of educational outcomes. Although their misuse has been criticized from many angles,[6] they have particular limitations when evaluating students in special education, since the tests are based on psychometric assumptions that do not always hold for these children.

One of the primary assumptions is that students' abilities to perform the tasks required by the tests themselves are more or less equal. However, just as one would not place much faith in an English-language test administered to a Spanish-speaking student, so one has to be cautious of written tests administered to students who have reading difficulties of any kind. Exceptional students may also have physical handicaps that interfere with their ability to produce written answers. Adaptations of the tests (preparing them in braille, for instance) are better than nothing, but still do not obviate the problem that one is measuring, in part, the student's ability to take the test. Another assumption of psychometric theory is that test scores are not overly influenced by motivational factors. There is much evidence, however, that students who have been labeled as handicapped, or whose mental retardation limits their ability to understand the nature and purpose of testing, have different test-taking motivations than other students. Factors such as persistence and speed are performance characteristics valued, and thus learned, in regular education. So it is not surprising that directly rewarding handicapped students' test performance has a much greater effect on improving their scores than it does for nonhandicapped students.[7]

A third assumption of many educational tests is that performance on the items reflects performance in real life. In competency tests, especially, it is thought that the items are closely related to the desired criterion behaviors. Imagine, for example, an item testing one's knowledge of the nutritional value of a given food product. A student's verbal knowledge, however, may have limited bearing on his or her purchasing habits. It is even more probable that for a student with limited cognitive ability, appropriate food shopping requires a variety of other skills (one that a nonhandicapped student might be assumed to possess already), such as to be able to get to the store or to communicate with the sales clerk, so that passing an item on a paper and pencil test does not reveal actual shopping ability. With excellent teaching it is sometimes possible to confound predictive validity in the opposite direction. Thus it is possible to teach a student with severe handicaps to buy specific items of nutritionally balanced food, without teaching general verbal information about health, how to shop for food, and so on. In this case the student would be more competent in real life than would actually be revealed by the test.[8]

The implication of this discussion is that the more traditional measures of pupil progress in regular education—achievement tests, competency tests, and completion of the designated curriculum—are not always suitable for assessing students in special education. Not surprisingly, program evaluations have turned to more direct measures of specific accomplishments, which in turn raises questions regarding what accomplishments are most important, how standards within and across these skills should be determined, and the best ways to measure them.

ESTABLISHING MEANINGFUL EDUCATIONAL GOALS

Consensus over goals still eludes special education. When asked what they saw as the goal of special education, the administrators in our survey all commented that the goal should be for the student to be able to reach his or her maximum potential: "I think the focus of special education is to achieve at their maximum potential and not to see their handicap as an excuse." A very prominent secondary theme in the replies to this question was that students' self-concept was of great importance, that they should be able to feel good about themselves:

A sign of success? Probably that they are able to survive as much as possible in the normal mainstream without calling attention to themselves, so they don't have to cope with that feeling of being separated by their handicap.

As one person remarked: "The biggest concern that I have—not to be a bleeding heart—is to deal with some of the feelings that people have that cause a lot of sadness in their lives."

Similar results were obtained in a parallel study of a group of parents. The parent panel was asked to list what they considered to be the major goals of special education, and they generated the following (in order of importance): for the student (a) to reach his or her potential, (b) to live independently, (c) to be part of the community, (d) to be prepared vocationally, and (e) to achieve satisfaction with life.

Admirable as these goals toward normalization are, some of them are not formulated in terms of tangible attainments that could be objectively measured. On the other hand, some of the goals (like living independently or having a job) are tangible but depend on factors other than the quality of the special education program (e.g., economic climate, or type of adult services available). Thus, the best way to express specific goals would be in terms of individuals' skills and competencies that might allow them to achieve the greatest possible blending into the social mainstream. Naturally, when probed a little further, the parent group identified as the major outcomes that should result from special education such topics as job skills, community living skills, and leisure skills, more or less in that order of importance. Similarly the administrators, when asked for more specific goals, made such comments as:

> We should be preparing students to be competent when they finally leave school. . . . But I'm not sure how many are, or how many can exist without support from institutions. How many can go out and find an apartment that's going to be adequate?
>
> Being able to communicate in whatever way they can, and do as much self-help—taking care of themselves—as best they can. That is important.
>
> One of the things I am very concerned about is that we are not focusing sufficient time and effort on, well, call it *life skills*, or call it *how to cope*.
>
> I happen to believe in expanding the mind; I don't think exposure hurts. But in special ed., expecting the child to master academics, I think that is ridiculous. I think we should be teaching them *at* the grocery store—real numbers, math that is useful.
>
> One of the major goals should be to develop social skills. These are the skills to get along in society.

It is interesting to note that both the parents and the administrators were essentially endorsing a concept that has become prominent in technical analyses of special education, namely, the importance of focusing on functional goals. It can be asserted, then, that *functional competencies*, or life skills, represent the most meaningful level for depicting individual pupil outcomes. This does not mean that other more basic skills (such as the traditional domains of language, fine motor dexterity, cognitive and perceptual processes, or academic content such as reading, writing, and math) are not important. Rather, the argument is that all new learning serves as a means toward some end, with psychological processes enabling academic learning, which in turn enhances functioning in the practical world, which in turn permits achievement of complex personal feelings and social relationships. On this continuum, just measuring the basic processes of the academic skills is insufficient because those measurements will not necessarily translate, particularly with more handicapped students, into functional skills. So too, trying to measure intangible long-range outcomes like personal satisfactions is too global to serve a useful function for educational evaluation despite their being agreed upon as ultimate objectives. Like the baby bear's porridge, it is the middle of the continuum—functional life skills—that is just right when it comes to evaluating special education's effects.

STANDARDS FOR MEASURING FUNCTIONAL COMPETENCIES

If we accept that the critical outcomes for students with more severe handicaps to achieve are everyday functional competencies, certain important concepts follow.[9] One of the central considerations is the notion of critical effects, or mastery. If a skill is to have value it must be performed with sufficient ability so that it actually serves its intended purpose. In other words, if the behavior of interest is buying candy at a store, the critical effect is that you leave the store with candy (and with less money than when you walked in!). Obviously, the actual behavior of buying candy varies greatly. It could be achieved by handing the storekeeper a picture of the desired candy bar or asking for it verbally. We usually refer to skills that are effective as *competencies*, and to those that are most useful as *functional competencies*.

In measurement we need to focus on the achievement of the critical effect and not worry too much about greater skill levels beyond that point. Conversely, if the student's behavior fails to achieve the desired outcome, it is not particularly valuable to possess some parts of the chain without the quality necessary to produce results. For instance, if one can catch the right bus, pay the correct fare, but not get off at the desired stop, those other components are not of much use. Of course, having these elements would be useful in that it leaves only getting off the bus as the component still needing to be learned. Measuring step-by-step acquisition would therefore be helpful in monitoring student progress, but not for evaluating outcomes. For a teacher planning a program to develop bus-riding skills, it would be important to know that the pupil has two-thirds of the appropriate steps of the tasks, but in evaluating the program's effectiveness, that finding would force us to consider the program unsuccessful.

Outcome measure, therefore, should focus on a relatively small number of competencies judged by very high standards. By the same reasoning, all of the competencies should be seen; that is, a certain minimal criterion needs to be reached, regardless of what the average child is capable of achieving. To illustrate some of the strengths and weaknesses of these "criterion referenced" measures, we will briefly mention the evaluation of early developmental intervention. When early childhood education programs became more widespread and there was a mushrooming of neighborhood infant stimulation programs to give high-risk preschoolers the cognitive boost that might avoid special education services, evaluation became a major concern. Because there were so few suitable measures, many projects devised their own. These usually consisted of a menu of self-help, motor, language, and other cognitive skills ("can tie shoes," "can hop on one foot," "can understand prepositions *on* and *under*," "can match shapes"—to give an example from each category). The child's attainment of these skills would be determined through direct observation of his or her classroom behavior, or indirectly from parent and teacher reports. Although sometimes the items were ordered according to difficulty or developmental sequence, the measures were not used to evaluate students relative to some norm, but to evaluate the program's success in imparting these specific skills to the youngsters.

The limitations of this approach are twofold. One is that, without a comparison group not enrolled in early education, it could not be determined whether the gains were due to the program or were the natural gains to be expected from any maturing child. Well-standardized, norm-based instruments could show that the gains were greater than would be expected from maturation, but young children with handicaps are well behind these norms anyway and the expected developmental rates for such children are not known. The other limitation is that the items may be commonly observed features of developing children. But are they the important ones? Did the instruments focus on relatively trivial skills like shoe-tying (less critical in the days of velcro) or the more important "survival" skills like being able to solve a problem or follow a teacher's directions that would be expected of children in a regular first grade?

It can therefore be argued that the best way to measure improvement is not in terms of where children are now relative to where they once were, but where they are now relative to where they need to be. The survival skills needed by school leavers might be very different from those needed when making the transition from preschool to kindergarten, but the concept of preparing for the future is essentially the same.

Evaluation of Programs

Thus far we have been discussing the need for highly veridical and direct measurement of skills we expect students in special education to learn, and how we decide that these competencies are the most important. Ultimately, judging the effectiveness of a program requires documentation that these important outcomes are being achieved. We have considerable professional agreement that certain educational practices are more likely than others to produce positive outcomes;

thus, it is possible to evaluate programs themselves in terms of the degree to which they meet current standards of practice. We may view this as the investigation of process variables whereby the educational program is supposed to work. In this next section we will discuss the evaluation of these processes such as instructional methods, the curriculum, and the characteristics of the teachers.

It is important to remember that although these aspects of the educational process often constitute the subject of evaluations, they should never be seen as ends in themselves. They are considered important *only* because it is believed that they will have the greatest benefit to students in terms of tangible outcomes. Yet the exact benefits of what professionals consider desirable practices are not always known. Generally we have to take it on faith that some practices are more effective than others, and there may be factors unique to individual schools or programs that would necessitate some modification of the general rules. To illustrate, a general rule might be that a student with moderate or severe handicaps should be taught adaptive skills in their natural context; but for one individual pupil, drill on a particular aspect of the skill (which may preclude the natural context) might be indicated.

Thus, we emphasize the need to attend to the educational or social principle underlying any suggestions regarding effective procedural variables. It is unfortunately easy for good educational ideas to get translated into rules which no longer capture the essence of the original suggestion. For instance, the principle that parents of children with handicaps should be included when selecting educational priorities has become translated into the policy "rule" that parents must attend IEP meetings and sign the IEP. Yet it is well documented that parents often have little real input at IEP meetings.[10] Parents are sometimes handed a virtually completed IEP that they are expected to sign. An administrator evaluating the procedures of the special education program might be tempted to check on some compliance monitoring form that parents in his or her school do sign the IEPs. However, if really interested in the principle of involvement in decision making, it would be necessary to ask all parents (in nonthreatening circumstances) whether they feel their educational priorities have been taken into consideration.

CHECKING PROGRAM QUALITY

The other chapters in this book discuss many special education practices that are currently considered state of the art processes, and obviously there are now many attributes needed to characterize a program as exemplary. To help educators appraise their own programs in the light of these criteria, there have been some attempts to codify all the "best practices" that have been recommended by pedagogical scholars and researchers. An example of such a list set has been developed in the form of a checklist of desirable practices by Meyer.[11] The checklist covers six program components (philosophy, design, instruction, parental involvement, staff development, and facilities), within which a series of individual items represent features of the program that have been recommended by researchers and experienced experts, generally on the basis of empirical data, but sometimes reflecting informed professional opinion. The items have been socially validated independently by representatives of various professional and consumer advocacy organizations.[12] Some sample items are as follows:

The program philosophy emphasizes the goal of social acceptance and adjustment.

Students attend different subject area classes throughout the day, according to patterns typical for same-age regular education peers.

Each student receives appropriate positive reinforcement and feedback (e.g., 75 percent positive to 25 percent corrective in the classroom).

Parent training is available and parents might be asked for assistance in working on skills with their child at home.

The school principal has received training directly relevant to the disability areas served in the school.

Classrooms are close by those for same-age nonhandicapped peers.

Utley and Evans developed a checklist of desirable program characteristics (based on common consensus) that was used in a statewide evaluation of services to severely handicapped deaf-blind students.[13] Information obtained by using the checklist in classroom observations was intended to provide the state education department with a sense of how well its program for deaf-blind students was conforming to ideal procedures. The features of an ideal program were organized in the checklist under the following headings: administration; diagnosis, evaluation, and placement; program elements (school, classroom, curriculum, programming, related services, evaluation); parents and families; long-term planning (individual, system). Examples of items under each of these categories are:

Administration
There is coordination between state department of education consultants responsible for deaf-blind services and the local districts.

Diagnosis, evaluation, and placement
Early screening and identification programs are in place.
IEPs show evidence of periodic review and update, not just annually.

Program elements
School: All school programs and facilities are accessible to students with combined visual and auditory handicaps.
Classroom: Noncategorical grouping of students is encouraged.
Curriculum: There is an emphasis on functional competencies.
Programming: Choice and independence are both encouraged.
Related services: Different therapists do not work separately or in isolation with individual children.
Evaluation: Technically sound procedures are used to measure student progress on individual programs.

Parents and Families
Parents evaluations are always included in program planning.

Long-term Planning
Individual: Community-based instruction is used to aid transition to new environments.
System: State education agency anticipated future needs based on incidence figures.

Again, it is important to stress that when evaluating procedural variables, primary focus should be on the principles involved. Integration, community based instruction, functional skill building, and other fashionable procedures sometimes need to take second place to other vital considerations. For instance, is *this* particular child benefitting? Are the students enjoying school? Are activities fun even if not always age-appropriate? Does parental involvement consider the level of change a particular family can handle?

One of the advantages of thinking about process evaluation is that the measurement procedures needed to check on the flexible implementation of sound principles do not need to be very sophisticated in order to provide useful information. Generally speaking, the task is really to insure that program components are in place and occurring as planned. This confirmation is known as "treatment integrity"[14] and simply refers to some method of checking that programs are being implemented as designed. One useful technique is in terms of products. For example, if teachers are attempting to implement community intensive instruction, then there should be requests from those teachers for transportation money or permission to leave school grounds. If effective communication has been established with parents, a product might be a log of positive calls to the principal's office, relative to the number of complaints. Another product that would reflect successful integration of handicapped students might be photographs in the annual yearbook that depict special students interacting with peers only in normal situations.

Another type of informal evaluation of process is in terms of consumer satisfaction. This has become a widely used technique for evaluation. For instance, college students may rate a professor's course, or participants at a workshop may complete a simple rating of the value, organization, or clarity of the presenter's materials. Clearly, people might enjoy a workshop but not actually have learned anything, so satisfaction ratings have serious limitations. Nevertheless, they are easy to gather and can provide parents, students themselves, and other consumers a chance to express concerns about programs that could be very easily rectified. An additional area where it is quite straightforward to gather good information for improving the process of instruction is through observation of classrooms. Most of us feel somewhat threatened when formally observed for purposes of evaluation; however, principals and other administrators are in and out of classrooms often enough to allow some quick impressions of classroom atmosphere variables.

In various places in this section we have admitted that formal data from research cannot necessarily guide good educational processes. This is why it is so important for special educators to engage in an active and open process of self-examination. Fortunately, this ethic is generally taught to special education student teachers, especially those working with the severely handicapped. The more handicapped the pupil, the more crucial it is to implement effective teacher strategies. Many of these have evolved from principles of behavior modification[15] where there is a strong tradition of gathering data to guide decisions. To be really effective in solving difficult instructional problems, teachers may have to gather formal baseline data and conduct functional analyses of behavior. This is time consuming and difficult, so there is a need in the field for somewhat more straightforward methods. Evans and Meyer, for example, provide a variety of forms for gathering useful information.[16] Teachers are also encouraged to conduct self-evaluations by such strategies as inviting other respected teachers to their classrooms to observe, or to keep a log of how much instructional time they are actually devoting to a particular student's program. Based on these formative evaluations, decisions can be made about changing programs.

USING EVALUATION INFORMATION TO CHANGE PROGRAMS

There are various "models" available to guide administrators in the evaluation of special education programs. In our opinion some of these are needlessly complicated, providing formal guidelines for every aspect of the procedure. Four of these complex models have become better known and respected because a few years ago they themselves were evaluated in a project cosponsored by the Council of Administrators of Special Education and the Office of Special Education Programs of the U.S. Department of Education. The four evaluation models selected for trial use in local districts interested in evaluation were:

1. The *California Statewide Cooperative Program Model for Special Education Programs*, which provides a detailed manual for a district to use in gathering information about student performance, degree of least restricted environment, consumer attitudes about services, and the like.

2. The *Massachusetts Special Education Program Evaluation Model*, which is also based on a state education department's efforts to gather consumer satisfaction information and to report findings back to the local school districts.

3. The *SPEED/SMA Special Education Total Program Evaluation Model*, which evaluates according to the "quality, sufficiency, and cost effectiveness" of all aspects of special education services, including teachers, physical facilities, transportation, and program philosophy by comparing "what is" with "what should be."

4. A *Systems Framework for Special Education Program Evaluation*, which was developed by Maher and Bennett[17] and is more of a methodological approach than a formal model, with no specification of particular instruments.

In the study of the usability of the four approaches, Danielson and Greenburg reported that each participating district strongly endorsed the model they had used, but that on comparison the California and Massachusetts models seemed quicker and easier to use, and were also cheaper, in terms of professional consultation required.[18]

While we would encourage any district to implement a prefabricated evaluation model, there are some features of these formal approaches that render them difficult to understand and hard to use.

The logic of formative evaluation, as we have described it, is that program planning and change decisions should be based on, and further modified by, objective data. However, the connection between what has been discovered and what should then be changed is not always obvious. Let us imagine that an outstanding evaluation of a high school program for students with learning disabilities revealed that the pupils lacked important work skills and after graduation were not holding jobs for any length of time. Should there be a change in the curriculum, making it more functional? Should there be an increased focus on instruction in specific community and work environments? Should the LD resource room model be dropped in favor of an Adaptive Learning Environments model?[19] Or should the elementary school LD program be intensified to ensure that cognitive and social deficits in the students are rectified before they actually reach the high school level? If the answer is in the affirmative to all of these, then clearly the evaluation is not of much use, just as the psychological evaluation of an individual child is of little use if it does not lead to clear differential prescriptive recommendations for the teacher.

Assuming the evaluation model does suggest some foci for change, it is obvious that not all possible changes are equally mutable. Some things are easier to change than others. This might be due to practical and logistical factors, or to social and psychological factors. For instance, parental dissatisfaction with a special education program may reflect inadequacies in the skill level of teachers in relating to families. This represents a practical problem in teacher training over which the individual district has little control (although the district could work with local universities to enhance student-teacher practicum training in the area of parental interaction).

In general, then, the formal evaluation models focus on the *acquisition* of information, not its use as a monitoring procedure or in decision making. The figurative description of formative evaluation as the "fine-tuning" of programs is often used, but rarely specified with any precision. An analogy with the data-based model of teaching might be helpful, since the evaluation of an entire program is really an extension of the process specified under PL 94-142, in which the IEP is supposed to include procedures for assessing a student's progress toward the identified goals. Thus, special education instruction is mandated to be data-based, and performance measures affect decisions to change, delete, or add educational programs to the individual student's total plan. Precision teaching, or a discrete trial approach, provides immediate data on acquisition (teacher recorded success or failure on a given trial) that determines when that activity has been learned and when one can move onto the next. A good example of this strategy can be found in the West Virginia System,[20] which allows the teacher to graph progress at the same time the data on correct responding are being gathered. The implication at the systems level is that information on accomplishment be transmitted to the next phase of the program so that time is not spent on teaching previously acquired skills. In our survey of one district, no such mechanism was in place and only if the individual teacher made the effort was useful information on student learning ever passed on to the next teacher.

A more detailed decision model for when the teacher should change strategies has been proposed by White and his colleagues.[21] The teacher plots an "acceleration" line and then estimates whether, at the present rate of progress, a student will achieve the goal within the available time. More global decision rules of this kind are specified in the Data Based Program Modification Model,[22] which results in pupils knowing their own progress on specified goals. For the administrator the implication is that the district needs to have a school life-span perspective. Teachers of all age levels have to meet to specify what the desired competencies at school leaving should be, set up landmarks to check whether students are on track, and make decisions on what student accomplishments need to be concentrated upon if the milestones are not being reached. This is the program support needed for the concept of the criterion of ultimate functioning.

An interesting aspect of the precision teaching model is the focus on what to change in an instructional strategy if the student is not acquiring the behavior. Our research knowledge of enhancing motivation, breaking the task down into more fine-grained steps, using appropriate and natural eliciting cues or prompts, teaching metacognitive strategies, compensating for fundamental deficits by means of prostheses—to name but a few—is now very sophisticated. There are also system-wide equivalents of these learning methods, and the following examples are matched to this list of instructional strategies: enhancing motivation through special diplomas and merit awards, rather than limiting them to the most intellectual students; creating opportunities for partial assistance for learners who have not yet acquired a complete routine; ensuring practice of new skills in the total school environment, not just in the isolated special education classroom; supporting academic learning with life-skills training opportunities; and ensuring that the school environment is accessible to all disabled students through architectural design. This level of implementation of effective programs is the responsibility of the senior administrators. It should not be too difficult to relate improvements in educational outcomes to such provisions in much the same way as the teacher has to modify instructional techniques to guarantee that the student's baseline of performance is steadily rising.

Conclusions
PROGRAM EVALUATION AS APPLIED SCIENCE

If special education were a technology, then our professional responsibility would be limited to ensuring that the latest techniques and procedures, validated by basic research, are introduced and correctly used. However, we all know that this is not the case. It is true that basic and applied research can provide important suggestions regarding effective practices. For instance, basic learning research on reinforcement and on stimulus control has provided behavior modification methods that have generated highly effective educational methods for the most severely disabled students. But often the learning principles have been translated from the laboratory to the classroom without proper consideration of other valid principles (such as functionally analyzing behavior before trying to change it), or of other social standards and values (such as not depriving students in order to generate artificial reinforcers). As a result, therefore, punitive procedures have been introduced into some settings in lieu of a fully comprehensive educational program for the students.

Similarly, the classic experimental study of some educational method rarely reveals the absolute superiority of one tactic without consideration of related variables, such as the type of student or the personality of the teacher. Weld and Evans, for example, recently showed that the often recommended practice of teaching a whole task rather than teaching each of the parts separately, was superior only for moderately handicapped students, not the more severely handicapped teenagers.[23] The multitude of similar studies in special education, if properly interpreted, do not leave the practicing educator with a set of specific procedural rules, but only suggestions about practices that might be worth attempting if suitably monitored and adapted to the individual.[24]

By the same token there are general philosophical trends in special education that become professionally accepted but which do not yet have—and may never get—direct empirical support. Often the endorsement comes from undocumented but persuasive experiences and from valued higher principles, such as the dignity and worth of the individual. There is no point, therefore, in waiting and hoping for unequivocal empirical support for practices that are actually prized on the basis of general educational and humanitarian values. Integrated education, for example, has some documented outcomes that most of us would consider beneficial (e.g., improvement in the attitudes of nonhandicapped students[25]), but is largely driven by moral arguments for rights to equal educational opportunity.[26] It is arguable that the extent to which a school district is able to minimize the differences between handicapped students in terms of goals, values, and standards of educational excellence, is the measure of their success in implementing the true spirit of PL 94-142. Even if the benefits of integration could somehow be scientifically proved, its implementation without concern for the moral principle might be quite unsuccessful; simply attending the same school, for example, does not ensure that handicapped and nonhandicapped pupils are socially integrated. Compliance with the law is necessary, but the formal regulations must be transcended by an ethic that emphasizes not the specialty of children with disabilities but their commonality with the other children in the educational system.

This ethic is strongly based on the theory of "normalization," which asserts that a quality program is one that "enhances a person's social image or perceived value and enhances their competencies."[27] Our interviewees, by advocating such goals as "being able to survive as much as possible in the normal mainstream . . . so they don't have to cope with that feeling of being separated by their handicap," and "to develop functional skills and be useful in society," were endorsing the basic principles of normalization. It behooves the program evaluator to be aware of the idealism behind the terms "least restrictive environment," "integration," and "education for all handicapped," since it provides a strong conceptual base for any judgment of quality.

As special education practice cannot wait for empirical findings to translate directly to procedures, ongoing program monitoring becomes essential. And if scientific proof continues to elude the research field, then the monitoring required does not need to have the same rigor as formal evaluation methodologies that hope to make generalizations regarding the worth of some general method. This argument means that programs should be less daunted by scientific standards developed for evaluation, and should concentrate more on responsivity to feedback. If programs could become more self-critical, examining their activities in as objective a manner as possible, and be willing to adjust their efforts on the basis of accurate information (not fixed belief, personal bias, educational fad, or state regulation), then program evaluation would represent an exceptionally constructive approach for achieving educational quality.

THE IMPORTANCE OF EVALUATION

We feel that it is necessary to be wary of assuming that evaluation is carried out in order to *justify* education programs. It is not appropriate to try to place a financial value on services themselves. As one of our school board members said in the interview: "We see the dollars going up, up, up, but if you talk against special education you might as well be against motherhood." The Director of Special Education also remarked: "the costs for special education have increased roughly 50 percent in the past four years, yet I haven't heard anyone question that we have got to provide the programs, or question what they cost." Special education does not require any more (or less) justification than regular education, despite various calls for accountability. A monetary value should not have to be placed on special education. It is necessary only for individual programs to use their pupil data as the standard by which to demonstrate continued progress. We have argued that there is a need to move away from traditional, norm-based achievement and competency tests in favor of more direct behavioral measures of the extent to which educational goals have been met. In fact, in some contexts, this may turn out to be a necessity for evaluating outcomes of nonhandicapped students as well. Vocational training programs, as one example, require direct measurement of such skills as getting along socially with co-workers, interacting with authority figures, and proper use of equipment. Interestingly, in one investigation we found that both nonhandicapped students in occupational education and students with mental retardation in a work study program agreed that those are important goals of training.[28]

Students' own perceptions of their educational experiences are informative in evaluation. The obvious reservation is that enjoying a program and appreciating its utility for one's personal goals are not always congruent feelings. For whatever reason regular education students may experience dissatisfaction, they at least have some control over their educational opportunities. Boys and girls in regular education can opt for novel courses, elect to change schools, complete or not complete their homework, and in general exert a considerable amount of personal (or at least family) responsibility for their education. Until the passage of PL 94-142, on the other hand, parents of children with disabilities had to be grateful that any school program was available. It is for this historical reason that ensuring the quality of special education today is so vitally important. What typifies mental retardation is a lessened ability to profit from the normal, haphazard learning experiences of our environments—at least nonhandicapped children acquire *some* knowledge when saddled with less gifted teachers. Special education, therefore, is more directly responsible for what a handicapped child does or does not learn.

In practical terms, the implication for educational administrators is the importance of ensuring that the time a handicapped child spends in school is time well spent. When one thinks how slowly youngsters with mental retardation learn, the poor lesson plan, the bad IEP, the repetitive task, or the unavailable special service cannot be rationalized away by saying there's always next week, or next year, or the next school, or adult services. Lost learning occasions represent a vital percentage of a student's total learning opportunity. It is tempting for school administrators to perceive in an adversarial light those parents who demand much from public schools and who advocate vociferously for maximum services, but given the importance of maximizing educational time, schools have an ethical responsibility to ally themselves with such advocates. By the same logic, our professional role demands that parental satisfaction cannot be the sole standard whereby a program is judged. We found that parents of older, severely handicapped students reported more satisfaction with the quality of educational services than the parents of younger children, probably due to the former's unwillingness to be too critical of services they remember having fought to obtain.[29]

With such a vast range of possible satisfaction, progress, and outcome measures available, program evaluation can seem a little daunting. When evaluation becomes stuffy and overly complex, educational administrators begin to shy away from what is in fact a relatively simple exercise they are already quite familiar with, namely, developing measures that allow for continued program redesign and improvement. The purpose of our chapter is to reduce avoidance by arguing that good evaluation requires adherence to only simple principles of measurement and logic. The burden of proof for self-evaluation does not have to be as demanding as in an experiment, but there are standards for what would constitute a meaningful evaluation and what can reasonably be surmised from a less than perfect measure.

Poking one's head into the special education resource room might give one some useful information about the program that could result in helpful suggestions to the teacher. But it would not be as informative as systematically asking students if the special education program was preparing them for their future lives. Similarly, that sort of information is subject to too many errors to try to reform the entire program on the basis thereof. Major program revision might not be initiated until there is a clear evidence, for example, that students are not getting jobs after leaving school.

Program evaluation is designed to inform decision making. If it does not do so it is of no use to anyone. The more costly the decision—in terms of its impact on students—the more critical is the quality of the data and the correctness of their interpretation. All measurement contains error, but the more directly one measures what it is one wants to know about, the more likely one is to obtain the type of information needed to modify the educational practices in a constructive direction. Program evaluation is as simple (or as complex!) as that.

FOOTNOTES

1. Donald T. Campbell and John C. Stanley, *Experimental and Quasi-experimental Design for Research* (Chicago: Rand McNally, 1966).

2. Luanna H. Meyer, Joanne Eichinger, and Seunghee Park-Lee, "A Validation of Program Quality Indicators in Educational Services for Students with Severe Disabilities," *Journal of the Association for Persons with Severe Handicaps* 12 (Winter 1987): 251-63.

3. Ian M. Evans, "Individual Expectations and Outcome Evaluations: A Strategy for Judging the Benefits of Special Education," Technical Report No. 9 (Binghamton, NY: Project SPAN, SUNY, 1985).

4. Mark L. Wolraich and Gary N. Siperstein, "Assessing Professionals' Prognostic Impressions of Mental Retardation," *Mental Retardation* 21 (February 1983): 8-12.

5. Valerie Owen and Keri A. Weed, "Perceptions for the Future: Mothers' Perceptions of Regular and Special Education Curricula Services," Technical Report No. 8 (Binghamton, NY: Project SPAN, SUNY, 1985).

6. Edward Burns, *The Development, Use and Abuse of Educational Tests* (Springfield, Ill.: Charles C Thomas, 1979).

7. Ian M. Evans and Rosemery O. Nelson, "Assessment of Child Behavior Problems," in *Handbook of Behavioral Assessment*, ed. Anthony R. Ciminero, Karen S. Calhoun, and Henry E. Adams (New York: Wiley, 1977).

8. Ian M. Evans and Fredda Brown, "Outcome Assessment of Student Competence: Issues and Implications," *Special Services in the Schools* 24 (1986): 41-62.

9. Ian M. Evans, Fredda A. Brown, Keri A. Weed, Katherine M. Spry, and Valerie Owen, "The Assessment of Functional Competencies: A Behavioral Approach to the Evaluation of Programs for Children with Disabilities," in *Advances in Behaviorial Assessment of Children and Families*, ed. R.J. Prinz (Greenwich, CT: JAI Press, 1987).

10. Ann P. Turnbull and H. Rutherford Turnbull, "Parent Involvement in the Education of Handicapped Children: A Critique," *Mental Retardation* 20 (June 1982): 115-22.

11. Luanna M. Meyer, *Program Quality Indicators (PQI): A Checklist of Most Promising Practices in Educational Programs for Students with Severe Disabilities* (Syracuse, NY: Division of Special Education and Rehabilitation, 1987).

12. Meyer, Eichinger, and Park-Lee, "A Validation of Program Quality Indicators in Educational Services for Students with Severe Disabilities."

13. Bonnie Utley and Ian M. Evans, "*Educational Evaluation of the Services to Deaf-Blind Students in the State of New Hampshire*," unpublished report (Syracuse, NY: TASH Technical Assistance Project, Syracuse University, 1985).

14. William H. Yeaton and Lee Sechrest, "Critical Dimensions in the Choice and Maintenance of Successful Treatments: Strengths, Integrity and Effectiveness," *Journal of Consulting and Clinical Psychology* 49 (April 1981): 156-67.

15. Robert J. Gaylord-Ross and Jennifer Holvoet, *Strategies for Educating Students with Severe Handicaps* (Boston, MA: Little, Brown and Co., 1985); Martha E. Snell, ed. *Systematic Instruction of the Moderately and Severely Handicapped* (Columbus, OH.: Charles E. Merrill, 1983).

16. Ian M. Evans and Luanna H. Meyer, *An Educative Approach to Behavior Problems: A Practical Decision Model for Interventions with Severely Handicapped Learners* (Baltimore, MD: Paul H. Brookes, 1985).

17. Charles A. Maher and Randy E. Bennett, *Planning and Evaluating Special Education Services* (Englewood Cliffs, NJ: Prentice-Hall, 1984).

18. Louis C. Danielson and David E. Greenburg, "Facilitation of Local-level Special Education Program Evaluation," unpublished manuscript (Washington, DC: Office of Special Education, U.S. Department of Education, 1984).

19. Margaret C. Wang, "Adaptive Instruction: Building on Diversity," *Theory Into Practice* 19 (Spring 1980): 122-28.

20. John D. Cone, *The Pyramid Scales* (Austin, TX: Pro-Ed, 1984).

21. Owen R. White and Norris G. Haring, "Evaluating Educational Programs Serving the Severely and Profoundly Handicapped," in *Teaching the Severely Handicapped*, Vol. III, ed. Norris G. Haring and Diane Bricker (Seattle: AAESPH, 1978).

22. Louis Fuchs, Stanley Deno, and Phyllis Mirkin, "Teacher Efficiency in Continuous Evaluation of IEP Goals," *Research Report* No. 53 (Minneapolis: Institute for Research on Learning Disabilities, University of Minnesota, 1981).

23. Elvera M. Weld and Ian M. Evans, "The Effectiveness of Part Versus Whole Teaching Strategies for Students with Moderate and Severe Handicaps," (Binghamton, NY: Psychology Dept., SUNY, 1987).

24. Luanna M. Voeltz and Ian M. Evans, "Educational Validity: Procedures to Evaluate Outcomes in Programs for Severely Handicapped Learners," *Journal of the Association for the Severely Handicapped* 9 (1983): 3-15.

25. Luanna M. Voeltz, "Effects of Structured Interactions with Severely Handicapped Peers on Children's Attitudes," *American Journal of Mental Deficiency* 86 (January 1982): 380-90.

26. Douglas Biklen, *Achieving the Complete School: Strategies for Effective Mainstreaming* (New York: Teachers College Press, 1985).

27. Wolf Wolfensberger, *The Principle of Normalization in Human Services* (Toronto: National Institute on Mental Retardation, 1972).

28. Fredda Brown, Keri A. Weed, and Ian M. Evans, "Students' Perceptions on the Importance and Utility of their High School Curricula," Technical Report No. 13 (Binghamton, NY: Project SPAN, SUNY, 1985).

29. Christine Salisbury, Keri A. Weed, Valerie Owen, Fredda Brown, and Ian M. Evans, "Parents' Perceptions of Educational Outcomes: A Comparison of Regular and Special Education Services," Technical Report No. 7 (Binghamton, NY: Project SPAN, SUNY, 1985).

Section Four
CONCLUSION

CHAPTER XI

Elements of Integration

DOUGLAS BIKLEN, ALISON FORD, AND DIANNE FERGUSON

When we conceived of this book on schooling and disability we did so with certain assumptions about the field of special education and the experiences of students classified as handicapped. We assumed, for example, that it would be helpful not to take the prevailing ways of thinking about and organizing special education for granted, or uncritically. We assumed that an understanding of special education required an awareness of critical issues for all education. For example, the nature of professionalism, the place of gender, race, and class in education, relations between parents and schools, philosophies of education, and the purposes of schooling cross the arbitrary boundaries between special and regular education, informing and challenging both in similar ways. Perhaps most importantly, we believed that in order to explore issues of disability and schooling we must also examine the meanings of disability in culture.

This final chapter reflects our assumption that a disability, whether retardation, learning disabled, deafness, emotional disturbance, or other classification, is never experienced apart from its social and cultural context. Disability, like other personal qualities, derives its meaning from the ways people respond to it, interpret it, and experience it. In this chapter we explore some of the major themes of

---

This chapter was prepared with support of the Research and Training Center on Community Integration, funded by the National Institute on Handicapped Research, U.S. Department of Education (Cooperative Agreement No. G0085C03503). The opinions expressed herein are solely those of the authors and no official endorsement by the U.S. Department of Education should be inferred.

disability in school culture and suggest broad strategies for transforming the meaning of disability in schooling.

Themes of Disability in School Culture

SEEING THE PERSON

Disability often obstructs people's views of each other. A person's blindness, for example, is rarely simply an observable fact (e.g., an inability to see); it usually evokes a social interpretation, "the poor soul," or "she's amazing, she's succeeded despite being blind." There is nothing inherent to disability that justifies stereotyped responses. A more humanistic alternative would be to evaluate people for qualities over which they have some control, like being humorous or boring.

It may seem both trite and unhelpful to say that educators should try to see and appreciate the person apart from disability, or with disability relegated to a position of being just one of many personal qualities. Nevertheless, a few specific practices can suggest *how* to see the person. Schools can look to adults with disabilities as experts on the disabled school experience, able to point out some of the ways the nondisabled world, however unintentionally, stereotypes a person with a disability. Secondary school can make disability a topic of investigation and discussion in the same way that some schools explore issues of sexism and racism. As a matter of policy, schools can make the school life of a student with a disability as "least special" as possible, providing specialized supports only when necessary and providing them as unobtrusively as possible. One way that some schools accomplish this, for example, is by infusing certain kinds of assistance, such as sign language instruction or language development and reading instruction, into the subject areas of the general curriculum. Another way involves continual awareness by staff of their role as models for students. Staff members who relate to each person as an individual and actively discourage preconceived notions of how a disability affects one's life, set positive examples for the students who seek to emulate them.

An aspect of such teacher and staff modeling would be how they speak about programs and services. Do they use ordinary educational terms? Instead of terms like "training" or "treatment," do they use words like "teaching reading," "community living," "social skills," and "social studies"? School administrators might refer to classrooms by grade level and classify teachers by subject areas rather than by disability categories. A logical result of such new practices may be to eliminate the need for parallel systems of education (i.e., special and regular) and to rid schools of traditional disability labels.

WHERE THERE ARE NO INSIDERS AND OUTSIDERS

A resource teacher recently came to talk to one of us about leaving teaching. She aired a common complaint of all teachers, but especially of special education teachers: she was lonely. She felt isolated. As she put it: "When I walk down the hall, they (the other teachers) don't see me. They see one of my kids, the kids they wanted to get rid of. In their minds, I'm associated with the kids they've rejected." Even special education teachers who provide resource assistance to students within the regular class feel isolated and lonely. It is an isolation and loneliness exacerbated by the fact that special education teachers function as the safety valve or repository for surplus students.

Schools that want to integrate disabled students also need to integrate teachers. Instead of organizing the teaching staff into insiders (regular teachers) and outsiders (specialists), the school needs to develop teams of teachers that include generalists and specialists who meet and collaborate to develop curricula, share teaching strategies, and teach lessons where each teach both classified and nonclassified children. Responsibilities must not lie entirely with one or the other teacher; rather, they must always be shared. As suggested by several of the examples in the introductory chapter and in the chapters on curriculum and classroom organization, there are many initial steps that can narrow the gulf that separates the specialist from the generalist, to ensure at least a modicum of communication between them. We have observed such concrete strategies in use. In one program, specialists and generalists exchange roles periodically during each year, and then share their adopted role experiences during scheduled meeting times. Other programs use team teaching and consulting teaching models which facilitate special programming in the typical classroom setting. Some programs also use staff development strategies that prepare the regular educator to serve certain specialist functions in the typical class.

NO TESTS FOR ACCESS

Educators rely heavily on tests. We use them to help us decide what to teach, to measure progress, to compare scores, and to understand learning difficulties. We also use tests to determine *eligibility and access*. Some students must pass our tests to become eligible to reenter a regular classroom. Other students must meet our criteria before being allowed to enroll in a regular public school. Still others are required to prove that they can benefit from education at all. We decide whether they are eligible, whether they are qualified to participate in learning opportunities freely afforded their peers. We will provide two examples to describe this phenomenon.

What is the test for regaining entry into a regular classroom? William knows. Years ago he was removed from a regular sixth-grade class because of his "failure to attend" and his occasional "disruptive behavior" (i.e., talked to his peers, mimicked the teacher, and moved about the room without permission). He was placed in a self-contained classroom with other students who shared his newly acquired label of "emotional disturbance." This "ED" program devoted a significant amount of time and attention to the development of prosocial behaviors. When he was not role playing, practicing coping skills, or charting his behavior, he received tutoring on his academic work. The months passed without any change in William's placement. Over time, he found himself in an all too familiar predicament. A few behaviors caused his removal from regular classes but the criteria to reenter involved much more. He had to prove that he could perform at grade level (or near grade level) in each of the regular subject area classes before reentry would even be considered. William was never really a strong student and during the year or so he spent in a self-contained program he seemed to lose ground academically, falling approximately two grade levels behind. Today his teachers no longer talk about what it will take for William to reenter the regular science, mathematics, English, and social studies classes. It seems that the new test requirements are beyond his reach. William used to warn his teachers that, "Once you're out, you can't get back in." It seems that he understood, perhaps better than most, the toughness of the tests for reentering regular classroom settings.

The test for access came much earlier in Alex's life. At the age of five his mother brought him to the neighborhood school to register for kindergarten. Even at this early age many of Alex's disabilities were obvious to school officials. Alex rarely spoke, and when he did, he used only one word utterances. He moved with an unsteady gait, had many awkward body movements, and waved his hands repeatedly in front of his face. On the basis of these and other initial observations, the school district decided that Alex should be "tested." Following an evaluation session during which he was given four standardized tests, the conclusion was reached that Alex was eligible for a special school placement. As his parents soon learned, being eligible for a special school actually meant being *in*eligible for a regular school.

After much negotiation, the parents succeeded in enrolling Alex in a classroom for multiply handicapped students in an elementary school. Once he achieved regular school placement his parents thought the eligibility question was laid to rest. But as long as there was a special school nearby, teachers and administrators seemed compelled to ask the question, "Wouldn't Alex be better off in the special school?" Eventually the school district felt they had gathered enough data to show that regular school placement did not satisfactorily meet Alex's needs. The recommendation to send him to a special school concluded that: (1) significant progress has not been made in certain developmental and/or educational areas; (2) his need for supervision and a protective environment is such that placement in a public school is more restrictive than placement in a sheltered environment; (3) Alex could profit from educational experiences in an environment where he is not the weakest pupil in the building, and (4) Alex could profit from a variety of contacts with developmental peers. Remaining in the regular school now depended upon his ability to make significant progress, to function without supervision, to alter his perceived status as the weakest pupil in the school, and to find developmental peers with whom to interact.

The fairness of these criteria became the subject of a due process hearing. The hearing officer concluded that the school district could not exclude Alex from a regular school on the basis of these criteria and recommended that the district design a program that would more appropriately support Alex's learning there. Since that time Alex has not been asked to prove that he can benefit from an education that takes place in a regular school setting, but many of his disabled peers continue to be asked to pass "tests for access." Like Alex, many of them fail.

It may be that Alex's hearing officer was persuaded that he deserved the right to be educated with his peers. It may also be that the hearing officer understood, as did Burton Blatt that "educability is a two-edged sword." Explaining the two-edged sword, Blatt refers to the experiences of Helen Keller and Anne Sullivan:

Anne Sullivan accepted the responsibility to teach Helen Keller not because she expected Helen to become a world-famous inspiration to people in every walk of life. The "miracle" of the Anne Sullivan-Helen Keller saga was exactly that no one expected things to turn out so marvelously well. By definition, that's the ingredient required for a miracle. The paradox of the Anne Sullivan-Helen Keller saga, the paradox of any miracle, is that it must be unexpected. Anne Sullivan necessarily had other reasons for assuming responsibility for Helen, or there would have been no miracle, no story, no demonstration of educability. Educability is a two-edged sword: Even if educability cannot be empirically verified, the clinician must behave as if it has been verified.[1]

Why should opportunities for learning in groups with nondisabled students, socializing with nondisabled students, and participating as equal members of a school depend upon a student passing a test? Why should even the chance for students with and without disabilities to make friends with each other be dependent upon whether some of them have passed the tests that allow them to be present.

Clearly William and Alex's experience justifies a different approach. They challenge us to assume that all children can learn, need variety in their lives, and deserve respect and consideration. They also force us to admit that the burden or test should be for professional educators to discover ways of making education work. This means, of course, that schools should struggle to find ways of integrating disabled and nondisabled students, not because students with disabilities have proved themselves capable, but because it is important. Tests would not be used to determine *whether* a student could benefit from an education or a placement in a regular school or class, instead they would be used to determine how a student with disabilities could participate more fully in school life.

OF EQUAL IMPORTANCE

A school district that we shall call Aurora is well known for its innovative approach to educating mildly impaired students. A team of three teachers, including one certified in special education, share the space of two classes and educate a group of seventy-five students. The students and teachers move around within the space in accordance with students' needs for instruction in mathematics, reading, and social studies. A student might receive small-group instruction in reading, but not for any other subject. Another might be in small groups for all subjects. A teacher might teach a small group for science, but not for reading or mathematics. And so it goes, students and teachers assigned in an individualized and fluid fashion. The Aurora model reveals an exceptional degree of coordination and team cooperation by teachers. There is an underlying, unstated assumption that the program must adapt and bend to meet the needs of the diverse group assigned to the three teachers. School officials take pride in the academic success of the program. The reading program coordinator, for example, expresses an unusual knowledge and pride in the performance of mildly disabled students in Aurora's combined classes.

But when asked about more severely disabled students (Do you have any students with severe disabilities in the school? Where are they served?), the regular educators cannot respond. Their silence reveals that severely disabled students are really not known to the school. At best, such students are an afterthought; at worst, they are forgotten altogether. The reading coordinator tells us, "You'd have to ask Ralph (Director of Special Education). I think some go to BOCES (Board of Cooperative Educational Services, an intermediate school system)."

A district that *would* include all students would need to treat the education of each group and individual as an indispensable part of the whole. In such schools it would be as unconscionable to send away students with disabilities or to otherwise ignore their education as to exclude students with average or above average ability or to ignore their education. In such a district, students with disabilities would be seen as peers of nondisabled students. The education of each would be equally valued, equally memorable. Similarly, decisions over limited resources would not automatically evolve to resource stealing from one or the other group but would be seen as community concerns. As one superintendent explained to us, for example, when faced with increasing enrollments and therefore diminishing classroom space, he asked the School Board to approve purchase of a modular unit to house a music program. When we asked if the school board had ever considered relocating a special education class, he responded, "there are some decisions that you do not give the school board as a choice to make."

STUDENT VS. PATIENT

Assessment and classification, diagnosis and treatment, disorders and syndromes, therapy and intervention are all terms that bespeak the medicalization of special education. They represent a language of student-as-patient. As we discussed in the first chapter, these words and the approach they represent imply that the purpose of special education is to fix students' problems. They suggest that difficulties in schooling belong to the student instead of being a product of school and student interaction.

An alternative view seeks to balance the inherent tension between fixing the student and allowing the student to participate in the social setting of schooling. Adrienne Asch offers a former student's perspective on the dilemma and remedy. "I'm leery of professional overkill" she warns. "Students want a chance to display their sameness (read ordinariness or the chance to escape patient status), to say that they like the same rock music and haircuts, and share the same distaste for parent-imposed curfews." In order to escape the different, patient, or client-like role in schools, students with disabilities need to be allowed to be treated "the least differently as possible." This does not have to mean a student needs to deny his or her disability. It is rather that special services need to be offered in a normal manner.

In schools that minimize the view of students as patients, education is seen as interactional. Every student's experience, whether positive or negative, is seen as tied to the social experience of school. Students are not either right (healthy) or wrong (sick). Nor should they be viewed as objects, waiting for the next new technology, treatment, or intervention. Rather, they are people who have ideas, feelings, skills, and knowledge; they are people who can participate in education and not merely be acted upon. Such schools teach students how to interact with each other, how to participate, how to show their strengths, how to listen, how to question, and how to think. They teach students how to appreciate each other, how to make friends, how to be supportive, and how to be assertive. In short, they are schools in which there is a sense of community and participation.

MAKING FRIENDS

A principle debate over whether or not to integrate disabled and nondisabled students has been the degree to which students with disabilities will find acceptance in regular schools. Will their nondisabled peers accept them? Will they interact? Or will students with disabilities feel rejected? Is integration worth the price of prejudice, stereotyping, discrimination, and isolation?

Nonacceptance has been well chronicled by students themselves and by parents. The feeling of having to make an extra effort to be accepted and to have friends is a common recollection in disabled adults' accounts of their school experiences. Adrienne Asch, for example, remembers how helpful it was that her parents told her that she might have to invite students to go to the movies with her. She also recalls her parents' fight to get her access to the school music programs, as well as to other social situations in school where she would have a chance to make friends. "From very early on, I didn't want to be just in class. I wanted to have friends." Of course, parents can support and teach their children not to internalize prejudice, to confront it or ignore it perhaps, or to work their way around it.

Schools, like parents, can try to prevent bad attitudes by instilling positive ones. Their methods typically include changes in curriculum to include explanations of disabilities, exposure of students to adults with disabilities who may be seen as role models, puppet shows about disabilities that encourage students to explore their feelings about differences and help students appreciate the sameness of students, childrens' stories or other content that teach about people with disabilities, and disability awareness campaigns. Such attitude change events and curricula can also create problems. Even if done sensitively, they may highlight differences and communicate only superficial awareness of the disabled experience. Because they are special events they may be perceived as temporary. They may excuse daily noninteraction.

Schools cannot promise friendships, and they certainly should not try to make a science of friendship building, but they can facilitate them through a few simple strategies. Schools can assure physical proximity, teach listening, value people with disabilities, encourage cooperative teaching and learning, and make it a practice to look for what Judith Snow calls each student's *gifts*—those best and special qualities that transform difference into uniqueness.

In their chapter on what parents and people with disabilities want from schools, Ferguson and Asch mention the value for students with disabilities of having allies. It is certainly no accident that they speak of "allies" rather than simply "people who care" or "experts concerned about children's best interests." Had they wanted "caring individuals" they might have encouraged schools to develop big brother/big sister relationships, and adopt-a-student programs. Perhaps they realize only too well the potential problem in these types of relationships, especially those conceived of as a kind of charity. One person typically is the benefactor and the other a recipient. The benefactor identifies what the recipient needs and gives with the expectation of being thanked or at least thought well of for the good deed. Ferguson and Asch obviously have something else in mind.

What are the characteristics of the ally? From the perspective of a student with a disability, an ally could be another student, the student's parents, and possibly a teacher. Allies are friends. They come together out of mutual interest, not for charity and not to give treatment. Similarly, most friendships are not founded on a sense of obligation to public service. Strully and Strully note with some pride that there is a real difference between a friendship or alliance and charity or service. They describe what happened when a school principal wrote to their daughter's friend Tanya telling her how proud he was of her "community service" to the Strullys' daughter Shawntell.[2] Tanya wrote back: "I want to thank you for sending me the note, but I do not consider this friendship a community service. It's just a friendship."[3] Thus, not all peer tutor matchings or buddy systems would be alliances. Implicitly, allies see each other as peers, as equals; and they try to understand one another's needs, interests, and perspectives. Being an ally is a little like being an ethnographer. One must be sensitive to the other person's ideas, receptive to their feelings and thoughts, and willing not to impose assumptions on the other person about what he or she should think, feel, or do. Neither member of the relationship is in charge, both participate and contribute, both benefit.

A person who befriends or becomes the ally of a person with a disability faces the special challenge of dealing with society's response. Allies of people with disabilities may find themselves the objects of negative attitudes, often captured in unashamed, and often uninvited, comments like "Don't you have to be awfully patient?" or "Doesn't it depress you?" Another common remark sounds more positive but reflects underlying rejection of people with disabilities: "It's so good of you to give up your life to work with those people."

Of course, it is not self-denial or sacrifice that motivates allies and friends. Friends are motivated by the good feelings of a friendship. Allies who are also friends are likely to be motivated by the desire to make the school a different kind of place, a better community. Allies who seek a role in this kind of broader change also must bear the sting of society's reluctance. They may find themselves at odds with some of the other people in the setting, perhaps with other students or with teachers, the principal, or other parents. After all, change agents in schools are not unlike whistleblowers. If the change they seek involves changing standard operating procedures or traditional ways of doing things, they may provoke others resentment. It is not always a comfortable role.

Students with disabilities are often in situations where they have fewer allies than other people. This is true because of their marginal status within the culture. It is particularly true in schools where students are evaluated in terms of their abilities to meet specified expectations or norms. Students will tend to be more isolated than others if they are thought of as less competent, as possessing problems of thinking, moving, behaving, or looking, and as challenging the standards. Among peers, students with disabilities may be seen as different. And those who might want to befriend them may feel pressured not to because "It's not cool." Despite such powerful forces discouraging alliances, schools can take measures to support students in building alliances, in making friends, and in being less isolated.

Some schools find that alliances occur naturally when given the opportunity. The presence of handicapped students in a variety of regular classes, common curricula, innovative instructional practices and the constant support and engagement of all students' families are a few of the practices that create a climate which supports the development of alliances. Some schools find it helpful to employ a systematic approach to ensure that all students find allies. One such approach has been developed by Forest, Snow, and their colleagues, the McGill Action Planning System (MAPS),[4] a consciousness-raising strategy that enlists the active participation of student peers and teachers in *mapping* out ways that students can become allies in helping a student become part of the school community.

Strategies of Integration

The six themes discussed above suggest that achieving full integration is a complex, difficult, and yet achievable task. Good integration is simply a part of good education. Where it works, integration is a constant presence. It is not an IEP objective that can be operationalized, measured, and achieved for ever after. Nor is it a special event or episodic occurrence that can be added on to an otherwise segregated organizational structure. It cannot be achieved through annual involvement in Special Olympics, a week-long series of attitude change workshops, or a disability awareness day. Also, it would be wrong to think of integration as achievable merely through the introduction of a new curriculum or concept. Rather, integration is a fundamental, constant, part of people's professional perspective, personal beliefs, and daily life. The nature and quality of school integration for students with disabilities is inexorably linked to the nature and quality of schooling in general.

A school's experience with integration reflects other aspects of the school culture such as the overall commitment to problem solving, the style of interaction between students and teachers, the concern for affective as well as academic education, the sense of school community, a common set of rules and expectations as well as rewards and support, and the degree to which every student is regarded as a valued participant. The way a school community responds to the issue of integration depends upon the way it thinks about schooling. The promise and problems of both special education and regular education inform and affect each other, linking the integration of children to the integration of adults, and eventually, to the larger community.

At another level, integration for all students, including members of minority groups other than students with handicaps, is linked to the approach of society generally to those groups. As we have emphasized in various ways throughout this book, some groups are thought to be unacceptably different, devalued, and especially eligible for discrimination in other social arenas. And unfortunately schools and education mirror these broader social inequities. The security of educational integration of students with handicaps will never be complete until all social and cultural institutions assure the presence and participation of all devalued groups. Given the subtle, but powerful, nature of the cultural themes and beliefs that would divide students by perceived ability, those who strive to achieve integration must be constantly vigilant. Integration hard won is also fragile.

Admittedly, analyses like this which make everything connect to larger and larger spheres of social and community life, can make it seem that any individual, or even group effort will have negligible effect since the problem is really an overarching one. A more accurate and helpful interpretation is that small changes, through their ripple effects, actually create broader social change. Thus, integration efforts, in the relatively small sphere of public schooling, can potentially further larger social goals in important ways. This seems particularly persuasive considering the powerful influence of schools on the beliefs and practices of future generations. Making integration a constant presence by linking the best of regular and special education, and maintaining constant vigilance on both the spirit and the fact of an integrated community promises an eventual society in which integration would be an unnecessary concept because segregation would no longer exist.

THREE BROAD STRATEGIES

In chapter 1 we remarked on the fullness of integration that people with disabilities envision as achievable. We also noted that communities and groups have sometimes attained this level of full integration. In these cases, disability is unremarkable, certainly not cause for segregation, labeling, or treating a group of people as substantially different or unworthy. We can find such positive integration experiences in some intentional communities such as the L'Arche community living homes and in a number of small home living arrangements that have emerged in recent years. We can also find them within the self-help/disability rights movement where people with and without disabilities work together for social change. In chapter 1 we also pointed to the fully integrated, mutually supportive, and interdependent experiences of families with disabled members.

The fact that such relationships and communities exist is important. Their presence in our lives promises that other groups and communities can find similar levels of acceptance and interdependence based as much on people's desire to affiliate and participate as on their need to rely on others. More than merely fostering optimism, however, the extant cases of integrated cultures suggest to us some of the conditions essential to integrated societies. There are many: respect for each person, opportunities for everyone to make choices about their own lives, self-determination, equal access to opportunity, chances to be valued, and opportunities to share and participate. Three of the most critical elements are also exceptionally obvious.

Creating the commitment to integration. As we have said elsewhere, perhaps the most critical element in achieving integration is first to decide to do it.[5] The signs and symbols of commitment are multiple. An explicit policy of integration is obviously one important ingredient, but so is articulating the goals of schooling and developing a curriculum framework that "works" for all students. Efforts to educate the community surrounding the school about the all-inclusive goals, and involving all levels of the school community in the responsibility of planning for integration are other important signs of commitment.

Creating opportunity and capacity for integration. Of course, wishing does not make it so. Successful integration efforts employ a variety of strategies for creating both the opportunity and the capacity for all members of the school community to work toward integration. These range from relatively obvious one-time changes like renovating a building to make it completely architecturally accessible, or locating students with handicaps in the midst of age peers; to ongoing strategies for cross-disciplinary communication, collaboration, and team teaching. Important structural changes in the bureaucracy are frequently necessary to create the capacity for integration and might include fiscal incentives, a single administrative structure for all students and faculty, equitable distribution of space and resources, and specific student and faculty policies that apply to all.

Nurturing the themes of integration. Nurturing and confirming integration's constant presence requires identifying those strategies that will work in the particular setting. Understanding the themes of integration might encourage one school to use a structured planning approach like MAPS, while another focuses on creating curricula that are future-oriented, reflect students' interests, and place students in valued roles. Still another school might find a focus on innovative instructional strategies and teaching styles that promote interaction, a critical feature in the achievement of integration.

Many schools use the same strategies. We conclude this volume by listing some of these strategies and signs that seem to occur most frequently in those examples of more complete schools. We would point out, however, that the real message for achieving integration lies not so much in the specific strategies as in the way in which such strategies are generated. Having a vision of integration and understanding the themes that characterize it increase the likelihood that the strategies will fit the setting and will work.

1. *Creating the commitment to integration*

   Philosophy and stated policy showing commitment to educating all students within their community school.

   All students attend schools with students of their own age.

   Community education about the goals for all students' education.

   School level planning for integration; in other words, the responsibility for accomplishing integration should not be left to committees on student placement.

2. *Creating the opportunity and capacity for integration*

   Guarantee that students in a particular elementary school can anticipate moving to the next level secondary school with their peers.

   Single administrative structure for all student programs rather than a two-track (i.e., special and regular) system.

   Common transportation for all students.

   Architectural and other access; access is seen as an essential part of normal planning and maintenance throughout the school.

   Organization of educational staff that encourages communication between disciplines and areas of expertise; specialists participate on subject or grade level teams rather than in their own separate groups.

Funding practices that encourage integrated education.

Teaching that promotes interaction; e.g., group activities that allow students of different abilities to participate in different ways, cooperative learning.

Minimizing of laboratory, medical, or other professional language which may cause people to view the education of students with disabilities as fundamentally different from general education.

Environments, programs, and strategies that encourage students to learn from each other.

Grouping of students of different abilities throughout the school and classrooms.

Assurance that instruction and programs are sequenced to encourage growth or development of students.

Teacher to teacher interaction through consulting teacher services, team collaboration, problem-solving groups, program idea groups, team teaching, teaching demonstrations, etc.

Integration of adaptive physical education, language education, vocational education, and other special programming into the regular curricula.

3. *Nurturing the themes of integration*

Clearly stated and universally applied policies on student and teacher expectations, including behavior rules.

Labeling of programs by grade level, subject area or other useful identifier and not by disability or other individual qualities (e.g., slow learner, gifted); of course, labeling by personal qualities becomes moot as integration is achieved.

Equitable distribution of quality space and resources, including funding to serve all students.

Unified scheduling and other data management for all students and programs.

Recognition of teachers, parents, and students as critical thinkers, as people who must be encouraged to engage in the formulation of curricula and of the school environment.

Evaluating student progress, quality of instruction, and program effectiveness.

Activities that place students in valued roles, including helping roles.

Curricula that help prepare students for their future participation in community life.

Curricula that reflect students' abilities, needs, skills, interests, and choices.

Chances to practice learned knowledge or skills in real situations involving real problems.

Teaching and school atmosphere that maximizes independence with minimum supervision, yet recognizes natural interdependence.

Revisions of instructional strategies based on evaluation findings.

Parent participation through classroom observations, videos, discussions, classroom participation, communication via teacher/parent notebooks and telephone, planning meetings, parent support groups, parent/teacher study groups, and individual program planning.

Footnotes

1. Burton Blatt, *The Conquest of Mental Retardation* (Austin, TX: Pro-Ed, 1987), p. 356.
2. Jeff Strully and Cindy Strully, "Friendship and Our Children," *Journal of the Association for Persons with Severe Handicaps* 10, no. 4 (1985): 224-27.
3. Ibid., p. 226.
4. Marsha Forest, ed., *More Education/Integration* (Downsview, Ontario: G. Allan Roeher Institute, 1987).
5. Douglas Biklen, *Achieving the Complete School* (New York: Teachers College Press, 1985).

Name Index

Adams, Henry E., 253
Adkins, Winthrop R., 193
Adler, Mortimer J., 55
Agras, W. Stewart, 191
Albin, John, 230
Albright, Kathy Zanella, 59, 75, 166
Algozzine, Bob, 11, 12, 23, 24, 57, 85, 86, 103, 104, 105
Alloway, Edward, 105
Altbach, Phillip, 107
Anderson, Jackie, 229
Anyon, Jean, 56
Apple, Michael W., 55, 56, 58, 105, 106
Apsche, Jack, 190
Apter, Steven J., 190, 193
Argulewicz, Ed N., 105
Argyle, Michael, 193
Aronowitz, Stanley A., 55, 56
Asch, Adrienne, 4, 21, 108, 111, 112, 131, 138, 140, 264
Axelrod, Saul, 190

Baer, Donald M., 75, 165, 166
Bagnasco, Vincenzo, 227
Bandura, Albert, 171, 175, 191
Bank-Mikkelson, N. E., 147, 165
Bart, Deborah S., 105, 106
Barton, Len, 105, 106
Bastian, Ann, 55, 56
Bates, Paul, 166
Baumgart, Diane, 76, 153, 166
Beck, Clive, 190
Becker, Howard S., 138
Bedrosian, Jan, 75
Bellack, Alan S., 193, 194
Bellamy, G. Thomas, 58, 165, 229, 230
Bennett, Randy E., 254
Bennison, E. Anne, 103
Benson, Holly A., 57
Berman, Edward, 55
Bijou, Stanley W., 165
Biklen, Douglas, 1, 19, 23, 24, 56, 104, 206, 255, 256, 271
Binet, Alfred, 78, 79
Birch, James, 98, 107
Black, James, 19, 141, 165
Blatt, Burton, 5, 23, 166, 260, 271
Bloch, Alfred, 168, 190

Bogdan, Robert, 1, 2, 22, 105, 157, 160, 167
Boles, Shawn M., 230
Bourbeau, Phil E., 229
Bowe, Frank, 138, 139
Bowles, Samuel, 55, 57
Boyer, Ernest L., 25, 30, 42, 55, 57, 58
Boyte, Harry C., 138
Brady, Michael P., 57
Branston, Mary Beth, 165, 166
Brantley, John C., 76
Breen, Cathy, 231
Bricker, Diane, 57, 165, 166, 254
Bricker, William, 165
Brightman, Alan J., 2, 22, 139, 140
Brolin, Donn, 225, 231
Brown, Fredda A., 254, 255
Brown, Lou, 21, 40, 59, 61, 75, 76, 141, 157, 164, 165, 166, 167, 206, 207, 212, 221, 230
Brown, Steven D., 192
Browne, Suzanne, 139
Bryant, Bridget, 193
Bryson, Fred, 166
Bullough, Robert V., Jr., 58
Burns, Edward, 253
Butler, John A., 56

Calculator, Steve, 75
Calhoun, Karen S., 253
Callantine, Mary F., 191
Campbell, Donald T., 232, 253
Carlberg, Conrad G., 195, 196, 205, 206
Carledge, Gwendolyn, 107
Carney, Martin, 55, 56
Carrier, James, 105
Case, Charles W., 58
Certo, Nick, 24, 75, 165, 166, 206
Chapman, Hilary, 190
Charles, C. M., 190
Chasdey-Rusch, Janis, 229
Christenson, Sandra, 105, 206
Ciminero, Anthony R., 253
Clark, G. M., 231
Clements, Barbara S., 190, 207
Close, Dan, 230
Colavecchia, Betty, 190
Collins, Mary, 230

NAME INDEX

Cone, David D., 254
Conger, John J., 173, 191
Conger, R. E., 191
Conners, Deborah, 139
Cooper, M., 193
Coultry, T., 192
Courtnage, Lee, 57
Crawford, John, 190
Cronbach, Lee J., 193
Cutler, Barbara, 22

D'Zamko, Mary E., 206, 207
Danielson, Louis C., 246, 254
Davern, Linda, 165, 167
Dawson, Margaret M., 196, 206
Dean, Sidney I., 193
Dempsey, Patrick, 165
Deno, Stanley, 254
Diamond, Sondra, 116, 117, 139
Dickinson, Emily, 126
Doering, Kathy, 229
Donahoe, Clyde P., Jr., 191
Donnellan, Anne, 75, 165
Doris, John, 55, 103, 138
Duncan, Carl P., 191
Dunn, Lloyd M., 12, 23, 104

Edelman, Eric, 187, 194
Eichinger, Joanne, 253, 254
Elardo, P., 193
Ellis, Henry, 178, 191
Emmer, Edmund T., 190, 207
Epps, Susan, 12, 23, 24, 105, 192
Esveldt-Dawson, Karen, 191
Etzioni, Amitai, 58
Evans, Ian M., 15, 22, 166, 232, 243, 245, 249, 253, 254, 255
Evertson, Carolyn M., 190, 207

Falvey, Mary, 207
Fanning, Peter N., 166
Fantini, Mario, 190
Farber, Bernard, 89, 105
Featherstone, Helen, 23, 139, 140
Feinberg, Walter, 55
Ferguson, Dianne L., 7, 14, 21, 23, 25, 57, 92, 138, 221, 230, 256
Ferguson, Philip M., 4, 21, 108, 111, 131, 138, 139, 221, 230, 264
Filler, John, 57, 165, 166
Fleming, Donald, 181, 192
Flynn, Robert J., 229
Ford, Alison, 19, 75, 76, 141, 165, 166, 167, 256

Forest, Marsha, 57, 206, 266, 271
Forte, Joyce, 229
Franchild, Edwina, 116, 139
Franklin, Barry, 104, 106
Fraser, James, 229
Freedman, Barbara J., 173, 191
Freud, Sigmund, 79
Fruchter, Norm, 55
Fuchs, Louis, 254

Gagné, R. M., 193
Galassi, J. P., 192
Galassi, M. D., 192
Gallagher, James J., 104
Gartner, Alan, 57
Gaylord-Ross, Cory, 229, 230
Gaylord-Ross, Robert J., 166, 167, 208, 229, 230, 231, 254
Gee, Kathy, 229
Geiwitz, James, 191
Gelb, Steven A., 105
Gershaw, N. Jane, 191
Gideonse, Hendrick D., 58
Gintis, Herbert, 55, 57
Giroux, Henry A., 55, 56
Gitlin, Andres D., 58
Gittell, Marilyn, 55
Glasser, William, 190
Glick, B., 192
Gliedman, John, 138
Glynn, Ted L., 190
Goddard, Henry H., 79, 87
Goetz, Lori, 229
Gold, D., 192
Gold, Marc W., 165
Golden, N., 191
Golden, R., 182, 192
Goldman, Jeri J., 55
Goldstein, Alfred P., 168, 187, 190, 191, 192, 193, 194
Gonzalves, Linda, 87, 89, 103, 105
Goodlad, John I., 25, 55, 57, 159, 160, 167, 197, 206, 208, 229
Gordon, Lawrence R., 166, 219, 230
Granston, Mary B., 206
Grant, Carl, 107
Grant, M. Dilys, 190
Grasso, John T., 229
Greenburg, David E., 246, 254
Greener, Karen, 229
Greenfeld, Josh, 121, 139
Greer, Colin, 55
Grossman, Herbert, 104
Gruber, Ronald P., 192

Gruenewald, Lee, 75, 76, 165, 166, 167, 206
Guerney, Bernard G., Jr., 193
Guess, Doug, 57, 58, 155, 165, 166, 167
Gunter, Philip L., 57
Gunzburg, Herbert C., 191
Guzetta, Roberta, A., 182, 192

Hagie, Chris, 230
Hahn, Harlan, 140
Halpern, Andrew S., 223, 224, 228, 230, 231
Halvorsen, Ann, 229
Hammill, Donald D., 104
Hamre-Nietupski, Sue, 153, 164, 166, 206
Hare, M. A., 193
Haring, Norris G., 24, 166, 254
Haring, Thomas, 231
Harootunian, Berj, 190, 193
Hasazi, Susan D., 166, 219
Haskins, Kenneth, 55
Hawley, Isabel, 193
Hawley, Robert C., 193
Hawley, Willis D., 140
Hazel, J. S., 193
Heiman, H., 193
Heller, Kenneth, 193
Helsel, Elsie, 140
Hendrick, Irving, 103, 105
Heinrich, Edith, 140
Hersen, Michel, 193, 194
Heshusius, Lous, 106
Heward, William L., 24
Hobbs, Nicolas, 104
Holmes, D., 191
Holvoet, Jennifer, 166, 254
Horiuchi, Chiyo N., 166
Horner, Robert H., 229, 230
Hughes, Dana C., 139
Hull, Clark, 186, 193
Hummel, Jeffrey W., 192
Hunt, David E., 193
Hunt, Pam, 229

Irvin, Larry, 217, 230

Jaben, Twila, 57
Jablow, Martha M., 139
Jameson, Devi, 229, 230
Jennings, Rick L., 182, 192
Johnson, David W., 57, 58, 106, 206, 207
Johnson, F., 206
Johnson, G. Orville, 57, 104
Johnson, Mary, 140
Johnson, Robert F., 57
Johnson, Roger T., 57, 58, 106, 206, 207
Johnson, Susan Moore, 58
Jones, David, 221, 230
Jones, Reginald L., 56
Jones, R. R., 191
Jorgensen, Jack, 59

Kagan, Jerome, 191
Kanfer, Frederick, 192, 193
Karoly, Paul, 192, 193
Karuth, Denise, 2, 3, 23
Kauffman, James M., 104, 106
Kavale, Kenneth, 195, 196, 205, 206
Kaye, Nancy, 139
Kazdin, Alan E., 191
Keating, Thomas, 230
Keller, Harold, 190, 192
Kelly, Gail, 107
Kerr, Stephen T., 58
Kessler, Kim, 166, 230
Kiernan, William E., 228, 229
Killilea, Marie, 139, 140
Kirk, Samuel A., 57, 104
Klein, Nancy K., 58, 166
Klein, P., 191
Kohlberg, Lawrence, 183
Knoblock, Peter, 19, 24, 103, 138
Kohn, M., 191
Korinek, Lori, 85, 86, 104, 105
Kriegel, Leonard, 2, 23, 140
Kugel, Robert, 165
Kugelmass, Judy, 105
Kulik, Chen-Lin, 196, 205, 206
Kulik, James A., 205

Ladd, Gary, 185, 187, 193
Lane, M. P., 192
Larsen, Stephen C., 104
Larson, Magali Sarfatti, 58
Laski, Frank J., 165
Leavey, Marshall, 207
Lee, Mellanie, 231
Leigh, James E., 104
Lent, Robert W., 192
Levin, Henry M., 55, 56
Lewis, Jane F., 104
Lilly, M. Stephen, 107
Lincoln, Yvonna S., 56
Litwack, Stephen E., 181, 192
Lloyd, Lyle, 165
Loomis, Ruth, 75, 166, 230
Lussier, Andre, 140
Lynch, Kevin P., 228, 229

NAME INDEX

Lynn, Frances, 116, 139
Lyon, Steve, 206

MacKenzie-Keating, Sandra, 190
MacMillan, Donald L., 56, 103, 105
Madden, Nancy, 107, 196, 205, 206, 207
Magaro, Peter, A., 193
Maheady, Larry, 105
Maher, Charles A., 254
Mank, David M., 229, 230
Mann, M., 197, 206
Mar, Dave, 230
Mariampolski, Hyman, 139
Marston, Douglas, 205
Massie, Robert, 122, 126, 127, 139
Massie, Suzanne, 122, 126, 127, 139
Matson, Johnny, 191
Maurer, Steve, 166
McCarthy, Eileen, 75
McCarthy, Martha M., 55
McConnell, Scott, 191
McDermott, M. Joan, 190
McFall, Richard M., 191
McGinnis, Ellen, 191, 192
McGue, Matthew, 105
McLaren, Peter, 56
McNutt, Gaye, 104
McPhail, Peter, 190
Melton, David, 139
Mercer, Jane R., 104, 105
Mesibov, Gary B., 139
Messina, Rosalie, 76, 206
Meyer, John W., 56
Meyer, Luanna M., 57, 165, 166, 243, 245, 253, 254
Meyer, Marshall W., 56
Meyers, C. Edward, 56
Michelson, Larry, 193
Milburn, Joanne Fellows, 107
Miller, Wilbur C., 191
Mirkin, Phyllis, 254
Mithaug, Dennis, 166, 230
Mize, Jacquelyn, 185, 187, 193
Moore, Richard, 140
Moran, Mary, 102, 107
Morris, Richard J., 166
Musante, Penny, 230
Mussen, Paul H., 174, 191

Nau, Paul A., 190
Nelson, Niall C. W., 58
Nelson, Rosemery O., 253
Newmann, Fred, 190
Nietupski, John, 164, 166, 206

Nirje, Bengt, 147, 165
Nisbet, Jan, 75, 76, 166, 167

Oakes, Jeannie, 55, 56, 197, 205, 206
O'Brien, Jerry, 221, 230, 231
Olexa, Carol, 197, 206
Oliver, Donald, 190
Orlansky, Michael D., 24
Osgood, Charles E., 178, 191
Owen, Valerie, 253, 254, 255

Park, Clara Claiborne, 112, 139
Park, Hyun S., 229
Park-Lee, Seunghee, 253, 254
Parnes, B., 191
Patterson, Gerald R., 173, 174, 191
Paul, James L., 106, 139
Peters, Ann, 2, 23
Petrie, Hugh G., 58
Phelps, Allen, 229
Pieper, Elizabeth, 139, 140
Presland, Ian E., 190
Prieuer, Joanne, 229
Prinz, R. J., 254
Pugach, Marleen, 55, 106
Pumpian, Ian, 76, 165, 166, 221, 230
Pyne, Michael E., 228

Raiser, Lynn, 206, 207
Raleigh, R., 192
Raze, N., 205
Redl, Fritz, 194
Reid, John B., 191
Reiner, S., 192
Reynolds, Maynard C., 12, 23, 24, 57, 106, 201, 206
Rhodes, Larry W., 229, 230
Riessman, Frank, 138
Robinson, Catherine, 190
Roe, Cheryl A., 166, 219, 230
Roff, Linda A., 190
Rogan, Patty, 75, 166, 230
Roger, Blair, 231
Rogers, Dale Evans, 139
Rosenthal, Lisa, 191
Rosman, B. L., 191
Rossell, Christine H., 140
Roth, William, 138, 140
Rousso, Harilyn, 116, 117, 133, 139
Rubel, Robert J., 190
Rusch, Frank R., 229, 230
Russell, Robert, 139

Sachs, Lawrence, 140

NAME INDEX

Sagar, H. Andrew, 140
Sailor, Wayne, 58, 165, 229
Salisbury, Christine, 255
Sameoto, Dorothy, 190
Sanford, Julie P., 190, 207
Sapon-Shevin, Mara, 21, 33, 55, 77, 106
Sarason, Seymour B., 25, 54, 55, 57, 103, 138
Schaefer, Nicola, 140
Schafer, Walter E., 197, 206
Scheerenberger, Richard C., 103, 104
Schiefelbusch, Richard, 165
Schinke, Stephen P., 188, 194
Schlundt, David G., 191
Schnorr, Roberta, 165
Schofield, Janet W., 140
Schopler, Eric, 139
Schroeder, Jack, 76
Schumaker, J. B., 193
Schutz, Richard P., 230
Schwitzgebel, Robert L., 194
Scott, Robert A., 138
Searl, Stanford J., Jr., 103
Sechrest, Lee B., 191, 193, 254
Seligman, Martin, 58
Shapiro, H. Svi, 55, 57
Shea, James R., 229
Sheldon-Wildgen, J., 193
Shepard, Holly, 221, 230
Sherman, J. A., 193
Shevin, Mayer, 58, 77, 166
Shinn, Mark R., 105
Shiraga, Betsey, 75, 166, 230
Shive, R. Jerrald, 58
Shore, Eugene, 191
Siegel, Shep, 224, 229, 231
Siegel-Causey, Ellin, 57, 155, 166, 167
Simon, Theodore, 79
Singer, Judith D., 56
Siperstein, Gary N., 253
Sizer, Theodore, 55, 57, 58
Skinner, B. F., 147, 165
Skrtic, Thomas M., 56, 57
Slack, Charles W., 194
Slavin, Robert E., 107, 195, 196, 205, 206, 207
Sleeter, Christine E., 56, 104, 105, 106, 107
Smith, J. David, 105
Smith, Judy, 206
Smith, Marshall S., 55
Smukler, David, 167
Snell, Martha E., 254
Sniezek, Karen M., 149, 165

Snow, Judith, 264
Soder, Marten, 106
Sontag, Ed, 206
Spatz-Norton, C., 182, 192, 193
Spence, Susan H., 173, 191
Spradley, James P., 139, 140
Spradley, Thomas S., 139, 140
Sprafkin, Robert P., 191
Sprague, James, 229
Spring, Joel, 105
Spry, Katherine M., 254
Stainback, Susan, 19, 22, 23, 57, 58, 106, 107, 195, 206
Stainback, William, 19, 22, 23, 57, 58, 106, 107, 195, 206
Stanfield, James S., 150, 166
Stanley, John C., 232, 253
Stark, J. R., 228, 229
Stedman, Lawrence C., 55
Steffan, John J., 192, 193
Stein, Norman, 193
Stephens, Thomas M., 191, 193
Stern, David, 221, 224, 230, 231
Stern, George G., 193
Stern, Nanci, 139
Sternat, James, 206
Steward, Harry E., 230
Stokes, Trevor F., 75, 166
Storey, Keith, 229
Strain, Phil, 231
Strauss, Alfred, 80
Strickland, Bonnie B., 76
Strohm, Beth, 230
Strully, Cindy, 140, 265, 271
Strully, Jeff, 140, 265, 271
Swanstrom, Carl R., 192
Sweet, Mark, 75, 76, 166, 167, 230
Sykes, Gary, 56

Tawney, James W., 149, 165
Taylor, Josephine L., 108
Taylor, Steven J., 23, 56, 103, 206
Tharp, Roland G., 192
Thomas, John D., 170, 190
Thomas, M. Angele, 164
Thompson, B. J., 192
Thompson, R. Paul, 165
Thorndike, Edward L., 177, 191
Tjossem, T., 165
Todis, Bonnie, 191
Tom, Alan R., 58
Tomlinson, Sally, 6, 23, 105, 106
Towne, Richard, 105
Trief, P., 192

NAME INDEX

Trower, Peter, 193
Tucker, James A., 105, 206
Turnbull, Ann P., 76, 138, 139, 254
Turnbull, H. Rutherford III, 76, 138, 139, 254
Turner, James, 230
Twersky, Jacob, 139

Ungoed-Thomas, J. R., 190
Utley, Bonnie, 243, 254

VanDeventer, Pat, 59, 75, 76, 166, 230
Van Houten, Ron, 190
VanWalleghem, John, 153, 166
Voeltz, Luanna Meyer, 24, 166, 254, 255

Walberg, Herbert J., 12, 24, 206, 207
Walker, Hill, 191
Walker, J., 191
Walsmith, Charles R., 191
Wang, Margaret C., 12, 24, 57, 98, 106, 107, 197, 206, 207, 254
Warren, Frank, 139
Warren, J. M., 191
Weber, Wilford A., 169, 190
Weed, Keri A., 253, 254, 255
Weick, Karl E., 56
Weinstein, Gerald, 190
Weis, Lois, 56
Weiss, Lois, 107
Weld, Elvera M., 15, 22, 232, 249, 254
Werner, Heinz, 80
Wershing, Alice, 229
West, Elizabeth, 221, 230
Wetzel, Ralph, 192

White, Mary A., 190
White, Owen R., 254
Whitten, M. Elizabeth, 106
Wilcox, Barbara, 58, 165, 166, 206, 229, 230
Will, Madeleine, 12, 24, 99, 107, 219, 230
Williams, Gareth H., 58
Williams, Wes, 75
Willis, Paul, 56
Wilson, John, 190
Wilson, William, 229
Wineman, David, 194
Wolfensberger, Wolf, 138, 148, 165, 255
Wolraich, Mark L., 253
Wood, George H., 55, 56
Wood, Randy, 193
Woodworth, Robert S., 177, 191
Woronov, Naomi, 116
Worsham, Murray E., 190, 207
Wortis, J., 165
Wright, Beatrice, 118, 139

Yeaton, William H., 254
York, Jennifer, 75, 230
York, Robert 24, 165, 166
Ysseldyke, James E., 11, 12, 23, 24, 57, 103, 105, 166, 206

Zanella, Kathy, 19, 21, 230
Zimmerman, Don, 139, 182, 192, 193
Zittel, Gail, 229
Zivolich, Steven, 222, 230
Zollers, Nancy, 23, 104

Subject Index

Adaptive Learning Environments Model, 247
Adults with severe handicaps: employment options for, 219-22; economic conditions in relation to opportunities for, 222-24; problem of job retention for, 224-25; supported work for, 220-22
Aggressive children, deficits of, in prosocial psychological skills, 173-74
American Association of Colleges for Teacher Education, 100
American Association on Mental Deficiency, 80
American Orthopsychiatric Association, 79
A Nation At Risk, 25, 27, 28, 30-31
A Place Called School (Goodlad), 25, 159
Assessment: discrimination in, 88-89; procedures for, in vocational programs for severely handicapped students, 216-17
Association for Children with Learning Disabilities, 81, 82, 100
Association for Persons with Severe Handicaps (TASH), 37, 149-50
Association for Retarded Citizens, 82, 218

Battles v. Commonwealth of Pennsylvania, 148
Binet-Simon intelligence test, 78-79
Brown v. Board of Education of Topeka, 80, 90

Campbell v. Talledega County Board of Education, 149
Carl Perkins Act (1984), 209
Carnegie Commission, report of, on teacher education, 51
Character education movement, 170
Community-based learning experiences, for handicapped and nonhandicapped students, 43-44
Community-referenced curricula: concept of normalization in relation to, 147-48; conditions surrounding emergence of, 146-51; content of, 143; essential and negotiable activities in, 144; guiding principles for, 142-43; impact of litigation and legislation on rise of, 148-49; instructional practices in, 143-44; lessons learned from implementation of, 151-57; sample scope and sequence chart for (figure), 145; ways of incorporating, into the total school program, 159-64
Community Vocational Training Program for severely handicapped students, 210, 214-16
Council of Administrators of Special Education, 246
Council for Exceptional Children, 79, 100

Differences in children, needed changes in ways of viewing, 94-95
Disability, perception of, by nondisabled persons, 3-5
Disability categories, confusion regarding, 12
Disability labels, effects of, on school culture, 13
Disability Rights Education and Defense Fund, 124

Education for All Handicapped Children Act. *See* Public Law 94-142.
Egalitarian reforms, limited success of, 28-31
Emotional disturbance: definition of, 85; prevalence of, 85
Evaluation, of special education programs: educational administrators' views of, 234-35; importance of continuous monitoring in, 25-51; models for, 246, 248; unique features of, in evaluating individuals, 236-238
Evaluation and placement processes, in special education; discontent with, 12; studies of 11-12

Friendship and community support: parental perspective on, 126-28; personal perspective on, 128-30

Functional and nonfunctional skills: definition of, 66-67; standards for measurement of, 240-41
Functional curricula, for students with handicaps, 47-49

Handicaps, concept of, as internal deficits, 91-93
Hansen v. Hobson, 90
Heterogeneous grouping, procedures to accommodate diversity in, 198-205
High School (Boyer), 25, 30
Holmes Group, report of, on preparation of teachers, 51, 100
Homogeneous grouping: assumptions made in, 195; research on, 195-97

Identity, sense of: in persons with disabilities, 1-3; parental perspective on, 134-36; personal perspective on, 131-34
Individualized Educational Plan (IEP), 148, 233, 242; advantages and limitations of, 13-15, 44-47
Individualized Transition Plan, 74, 218
Integration (of special education students) with regular education: criteria for, 64-65; examples of, 17-21, 35-36, 41-42; principle of least restrictive environment (LRE) in relation to, 39-41; strategies for achieving, 256-71

Learning disability: definition of, in PL 94-142, 84; prevalence of, 84
Learning disabled/gifted, definition of, 91
Least restrictive environment (LRE): confluence of language on, in various Public Laws, 209; principle of, 39-41

Madison (Wis.) Metropolitan School District, studies of postschool outcomes for special education students in (1971-78 and 1984-86), 151
McGill Action Planning System, 266
Mental hygiene movement, 79
Mental measurement: effects of, 90; impact of, on special education, 87; use of culture-fair tests in, 88
Mental retardation: definitions of, 83-84; identification of levels of, 80; prevalence of, 83; socially constructed nature of, 89
Mild disability: categories of, 77; effects of proliferation of new categories of, 86-87; growth in all categories of, 81; primary focus on, in reforms in special education, 36
Morrill Act (1862), 208

National Coalition of Advocates for Students, 197
National Commission on Excellence in Education, 25
National Defense Education Act (1958), 209
National Federation of the Blind, 135
New Jersey Commission for the Blind, 125, 132
New York State Board of Regents, 159
Nonsheltered employment (for adults), Italian experience with, 226-27

Parent-child relationships: parental perspective on, 112-14; personal perspective on, 114-120
Peer relationships, between handicapped and nonhandicapped students, 42-43
Pennsylvania Association for Retarded Children v. Commonwealth of Pennsylvania, 148
Personal narratives, as sources of data on problems of persons with disabilities, 109-11
President's Committee on Mental Retardation, 84
Professionals, relationships with: parental perspective on, 120-24; personal perspective on, 124-25
Prosocial skills training: contribution of social learning theory to, 171-72; structured learning as an approach to, 172-73; utility of, for trainees of lower socioeconomic status, 172
Psychological tests, use of, to classify retarded children, 79
Public Law 94-142: 7, 13, 28, 44, 148, 212, 247, 250, 252; definitions of learning disability and seriously emotionally disturbed in, 84-85; effects of, 15-16, 34-36, 120-24; provisions of, 10, 34

Reform reports, of 1960s: analyses of, with reference to egalitarianism, 26-32; emphasis in, on excellence, 26; ignoring of, by special education, 26; lack of attention to special education in, 26; responses of critical theorists to, 31-32

SUBJECT INDEX

Regular Education Initiative (REI), 99-100

Schools: needed changes in structural organization of, 96-98; suggestions for, from the disabled community, 136-38
Severe intellectual disability: characteristics of educational programs for students with, 63-74; definition of, 60-61; learning and performance characteristics of students with, 61-63
Sheltered workshops, unacceptability of, for persons with severe handicaps, 213-14
Smith-Hughes Act (1917), 208
Smith-Sears Act (1918), 208
Social Darwinism, 29
Special education: assumptions underlying evaluation and placement processes in, 10; barriers to merger of, with regular education, 98-101; challenges to efficacy of, 81; clinical model of, in evaluation and placement, 9-10; effects of extreme professionalization on, 49-51; effects of shifting students in, 89; evaluation of programs in, 241-49; financing of, 8-9; functional competencies as goals of, 239; impact of consumer and advocacy groups on, 82; importance of evaluation of, 251-53; lack of consensus on goals of, 238-39; litigation regarding, 81-82; overrepresentation of black students in, 90; overview of history of, 78-82; preparation of teachers for, 52-53; relationship of, to regular education, 92; structural organization of, in schools, 7-8; two possible futures for, 102-3
Special education students: functional competencies (life skills) as goals for, 239; lack of consensus on goals for, 238-39; unique features in evaluation of, 236-38

Structured learning: aggressive-alternative skills in (table), 180; group procedures in, 188-89; methods of assessment in, 174-75; prescriptive utilization as enhancement of, 184-86; procedures of, for skill development, 175-77; research on, 181-83; selection of skills in, 188; trainee motivation in, 186-87; trainer-trainee relationship in, 187; transfer of training in relation to, 177-79
Syracuse City School District, 144
Syracuse University, 144
System of Multicultural Pluralistic Assessment (SOMPA), 84, 88

Teacher preparation, needed changes in, 52-53, 95-96

U.S. Office of Education and Rehabilitation Service, 149
University of Washington, 149
University of Wisconsin, 149

Violence, in schools: nature and extent of, 168; typical school responses to, 169-70
Vocational education: components of programs in, for students with mild handicaps, 209-12; criticisms of efficacy of, 211-12; definition of, 208; growth of, 208-9; programs in, for students with severe handicaps, 214-22; provisions for, in primary grades, 225
Vocational Education Act (1963), 209
Vocational Rehabilitation Act (1920), 208

Wechsler Intelligence Scale for Children, 80

INFORMATION ABOUT MEMBERSHIP IN THE SOCIETY

Membership in the National Society for the Study of Education is open to all who desire to receive its publications.

There are two categories of membership, Regular and Comprehensive. The Regular Membership (annual dues in 1989, $25) entitles the member to receive both volumes of the yearbook. The Comprehensive Membership (annual dues in 1989, $45) entitles the member to receive the two-volume yearbook and the two current volumes in the Series on Contemporary Educational Issues. For their first year of membership, full-time graduate students pay reduced dues in 1989 as follows: Regular, $20; Comprehensive, $40.

Membership in the Society is for the calendar year. Dues are payable on or before January 1 of each year.

New members are required to pay an entrance fee of $1, in addition to annual dues for the year in which they join.

Members of the Society include professors, researchers, graduate students, and administrators in colleges and universities; teachers, supervisors, curriculum specialists, and administrators in elementary and secondary schools; and a considerable number of persons not formally connected with educational institutions.

All members participate in the nomination and election of the six-member Board of Directors, which is responsible for managing the affairs of the Society, including the authorization of volumes to appear in the yearbook series. All members whose dues are paid for the current year are eligible for election to the Board of Directors.

Each year the Society arranges for meetings to be held in conjunction with the annual conferences of one or more of the major national educational organizations. All members are urged to attend these sessions. Members are also encouraged to submit proposals for future yearbooks or for volumes in the series on Contemporary Educational Issues.

Further information about the Society may be secured by writing to the Secretary-Treasurer, NSSE, 5835 Kimbark Avenue, Chicago, Ill. 60637.

RECENT PUBLICATIONS OF THE NATIONAL SOCIETY FOR THE STUDY OF EDUCATION

1. The Yearbooks

Eighty-eighth Yearbook (1989)
    Part 1. *From Socrates to Software: The Teacher as Text and the Text as Teacher.* Philip W. Jackson and Sophie Haroutunian-Gordon, editors. Cloth.
    Part 2. *Schooling and Disability.* Douglas Biklen, Dianne Ferguson, and Alison Ford, editors. Cloth.

Eighty-seventh Yearbook (1988)
    Part 1. *Critical Issues in Curriculum.* Laurel N. Tanner, editor. Cloth.
    Part 2. *Cultural Literacy and the Idea of General Education.* Ian Westbury and Alan C. Purves, editors. Cloth.

Eighty-sixth Yearbook (1987)
    Part 1. *The Ecology of School Renewal.* John I. Goodlad, editor. Cloth.
    Part 2. *Society as Educator in an Age of Transition.* Kenneth D. Benne and Steven Tozer, editors. Cloth.

Eighty-fifth Yearbook (1986)
    Part 1. *Microcomputers and Education.* Jack A. Culbertson and Luvern L. Cunningham, editors. Cloth.
    Part 2. *The Teaching of Writing.* Anthony R. Petrosky and David Bartholomae, editors. Paper.

Eighty-fourth Yearbook (1985)
    Part 1. *Education in School and Nonschool Settings.* Mario D. Fantini and Robert Sinclair, editors. Cloth.
    Part 2. *Learning and Teaching the Ways of Knowing.* Elliot Eisner, editor. Paper.

Eighty-third Yearbook (1984)
    Part 1. *Becoming Readers in a Complex Society.* Alan C. Purves and Olive S. Niles, editors. Cloth.
    Part 2. *The Humanities in Precollegiate Education.* Benjamin Ladner, editor. Paper.

Eighty-second Yearbook (1983)
    Part 1. *Individual Differences and the Common Curriculum.* Gary D Fenstermacher and John I. Goodlad, editors. Paper.
    Part 2. *Staff Development.* Gary Griffin, editor. Paper.

Eighty-first Yearbook (1982)
Part 1. *Policy Making in Education*. Ann Lieberman and Milbrey W. McLaughlin, editors. Cloth.
Part 2. *Education and Work*. Harry F. Silberman, editor. Cloth.

Eightieth Yearbook (1981)
Part 1. *Philosophy and Education*. Jonas P. Soltis, editor. Cloth.
Part 2. *The Social Studies*. Howard D. Mehlinger and O. L. Davis, Jr., editors. Cloth.

Seventy-ninth Yearbook (1980)
Part 1. *Toward Adolescence: The Middle School Years*. Mauritz Johnson, editor. Paper.
Part 2. *Learning a Second Language*. Frank M. Grittner, editor. Cloth.

Seventy-eighth Yearbook (1979)
Part 1. *The Gifted and the Talented: Their Education and Development*. A. Harry Passow, editor. Paper.
Part 2. *Classroom Management*. Daniel L. Duke, editor. Paper.

Seventy-seventh Yearbook (1978)
Part 1. *The Courts and Education*. Clifford B. Hooker, editor. Cloth.

Seventy-sixth Yearbook (1977)
Part 1. *The Teaching of English*. James R. Squire, editor. Cloth.

The above titles in the Society's Yearbook series may be ordered from the University of Chicago Press, Book Order Department, 11030 Langley Ave., Chicago, IL 60628. For a list of earlier titles in the yearbook series still available, write to the Secretary, NSSE, 5835 Kimbark Ave., Chicago, IL 60637.

2. The Series on Contemporary Educational Issues

The following volumes in the Society's Series on Contemporary Educational Issues may be ordered from the McCutchan Publishing Corporation, P.O. Box 774, Berkeley, Calif. 94702.

Case, Charles W., and Matthes, William A., editors. *Colleges of Education: Perspectives on Their Future*. 1985.
Eisner, Elliot, and Vallance, Elizabeth, editors. *Conflicting Conceptions of Curriculum*. 1974.
Erickson, Donald A., and Reller, Theodore L., editors. *The Principal in Metropolitan Schools*. 1979.
Farley, Frank H., and Gordon, Neal J., editors. *Psychology and Education: The State of the Union*. 1981.

Fennema, Elizabeth, and Ayer, M. Jane, editors. *Women and Education: Equity or Equality.* 1984.

Griffiths, Daniel E., Stout, Robert T., and Forsyth, Patrick, editors. *Leaders for America's Schools: The Report and Papers of the National Commission on Excellence in Educational Administration.* 1988.

Jackson, Philip W., editor. *Contributing to Educational Change: Perspectives on Research and Practice.* 1988.

Lane, John J., and Walberg, Herbert J., editors. *Effective School Leadership: Policy and Process.* 1987.

Levine, Daniel U., and Havighurst, Robert J., editors. *The Future of Big City Schools: Desegregation Policies and Magnet Alternatives.* 1977.

Lindquist, Mary M., editor. *Selected Issues in Mathematics Education.* 1981.

Nucci, Larry P., editor. *Moral Development and Character Education.* 1989.

Peterson, Penelope L., and Walberg, Herbert J., editors. *Research on Teaching: Concepts, Findings, and Implications.* 1979.

Pflaum-Connor, Susanna, editor. *Aspects of Reading Education.* 1978.

Purves, Alan, and Levine, Daniel U., editors. *Educational Policy and International Assessment: Implications of the IEA Assessment of Achievement.* 1975.

Sinclair, Robert L., and Ghory, Ward. *Reaching Marginal Students: A Prime Concern for School Renewal.* 1987.

Spodek, Bernard, and Walberg, Herbert J., editors. *Early Childhood Education: Issues and Insights.* 1977.

Talmage, Harriet, editor. *Systems of Individualized Education.* 1975.

Tomlinson, Tommy M., and Walberg, Herbert J., editors. *Academic Work and Educational Excellence: Raising Student Productivity.* 1986.

Tyler, Ralph W., editor. *From Youth to Constructive Adult Life: The Role of the Public School.* 1978.

Tyler, Ralph W., and Wolf, Richard M., editors. *Crucial Issues in Testing.* 1974.

Walberg, Herbert J., editor. *Educational Environments and Effects: Evaluation, Policy, and Productivity.* 1979.

Walberg, Herbert J., editor. *Improving Educational Standards and Productivity: The Research Basis for Policy.* 1982.

Wang, Margaret C., and Walberg, Herbert J., editors. *Adapting Instruction to Student Differences.* 1985.

Warren, Donald R., editor. *History, Education, and Public Policy: Recovering the American Educational Past.* 1978.